Un/German

Series Editor: Paul Fleming, Cornell University
Peter Uwe Hohendahl, Founding Editor

Signale | TRANSFER provides a unique channel for the transmission of critical German-language texts, newly translated into English, through to current debates on theory, philosophy, and social and cultural criticism. Signale | TRANSFER is a component of the series Signale: Modern German Letters, Culture, and Thought, which publishes books in literary studies, cultural criticism, and intellectual history. Signale books are published under the joint imprint of Cornell University Press and Cornell University Library. Please see http://signale.cornell.edu/.

Un/German

*Racialized Otherness in
Post–Cold War Europe*

Fatima El-Tayeb

Translated by Elisabeth Lauffer

A Signale Book

Cornell University Press and Cornell University Library
Ithaca and London

Originally published as *Undeutsch: die Konstruktion des Anderen in der postmigrantischen Gesellschaft* by Fatima El-Tayeb

Copyright © 2016 transcript Verlag, Bielefeld

English translation copyright © 2025 Cornell University
This translation is published by arrangement with transcript Verlag, Germany.

Cornell University Press and Cornell University Library gratefully acknowledge the College of Arts & Sciences, Cornell University, for support of the Signale series.

All rights reserved. Except for brief quotations in a review, this book, or parts thereof, must not be reproduced in any form without permission in writing from the publisher. For information, address Cornell University Press, Sage House, 512 East State Street, Ithaca, New York 14850.

First published 2025 by Cornell University Press and Cornell University Library

Library of Congress Cataloging-in-Publication Data

Names: El-Tayeb, Fatima, author. | Lauffer, Elisabeth, translator.
Title: Un/German : racialized otherness in post-Cold War Europe / Fatima El-Tayeb ; translated by Elisabeth Lauffer.
Other titles: Undeutsch. English | UnGerman
Description: Ithaca : Cornell University Press and Cornell University Library, 2025. | Series: Signale/transfer : German thought in translation | "A Signale book"—title page. | Includes bibliographical references and index.
Identifiers: LCCN 2024045088 (print) | LCCN 2024045089 (ebook) | ISBN 9781501780363 (hardcover) | ISBN 9781501781575 (paperback) | ISBN 9781501781599 (epub) | ISBN 9781501781582 (pdf)
Subjects: LCSH: Culture conflict—Germany. | Racism—Germany. | Romanies—Germany. | Islamophobia—Germany. | Germany—Ethnic relations.
Classification: LCC HT1521 .E466 2025 (print) | LCC HT1521 (ebook) | DDC 303.60943—dc23/eng/20241209
LC record available at https://lccn.loc.gov/2024045088
LC ebook record available at https://lccn.loc.gov/2024045089

Contents

Preface to the 2025 Edition   vii

Introduction   1

Part 1 Post/Colonial Capitalism

1. A Few Basics: Internalist History and Evolutionary Time   25

2. Internalism and Universalism: Where Are Europe's Borders?   53

Part 2 Post/Socialist Reckoning with the (Nazi) Past

3. Roma, Sinti, and the Question of German Guilt   83

4. "We Are the *Volk*": From Racist Terror to Terrorized Germans   102

Part 3 Post/Fascist Multiculturalism

5. Germany Is(n't) a Land of Immigrants   135

6. German Normalization, Islamophobia, and Muslim
   Antisemitism   160
Conclusion   196

Acknowledgments   223
Bibliography   225
Index   247

Preface to the 2025 Edition

The English translation of *Un/German* appears almost a decade after the publication of the German original in 2016.[1] This time gap initially had me somewhat worried about the relevance of its content, which in certain ways is tied to the particular historical moment in which it was written: right before and during the so-called refugee crisis of 2015, with Brexit on the horizon, a moment in which the narrative of Europe's successful and smooth post–Cold War transition seemed to suddenly be shaken to the core. In some ways, we are in a different moment now, various crises later, and in a different Europe—one in which the extreme right is playing a growing political role, not only in the continent's East, which is always under suspicion of not yet having shaken off its totalitarian legacy, but also in "core Europe," home to the nations that initiated

---

1. My sincere gratitude to Liz Lauffer, Paul Fleming, and Leslie Adelson for making this possible.

what has now become the European Union (EU) after World War II and that also claim to most represent the European values of democracy, freedom, enlightenment, and stability.[2] The prospect of war not far away but on the continent itself has become a reality that has led to an explosion of defense budgets and a shift in discourse—Germany recently introduced a national Veterans Day, something that would have been unthinkable in 2015, when peace was still considered the European norm and war the exception.[3] The COVID-19 pandemic and Russia's invasion of Ukraine have shaken the longtime belief in a European peace and prosperity that remains untouched by the chaos beyond its borders (even if the continent caused much of that chaos). Racialized communities, meanwhile, particularly Muslims, seem less "integrated" than ever and are in fact frequently seen as the cause of most of Europe's problems.[4]

Yet one of *Un/German*'s key arguments is that the 2015 moment of crisis did not arrive suddenly and unexpectedly but rather was part of a predictable (post)unification process, in which internal instability was managed through its externalization into repeated crisis moments, casting various racialized communities as the outside threat to Europe's integrity against which a deeply divided continent could unite. This externalization makes sure that the real root of the problem—a root that lies in the continent itself, in its navel-gazing view of the world, its insistence on a universalism that is not only deeply provincial but intrinsically tied to white (Christian) supremacy and structurally incapable of integrating those cast as Other—is

---

2. Of the nations that created the European Economic Community through the Treaty of Rome in 1957—Belgium, France, Italy, the Netherlands, (West) Germany, and Luxembourg—only Luxembourg has not seen a steep rise in the popularity of extreme-right parties in recent years.

3. Due to the nation's history of starting two devastating wars in the twentieth century, West Germany's army was legally restricted to strictly defensive purposes; this changed after German unification, and by now the Bundeswehr is a regular part of NATO missions (more on this topic in Part 3). For the introduction of Veterans Day, see Deutscher Bundestag, "Einführung eines nationalen Veteranentages."

4. "Racialization" is the act of attributing collective quasi-biological and/or cultural characteristics to certain groups, allowing for their perception as not belonging, even though they may be an established part of society. These characteristics, supposedly inherent in racialized subjects, are defined as both opposed to and incompatible with the dominant identity.

never addressed. As a result, the instability grows and the cycle of crises escalates, both in frequency and scope. The model of prosperity and peace at the expense of non-Europeans is not sustainable anymore, not even for Europe itself. If this seemed obvious when I was writing the book, it is even clearer now. Approached from this perspective, 2015 and 2024 have a lot in common and can in fact be seen as two comparable moments in a repeating pattern.

In spring 2024, just as in 2015, Germans held mass protests against racism for a few weeks, this time triggered by the uncovering of plans to forcibly "remigrate" racialized Germans and immigrants to North Africa should the extreme right gain power.[5] This seems a less unlikely prospect if we consider that the party behind the remigration plot, Alternative für Deutschland (Alternative for Germany; AfD), is currently coming second in national election polls, a trend

---

5. This came to light when a journalist from the investigative magazine *Correctiv* attended a secret meeting between members of Alternative für Deutschland (Alternative for Germany; AfD), neo-Nazis from Germany and Austria, and wealthy ultraconservatives (and, apparently, a few members of the Christian Democrats). The meeting's topic was the now infamous "remigration plan" (Bensmann et al., "Secret Plan"):

There are three target groups of migrants, he explains, who should be extradited from the country—or, as he puts it, 'foreigners' who should undergo 'reversed settlement.' They are: asylum seekers, non-Germans with residency rights, and 'non-assimilated' German citizens. It is the latter that, in his view, would pose the biggest 'challenge.' . . . The scenarios sketched out in this hotel room in Potsdam all essentially boil down to one thing: people in Germany should be forcibly extradited if they have the wrong skin colour, the wrong parents, or aren't sufficiently 'assimilated' into German culture according to the standards of people like [Martin] Sellner [an Austrian neo-Nazi]. Even if they have German citizenship.

The piece points out that this plan is tied to the "great replacement" conspiracy theory, cited not only by racist mass shooters across the world but also by Donald Trump and conservative politicians and media personalities in Europe and North America (Sellner was in communication with the shooter who killed fifty-one people in two mosques in Christchurch, New Zealand, in 2019). The conspiracy theory claims that evil entities (often Jews, Illuminati, woke liberals, or a combination thereof) try to replace white Europeans with African and Middle Eastern immigrants in order to destroy Western civilization (while proponents of the theory usually do not like to emphasize the connection, Hitler outlined a similar theory in *Mein Kampf*). The conspiracy claims gained renewed traction in 2011 after the publication of Renaud Camus's book of the same name, but they can be traced back to the late nineteenth century. See Southern Poverty Law Center, "The Racist 'Great Replacement.'"

that does not seem to have been broken by the quickly subsiding protests.[6] Instead, Muslims and other racialized communities are under growing surveillance, justified by a preemptive suspicion of antisemitism, which is increasingly equated with anti-Zionism (rather than being connected to the rise in white supremacist movements, the leaders of one of them, the so-called Reichsbürger (*Reich* Citizens), are currently on trial for planning a coup against the German government).[7] Communities of color are thus again cast as the biggest threat, as antagonistic to the nation, more than ever inviting the conclusion that their expulsion would reestablish an imaginary national unity. Whereas Chancellor Angela Merkel declared "We can do it!" about admitting refugees from Syria in 2015, her successor as leader of the Christian Democrat Union, Friedrich Merz, proclaimed in 2023 that "Germany cannot accept more refugees. We already have enough antisemitic young men in the country." Merz is thus both framing antisemitism as an issue of (Muslim) "foreigners,"

---

6. As in 2015, the German mainstream public seems more invested in celebrating itself for its performative antiracism than in actually practicing it in an impactful way. This assessment of millions of people taking to the street might seem cynical—and I was more generous in describing the 2015 demonstrations—but after the nth iteration of the same pattern without any meaningful changes, I feel justified in assuming that these demonstrations primarily work as a ritual that relieves mainstream Germans from any responsibility for the ongoing racist violence. The earlier mass protests were in part motivated by the rapid rise of the racist Pegida (Patriotische Europäer gegen die Islamisierung des Abendlandes or Patriotic Europeans Against the Islamization of the Occident—another reference to the "great replacement") movement, which held its own anti-immigrant and anti-Muslim mass demonstrations every Monday in 2014 and 2015, initially in the East German city of Dresden but later in other cities as well. As discussed later in this book, the protesters against Pegida perceived themselves as representing the moderate German majority, in opposition to a fringe of East Germans who had lost out in the transition to capitalism. In contrast to this, several studies show that the average Pegida supporter belonged to the same class as the counterprotesters, with above-average education and income and a self-identification as "center" or "moderate right." See Dostal, "Pegida Movement." We see a similar constellation now with protesters claiming to represent a German majority that has no sympathy for the fringe racism of the AfD, while the latter remains more popular than the center-left Social Democrats of Chancellor Olaf Scholz, coming in second in polls after the center-right Christian Democrats. See Wahlrecht.de, "Sonntagsfrage Bundestagswahl."

7. See Connolly, "Alleged Far-Right Plotters."

external to the German nation, and redefining racism and Islamophobia as anti-antisemitism.[8]

As in 2015, this threatens to undo the few moves toward more representation for the 29 percent of Germans with "migrant roots,"[9] who remain, in the majority's view at least, potentially un/German—and certainly so if they are not white or (culturally) Christian.[10] In short, my concern that the issues I addressed ten years ago would have lost relevance now appears to have been misplaced optimism. That said, I was writing from an explicitly 2015 perspective, occasionally referencing current events to a German audience who were intimately familiar with the issues I was talking about, because we were going through them collectively (albeit having very different readings of them). This caused some challenges for the translation, as this familiarity cannot be assumed for an English-language public, and we tried to address this by providing explanations and updates where necessary; overall, however, we kept the perspective as it was, so the "now" of the narrative remains 2015.

I used as a starting point the dramatic developments around the so-called European refugee crisis, which brought almost one million people, largely young men from Iraq and Syria, to Germany. I argue that the German reaction—a shift from a professed self-congratulatory "culture of welcome" to an escalating hostility, expressed in tightened asylum and immigration laws, hundreds of arson attacks on refugee centers, a mainstreaming of ethnonationalist positions formerly considered extreme, and the steep rise of a

---

8. Chancellor Merkel's controversial 2015 decision to admit close to a million Syrian refugees to Germany, rather than letting European border nations handle the influx as European Union (EU) law proscribes, is often referenced through her statement "Wir schaffen das!" (We can do it!). See Karnitschnig, "Merkel's Three Little Words"; Maksan and Serrao, "Friedrich Merz."
9. The German Federal Statistics Office defines the category of Germans with a "migrant background" (*Migrationshintergrund*) as all those who have been naturalized or have at least one parent who is a noncitizen, has been naturalized, received citizenship through adoption, or is a (*Spät*)*Aussiedler* (i.e., an "ethnic German" from Eastern Europe). See Statistisches Bundesamt, "Pressemitteilung No. 158."
10. For a critique of the concept as useless for capturing racism while contributing to the perception of this group as "foreign," see Will, "Migrationshintergrund."

new xenophobic, anti-European party, the AfD (yes, that same one)—was entirely predictable. While the media, politicians, and the public appeared utterly surprised by how things played out, they should not have been, since this had happened before, and more than once. The reaction was less that of a population overburdened by a sudden externally caused crisis than it was part of a longer pattern of creating a threatening Other in order to stabilize a changing national identity. This cycle of crises is not about integrating or fending off the foreign but about creating it, often through the mobilization of long-standing racialized tropes around gender and sexuality. That these tropes can be mobilized again and again is in large part due to a refusal to see the common pattern, treating each incidence as unprecedented and driven by unforeseeable outside causes.

We can trace this at least as far back as the "refugee crisis" of 1919, then attributed to the mass arrival of young Jewish men fleeing violence and persecution in eastern Europe but producing astonishingly similar reactions in the young Weimar Republic. The pattern repeated with the 1989 arrival of Roma refugees—also fleeing violence and persecution in Eastern Europe—into the just reuniting Germany and again with the 2015 arrival of Muslim refugees fleeing violence and persecution in the Middle East. In all cases, public resentment focused on the danger the refugees posed to German women, German culture, and the nation's economic stability (usually in that order). In all instances, the resentment led to lethal violence, followed by tightened migration laws. And in all cases, the refugees (and the larger communities they belonged to) were held responsible for crises around Germany's shifting national identity that began long before their arrival: the transition of a war-torn nation to democracy in 1919, the unification of formerly socialist East and capitalist West Germany in 1989, and in the last case the crisis following debates around Germany as a postmigrant society, that is, a society that accepts the reality of migration and its impact on what it means to be German.[11]

---

11. After tense debates, Germany introduced its first law regulating migration in 2004; until then, migration was legally treated as an exception—this despite the nation having invited large-scale immigration through the so-called guest worker agreements beginning in 1955. However, these labor migrants and their descendants were expected to "return." See Bade, *Deutsche im Ausland*.

While I focus on German developments, they in many ways can serve as a stand-in for the larger European unification process and the creation of a unified narrative of not only the continent's future but also its history. In order to break the cycle of denial, we need to understand the roots of this willful racial amnesia and come to a new, inclusive understanding of Europeanness. This also requires a new, inclusive understanding of the continent's past, however, rather than the ongoing aggressive repression of alternative memory discourses, especially those of marginalized communities. The uneven ways in which fascism, socialism, and colonialism are remembered as shaping Europe's past and present are reflected in the continent's ongoing inability to conceive of itself as multiethnic and multireligious, something that would require acknowledging as European the collective memories of those who remain Europe's Others. To achieve this, we have to understand the complex relationship between (our narratives of) the past, present, and future, which is far from linear and static. This is why I am referring to contemporary Germany as post/socialist, post/fascist, and post/colonial: the slash indicates the unstable and shifting temporal (and spatial) framework these three categories create for our current moment, neither still in nor fully out of socialism, fascism, and colonialism.

In *Un/German*, I apply a different lens to these constellations, one that makes visible their intersections and complex effects on contemporary German identity as well as on post–1989 narrations of its past. I do so by focusing on material manifestations of public memory—museums, monuments, exhibits, archives—and the controversies around them. This, I argue, shows how and why racialized Germans continue to be framed as un/German. Simultaneously within and outside of the national community, they are made to embody the inherent instability of "Germanness" and therefore their periodic expulsion through seemingly sudden and unconnected crises, which nonetheless follow the same pattern, creates the illusion of regained national stability—at least until the next crisis.

Public spaces, both in their material and virtual forms, are central sites of the reproduction of dominant structures and of the contestation of collective memories. Institutionalized memory makes visible which history has become part of "common knowledge" and which perspectives remain ignored. Alternative memory spaces in turn are usually temporary and ephemeral rather than institutionalized and often manifest as disturbances of dominant discourses. I focus on such disturbances of public rituals by racialized communities, bringing to the fore unresolved tensions around European- and Germanness. It is in these disturbances, I suggest, that we find promising seeds for a different, more inclusive narrative, one that lets go of the single story of enlightened European superiority, a story that is inextricably tied to a global regime that continues to destroy lives on a daily basis.

The complicated and complex production of hegemonic memory is particularly evident in post–World War II (West) Germany. The German example is quite unique in representing the attempt to produce a national memory that claims to be based not only on a common history, shared values, the overcoming of external persecution, and the fight for liberty and unity but also on the memory of Germans as perpetrators of genocide. This narrative was always controversial and met with demands to return to a more conventional, heroic form of national memory, such as by strictly separating Nazis and "regular Germans"—and, as I show, by discursively transferring the origins of fascism steadily toward the Orient/East. This happened first in the early 1980s through their attribution to the Stalinist Soviet Union, then in the early 1990s, after the end of the Cold War, through the rise of theories of totalitarianism and claims of the emergence of "new Hitlers" located at sites of NATO interventions in Iraq and Serbia, and finally through the trope of Islamofascism, which claims an ideological affinity if not a symmetry between National Socialism and Islamism.

The postunification claim of the incompatibility of Germanness and Islam is thus less seen as a continuation of the exclusion of racialized religious minorities than as a retroactive affirmation that Germanness really was always incompatible with antisemitism. This is currently playing out in the escalating debate around Muslim antisemitism, often presented as a reaction to the October 7, 2023 Hamas attack on Israel. However, as I trace in Part 3 of *Un/German*, the trope goes back to the earliest years of the united Germany and is arguably used to affirm postunification normalization not by erasing the Holocaust from national memory but by safely containing it in the increasingly distant past, ultimately as un/German as those who have not yet learned their lesson. Its root causes are thoroughly overcome by a new Germany, one ready to join, if not lead, its former enemies in the EU. The nation is only held back by its Muslim minority, which is framed as repeating Germany's historical antisemitism and thus needing to be educated and controlled by "real" Germans, who have overcome this history. This in turn aligns Germany further with its European neighbors facing similar issues with their Muslim populations. That the categorization of German Muslims as collectively backward, violent, intolerant, and thus not really German is so readily accepted, as is a quasi-natural link between Islam and antisemitism, has as much to do with repressed colonial histories as with the insufficient processing of European antisemitism—and with the end of state socialism, which also meant the end of the social market model in western Europe and the successive scapegoating of largely working-class Muslim communities.[12] The move negates how "historic" European antisemitism and contemporary Islamophobia are linked through the racialization of religion. The latter runs through Europe's history and certainly did not end in 1945 but is in fact experiencing a resurgence.

The aggressive identification of anti-Zionism with antisemitism allows the latter to be externalized, while statistics continue to show that the vast majority of antisemitic crimes are committed by the extreme right. This is the same faction that is busy planning to remigrate "unintegrated" Germans and replace the democratic system with a dictatorship, and the one responsible for the 2019 attack on a synagogue in the East German city of Halle that killed two people and the 2020 murder of nine people of Kurdish, Turkish,

---

12. Muslims form the majority of western Europe's racialized underclass, whether they or their ancestors were labor migrants to Germany, the Netherlands, or Scandinavia, (post)colonial migrants to France, Belgium, or Italy, or migrated from their eastern European ancestral homes in Bosnia, Albania, or Kosovo (in eastern Europe, this underclass is formed by Roma). See Horvath "Report Details anti-Roma Discrimination" and Connor and König, "Explaining the Muslim Employment Gap."

Afghan, and Romani descent in the West German city of Hanau.[13] And these are just the latest in a long line of often lethal racist attacks that momentarily shock the public but are erased from the collective memory with disturbing regularity and ease. One of the questions I explore is why the regularity of this violence never amounts to a national threat. I conclude that one answer lies in the perception of the victims as un/German, that is, not only "not really" German but actually opposed to "Germanness," a threat to the nation itself, purely through their existence. They are perceived as such not only by those who murder them but also by large parts of the public, the media, and the police—a pattern that was already obvious in the six-year killing spree by the so-called National Socialist Underground, a racist terror group responsible for murdering ten people and injuring forty-three.[14]

The German debate on Muslim antisemitism demonstrates one of the lasting effects of European colonialism and the negative consequences of excluding it from the collective memory. Paradoxically, the insistence on the uniqueness of the Holocaust, rather than using comparison to show this uniqueness, has frequently equated comparison with relativization, resulting in a prolonged resistance toward addressing Germany's colonial crimes, including the genocide of Nama and Herero in today's Namibia, and toward recognizing the

---

13. See ZDF Magazin *Royale*, "Davor, währenddessen, danach"; MDR Sachsen-Anhalt, "Die wichtigsten Fragen." Both terrorists were part of white supremacist online networks and announced/livestreamed their murders on social media (the Halle shooter stated that his attack on the synagogue was inspired by the Christchurch attack on two mosques that killed fifty-one). Nonetheless, they were largely portrayed as "lone wolves." This too is a long-standing pattern in the reporting on white supremacist terrorism.

14. Responding to the deep involvement of police and intelligence services in right-wing networks that came to light in the National Socialist Underground trial, the German domestic intelligence service published two studies (in 2020 and 2022) sharing the results of all investigations of members of the security forces for engaging in unconstitutional extreme-right acts (these forces include the police, customs, military, and domestic intelligence services). See Bundesamt für Verfassungsschutz, "Rechtsextremisten." Relatives of the people murdered in Hanau have long pointed to the multiple and ongoing failings in police responses to the shooting. See ZDF Magazin *Royale*, "Davor, währenddessen, danach."

Porajmos, the Nazi genocide of Roma and Sinti.[15] These exclusions produce an inability to constructively deal with contemporary conflicts that are based on diverging memory discourses. In dominant German debates, the anti-Zionist stance of many people of color and especially Muslims is understood exclusively in the context of the inner-European antisemitic tradition. But for contemporary racialized minorities in Europe, colonial racism and its aftereffects, in both the formerly colonized territories and the metropole, are key to understanding their ongoing marginalization; this is also a central framework through which they perceive conflicts such as the one in Israel/Palestine.[16] The rejection of this perception and the insistence on an internalist European concept of history, from which colonialism remains permanently excluded, enhances the resulting tensions instead of dissolving them.

The unified Germany's memory discourse excludes its citizens of color but places the nation back in the larger European narrative of defenders of democracy against external totalitarian forces: present-day Germany fights the rise of the new Islamofascists, and the history of East Germany is deployed as a narrative representing Germans as victims of an ultimately un-European totalitarianism in the form of Stalinism. This facilitates the integration of the united Germany into the emerging post–Cold War European memory, in which the shared experience of occupation by totalitarian powers, Nazi Germany and the USSR, is central. This narrative was formalized in a Europe-wide

---

15. The majority of Roma communities entered Europe from northwest India more than five hundred years ago. The term *Roma*, or *Romani*, serves both as an umbrella for all communities in Europe and as a distinction between the majority living in eastern Europe and smaller groups, such as the Sinti, present in Germany since the fifteenth century, or the French Manoush. Roma have historically been subjected to slavery, segregation, and pogroms across Europe and continue to experience extreme structural racism. See European Network Against Racism and European Roma Information Office, *Debunking Myth*; Horvath, "Report Details Anti-Roma Discrimination." For a discussion of German colonialism and its silencing, see El-Tayeb, *Schwarze Deutsche*.

16. Berlin is home to Europe's largest Palestinian community, largely concentrated in the working-class Neukölln neighborhood, which has been a constant target of media-induced panics around the Muslim underclass since it became a site of gentrification in the early 2000s. See Sharma, "Complete Censorship."

day of remembrance for the victims of totalitarianism, celebrated on August 23, the anniversary of the Hitler-Stalin pact. This both creates an overarching narrative for the whole continent and frames its West as a democratic victim of and liberator from Eastern totalitarian aggression (while failing to address the widespread collaboration with the Nazi occupiers in nations like France or the Netherlands, rooted in an antisemitism that remains unprocessed and projected onto the nations' current Muslim minorities).

Meanwhile, the victimization and occupation of colonized peoples by exactly these democratic European nations remains ignored, even though the resulting wars of liberation fundamentally shaped the continent's postwar history. Western Europe's history of colonial violence—and its current leading role in protecting its neocolonial economic dominance at the price of the lives of thousands at Europe's borders—remains invisible through the methodological lens of totalitarianism theories. The elephant in the room is structural racism; not only the United States but also Europe have shown that democracy and racial segregation are compatible: plans for a united Europe in the 1950s and '60s still included the continent's colonies, which were considered part of Europe in terms of free movement of goods but not of the colonized, who were certainly not conceived as equals to the citizens of the metropole.[17] In short, race remains the blind spot in theorizations of contemporary Europe. The failure to confront the colonial legacy—and it should be understood that all of Europe profited from colonialism—is made possible by a dominant ideology of Christianized secular colorblindness that claims race and racism are irrelevant and foreign to the continent. As a result, racialized communities are constantly reconfigured as external to a Europe that was homogeneously white until the 1950s, that is, the beginning of large-scale postcolonial and labor migration. This claim erases centuries of antisemitism that configured Jews as a fundamentally un-European, racialized population (and arguably the age of colonialism, the so-called age of discovery, started with the Reconquista, the expulsion of Muslims and Jews from Spain physically, which led to their ideological expulsion from Europeanness). It also completely negates that

---

17. See Hansen and Jönsson, "EU Migration Policy."

Roma and Sinti, the quintessential European minority of color, have been present in every European nation for over five hundred years, as they continue to face exclusion, mob and state violence, and structural racism across the continent. This includes their treatment in Germany, as I discuss in Part 2, despite the Porajmos, the Nazi genocide of over half a million Roma and Sinti, which is largely absent from German, and European, memory discourses.

The narrative of Europe's whiteness is convincing not because it is true but because it builds on a larger hegemonic story: that of Europe as the origin and natural home of human rights, democracy, and equality. In the last few years, the governments of the two most powerful nations within the EU, Germany and France, have both made plans to erase the word *race* from their constitutions (where it appears as a protected category).[18] This is meant to acknowledge that race is not a biological reality and arguably also to express the widely held belief that race as a social construct or political concept is of no relevance in continental Europe. Part 1 of *Un/German* deconstructs and contextualizes this narrative and its whitewashing of colonialism as well as of neocolonial economic violence, which is a major cause of the so-called refugee crisis. In dominant discourse, this crisis is associated with the year 2015, when it affected Europe, but in truth it began long before that and is still ongoing. It is mind-blowing that since 2014 between 22,000 and 30,000 humans have died preventable deaths in the Mediterranean and even more mind-blowing that this is not only thoroughly normalized in European discourse but is in fact enforced and escalated by EU policies.[19] Anyone imagining that this has nothing to do with race, with the fact that the majority of the dead are African or Middle Eastern and Muslim, should have been disabused of this notion by European reactions to the war in Ukraine.

The reactions to Vladimir Putin's invasion of Ukraine in February 2022 emphasized the exceptionality of the event, its disruptiveness and potentially massive global implications. World War II was a frequent reference point. Not since then, the understanding seems

---

18. See Witting, "Germany's Heated Debate"; Saget, "'Race' Out."
19. See Missing Migrants Project, "Migration."

to be, has Europe seen anything like it. In the Western press in particular, Ukrainian president Volodymyr Zelensky was frequently compared to Winston Churchill as the face and voice of the democratic powers resisting the onslaught of a merciless, totalitarian machine. In this sense, the reception of the war fits into the larger narrative analyzed in *Un/German*, a narrative that frames post–Cold War conflicts through the lens of World War II, with a now united Europe that includes Germany standing against new fascisms that always originate outside the continent's borders. The war also initiated immediate massive refugee movements from Ukraine toward the West. The reaction here, however, was strikingly different from the treatment of Jewish, Roma, and Muslim refugees mentioned earlier.

A closer look at Western media representations of those fleeing gives us an indication of why this was: Ukrainians were described as "people who look like us," "prosperous, middle-class people," "blond and blue-eyed," "[people who] look like any European family that you would live next door to," "not from developing countries," "Europeans leaving in cars that look like ours to save their lives."[20] White journalists could not seem to suppress their horror at people who looked like them, civilized Europeans, being subjected to a kind of suffering that only seems acceptable when experienced by Black and Brown peoples, for whom chaos and violence are apparently understood to be a quasi-natural form of being. The comments made two things very clear: Europeanness is still identified with whiteness and Christianity, and the "us" that the statements evoke is equally so. Those who are not white, Christian, or European are expected to share this perspective, the compassion for white refugees and the admiration for the heroic armed resistance of Ukrainians. Expressions of support, through demonstrations, blue and yellow flags on federal, state, and private buildings, and "Stop the war" slogans on buses and soccer stadium banners, were presented as apolitical, uncontroversial humanitarian gestures that any decent person would stand behind. The contrast with the

---

20. See Al Jazeera Staff, "Double Standards."

criminalization of calls for a ceasefire in Gaza could not be starker.[21] The disparity between which lives are considered mournable and worthy of protection and which are not is nothing new. The difference in the case of Ukraine was that here the value of whiteness was the explicit part, rather than the cheapness of non-white lives.

The German minister of the interior spoke for many when she declared, "This is a completely different situation than 2015. These are war refugees and Europe for the first time speaks with one voice. That also means that the borders have to be open."[22] Accordingly, the EU invoked a law passed after the failure to respond to the genocide in

---

21. The list of banned demonstrations, canceled events, and fired artists and academics is by now too long for them to be listed individually; for summaries, see Admoni et al., "Freedom"; Gessen, "In the Shadow." Among the canceled events was one that I was scheduled to participate in, titled "We Still Need to Talk—Towards a Relational Culture of Remembrance." Co-organized by Michael Rothberg and Candice Breitz, it was meant to continue conversations on German memory discourses around colonialism and the Holocaust but was canceled at the last minute by its sponsor, the Federal Agency for Civic Education, since "in view of the present political situation in Israel and the Gaza Strip, the necessary basic and security conditions are currently not given for a constructive debate within the framework of the planned symposium, which would be gainful for the discourse on cultures of remembrance in the German context" (according to the cancellation email to participants). One must ask when the right time would be for such a constructive debate, if not now. See Breitz and Rothberg, "We Still Need to Talk." However, overshadowed by the staggering bans and cancellations—which, bizarrely, disproportionally affect anti-Zionist Jews—is the devastating effect that these policies have on German communities of color, with multiple projects that address their ongoing marginalization losing their funding. See Hauenstein, "Germany Is Known"; Bax, "Neuer Radikalenerlass befürchtet." Schools, particularly in the largely Muslim Berlin neighborhood of Neukölln, have long been sites of racist panics around Muslim youths and have recently seen keffiyeh bans and the use of the text "Mythos Israel," which denies the Nakba, the violent expulsion of 750,000 Palestinians in 1947–49 (see "Mythos#Israel1948," Masiyot, accessed July 12, 2024, https://www.masiyot.de/mythos-israel1948). These measures that frame simply being of Palestinian descent as antisemitic show the inability of German society to tolerate its own growing diversity. See Sharma, "Complete Censorship." This also does not originate in the Hamas attack on Israel. The German government had already adopted the International Holocaust Remembrance Alliance's definition of *antisemitism*, criminalized support for the Boycott, Divest, Sanctions movement, and banned the annual march in commemoration of the Nakba as of 2018. Jegic, "Germany's Relentless Campaign."

22. Tagesschau, "Bericht aus Berlin."

Bosnia between 1992 and 1995 meant to unbureaucratically admit huge numbers of refugees.[23] The quick and unified EU reaction proves that it is logistically and politically possible to accommodate a huge and fast-growing number of refugees without disruptions, without closing the borders, without mass protests or hundreds of arson attacks on refugee centers—as long as the refugees do not challenge the existing racial order, which needs to keep Europe white and Christian, if not in reality than at least in ideology. There seemed to be widespread agreement that "we cannot take care of the whole world, but we need to take care of our own." And people of color are not part of that community of one's own—notwithstanding colonial narratives that claimed more connections between French people and Algerians than French people and Ukrainians, and notwithstanding that it is no farther from Tunis to Rome than from Kyiv to Warsaw.

This sends a clear message to those refugees whose fate Europe does not feel responsible for, even though it would often have every reason to: there is nothing you can do to receive the same treatment. While many Europeans rushed to the Ukrainian border to help transport people to Poland and Germany, they would have committed a criminal offense had they picked up someone fleeing from Afghanistan instead.[24] This also sends a clear message to racialized Europeans: you will never really belong, will always be less European, and are not one of us; no matter how long you and your ancestors have been here, your presence is preliminary and certainly does not give you the right to treat people who look like you preferentially when crisis strikes. That right belongs to real Europeans. This distinction has life and death consequences at Europe's borders: the evocation of shared

---

23. See European Union, "Council Directive 2001/55/EC." That the law was not used to admit refugees from Syria, Iraq, and Afghanistan not only meant that many were deported or continue to languish in camps at Europe's borders but also that those who were admitted faced numerous restrictions regarding education, employment, and housing that did not apply to Ukrainians, which then allows for a narrative contrasting the latter's successful integration with the former's failure, attributing this to their "cultural differences."

24. See Amnesty International, "Solidarity on Trial." In addition, while allowing in Ukrainian refugees (as long as they weren't Roma or Black), Poland, Romania, and Hungary continued their illegal pushbacks of asylum seekers from Syria, Iraq, and Afghanistan. See Trilling, "Dark Things."

values that allows for the accommodation of millions of Ukrainian refugees because they are white, Christian, and "civilized" also confirms the incompatibility of hundreds of thousands of Muslim refugees—or even that of a few thousand African, South Asian, and Middle Eastern students fleeing Ukraine. Without the immediate, tireless efforts of Black organizations, which built an extensive support network within days, many people of color fleeing Ukraine would not have made it safely to Europe (or would have been deported right away).[25]

Much has been made of the Russian attack as a wake-up call, forcing Europe and in particular its economic and political powerhouse, Germany, away from appeasement and toward the will to defend democracy with force if necessary.[26] Rather than a wake-up call, I see this as another instance of the dynamic outlined in *Un/German*, one that in all likelihood will be further enshrined: in order to insulate itself from the global consequences of its actions, Europe has been escalating its militarization, its defense spending had been growing faster than anywhere else before the Ukraine war.[27] After the war began, Germany doubled its military budget, which was already the seventh largest globally, and continues to do so, pointing to rising tensions in the Middle East (and to the prospect of a second Trump term making the United States an unreliable NATO partner). It is also one of the leading weapons exporters globally, and as stock prices of defense companies soar while investments in renewable energy continue to lag, there is a growing disparity between the nation's image as leading in sustainability and its actual economic and political practice.[28] The war also stabilized the position of the authoritarian and virulently anti-immigrant regimes of Hungary and Poland within the EU due to their growing role in fortifying Europe's eastern borders through illegal pushbacks, similar to Frontex's strategy in the Mediterranean. Meanwhile, the continent continues to contribute to people's reasons for flight

---

25. The collaboration led to the founding of the Tubman Network, which remains active. See their website, https://tubman-network.org.
26. See Barkin, "Europe's Sleeping Giant."
27. See Hasselbach, "Europe."
28. See Kranz, "Russia's War."

through military interventions, support of authoritarian regimes, and exploitative economic relations. NATO has left Afghanistan in chaos, and the European Commission has blocked even a temporary suspension of COVID-19 vaccine patents, while the EU is cutting deals with nations like Turkey, Morocco, Tunisia, and Lebanon, who are declared safe and paid millions to prevent migrants moving onwards to Europe, human rights violations notwithstanding (these are, by the way, the same nations that are the site of the right's fantasy of remigrating un/Germans). Europe needs to address and overcome its pathological investment in whiteness, to confront the violence inherent in it, rather than continuing to act it out. It's not difficult to imagine how our common future will play out unless there is a drastic shift away from a shared imaginary whiteness as the ticket to survival and toward European countries taking responsibility for our shared histories.

For Germany in particular, truly claiming responsibility for its genocidal past would require it to explore its roots and its afterlife in the core, not the margins, of German national identity, rather than continuing to project it outwards. Central to the trope of (German) Muslims as Hitler's heirs is not the protection of the Jewish minority but the protection of white discursive hegemony. Its aim is to refute attempts to take this Christian/Christian-socialized whiteness out of its unmarked hegemonic position, which allows it to claim objectivity while suppressing dissent. It is a means for the majority to maintain control of the discourse by pitting Jews against Muslims, shutting down not only criticism of Israel's policies but also the growing voices of scholars and activists analyzing these policies through the framework of settler colonialism while demanding a reckoning with Europe's colonial legacy. Claims of an inherent antisemitism in postcolonial studies, which are growing louder in European academia, are not rooted in analyses or data but in an attempt to keep these disciplines and their critique of European modernity out of the continent's universities.[29] The similarities to growing attacks in the United States on critical race theory (which, like postcolonial studies in Europe, functions as a catch-all term for

---

29. See Brumlik, *Post-Colonial Antisemitism*.

analytical approaches associated with "antiwhiteness") are not coincidental: both campaigns aim at undoing societal gains for racialized communities and at disqualifying analytical approaches that challenge hegemonic whiteness. And in both cases, narratives of the past are a key battleground.[30]

The desire of the white majority to not be held responsible for a structural violence that is not only past but also present is on display in Germany's unconditional support for Israel's war on Gaza. The relentless attack, with no discernible attempt to spare civilian lives, cannot in good faith be defined as a proportionate reaction to the Hamas attack of October 7, 2023, one necessary for the survival of Israel, or be justified based on that necessity. That does not mean that the narrative of an existential threat, an enemy who will not stop until all Jews are dead, until the state of Israel is wiped off the map, does not resonate with a population whose national narrative is built on having survived such an attempt at annihilation, no matter how obvious it is that the current situation is fundamentally different and that politicians like Benjamin Netanyahu cynically exploit this trauma. Understanding this, however, also does not mean that Palestinians are in any way responsible for this trauma or required to bear the brunt of it, or that one should not speak out against the inexcusable violence unleashed on them for decades. If any nation bears the responsibility of understanding this, it is Germany. The censorship, repression, and racism currently on display demonstrate an utter failure to recognize this responsibility. Acting out old patterns of violence again and again will not help end them, either in Israel, which will not have been made safer by producing a deeply traumatized, rightless, still occupied population, nor in Europe, which cannot escape the consequences of its inhumane violence by demonizing people of color within the continent and dehumanizing those outside of its borders.

My hope in writing *Un/German* was that by making visible the causes and effects of the repeating cycle of increasingly violent crises I could contribute to ending them. Ten years later, in 2024, on the eve of elections in the United States that threaten to return to

---

30. See El-Tayeb, "Undisciplined Knowledge."

power a former president who clearly stated his intention to disband democracy, and on the eve of German elections projected to bring huge wins for a party explicitly declaring racialized communities un/German, amid the rise of ethnonationalist movements globally, it is difficult to maintain hope. So I would like to end by expressing my gratitude to and admiration for the students at my university and on campuses across the United States and Europe who bravely model what it can look like to take responsibility for our entangled histories while standing in the heart of empire, building solidarity across communities, connecting struggles for freedom globally, and remaining peaceful and joyful in the face of violence and hate. Thank you for reminding us that this resistance, too, is part of the cycle, and our best hope for breaking it.

Un/German

Introduction

This book is not interested in those "objective" readers who peer down with a cheap and sour benevolence from the rickety towers of their Western civilization upon the near East and its inhabitants; who, out of sheer humanity, are struck with pity at inadequate sewage systems, and whose fear of contagion leads them to lock up poor immigrants in tenements where social problems are solved by simple epidemics. This book does not want to be read by those who would seek to deny their own fathers or forefathers if they happened to escape from such tenements. This book has not been written for readers who would blame the author for treating the subjects of his account with love, and not with that "scientific detachment" better known as indifference.

—Joseph Roth, *The Wandering Jews*

In a certain sense, this text functions as both a continuation of and a companion to my 2011 book, *European Others: Queering Ethnicity in Postnational Europe*. The earlier title examined specifically

European forms of racialization characterized in part by the conviction that structural racism does not exist in Europe: while other forms of inequality based on class, gender, or even ethnicity can be found here (albeit to a lesser degree than elsewhere), there is nothing that would amount to *racism*, because at the end of the day Europeans are "colorblind"—whether a person is white, Black, or green doesn't matter to them one whit. On the other hand, Europeans have a very particular concept of who counts as European and who does not. Here, too, color is key, with little nuance required. All it takes to determine continental belonging is distinguishing between white and non-white: if you're not white, you couldn't possibly be European. Far from attaching no significance to "race," the European self-image simply makes it impossible to call out racism. Differences between this racialized model of belonging and such "normative" racist systems as that in the United States do not make the former any less repressive or structural. Instead, the fixed notion of Europeanness as necessarily white and (culturally, secularized) Christian creates a peculiar positionality for racialized migrants, not to mention their offspring—these younger generations will never be European or, in this case, German, but will instead be categorized as "immigrants" or (to be perfectly politically correct) "citizens with a migrant background" or (if you want to be hip) NdH, which stands for *nichtdeutsche Herkunftssprache*, a mouthful that signifies a person's mother tongue is not German. The outcome is the same, comparable to freeze tag, like kids might play at a friend's birthday party: When a racialized person sets foot in the country, someone tags them and yells "Freeze!" That person and all their descendants, from there on out, are then frozen in the moment of having-just-arrived—at least in the eyes of true-blue Germans. They, whose right to belong is never questioned, meanwhile ponder when they might safely yell "Unfreeze!" to grant NdHs freedom of movement or, really, Germanness. (Spoiler alert: we haven't made it there yet.)

Invitation to a Postmigrant Kids' Birthday Party

Unlike giggling birthday party guests, those classified as "foreign" have not been caught for decades in a process of perpetual, repeated arrival; instead, they have been going about their lives, living out their own Germanness. In writing *European Others*, I was most interested in what this looks like, what it means to occupy a position that (as far as the dominant logic is concerned) cannot possibly exist, and what creative and radical means Europeans of color employ to deal with the paradox forced upon them. In *Un/German*, I look more closely at the "freeze/unfreeze" dynamic that not only traps racialized people in an endless loop with no way out but also subjects mainstream society to pathological, compulsive repetition: Time and again, society acts out the initial encounter with the foreigner (who always seems to materialize without warning) and the cycle runs its course, starting with panic, then moving on to optimism, aggression, and opposition; at first, society expresses readiness to engage, provided the foreigners yield to a few basic requirements (assimilation to German values chief among them). Before long, disappointment sets in that these humble demands have not been met, though it is unclear whether the foreigners can't meet them or simply don't want to. What *is* clear is that their inflexibility is to blame for changing German openness to antagonism.

The compulsion to repeat these patterns suggests either an endless influx of foreign masses into Germany or some real mental contortions (and the figures speak to the latter, with Muslims representing 5 percent of the German population and Germany [in 2015] coming fiftieth worldwide in terms of refugee intake relative to population). No sooner had panic about the Turkish minority quieted, with cautious debates asking if this group might actually be considered a *German* minority, than panic about Muslims arose. This was a group whose foreignness could be rediscovered anew, despite having already been met repeatedly with alarm, first as "guest workers" and then as "Turks." Integration is a pretty tall order if you are sent back to square one, compelled to prove the compatibility with

Germanness of yet another facet of your own alterity, just when you thought you could relax, when a sense of "unfreeze" filled the air and even the classic "Where are you from?" sounded more curious than combative. One might well suspect that this has less to do with a failure of those groups made out to be foreign than it does with mainstream society's refusal to relinquish the white/Christian image of Germanness, an image into which people like me will never be able to assimilate, no matter how German we are or how "post-migrant" society purports to be—or purported to be, until the latest wave of panic gripped the nation, this time unleashed by the so-called flood of refugees.

The topic of migration has been overshadowed in recent months by the "refugee crisis," which is now our own, German crisis—for others it began some time ago, but as long as it kept outside European borders, or at least south of Lampedusa, it was not of particular concern. This German refugee crisis seems to have triggered a German identity crisis that oscillates between a welcoming culture of Good People and open borders on one side, torched refugee housing and tightened asylum laws on the other. Most remarkable to me about this development was not the German soul in turmoil but the apparent amnesia the crisis and the questions of identity it elicited were met with, as though they were utterly unexpected phenomena, as though thousands of people hadn't been drowning in the Mediterranean every year for the last decade, as though the riots and hate crimes in Solingen, Mölln, or Rostock had never happened, nor the heartwarming candlelight vigils and *Mach' meinen Kumpel nicht an!* (Leave my buddy alone!) campaigns. Never mind the critical interventions of racialized and migratized groups and individuals, who have long called out the structural problems that rising numbers of refugees may amplify but have never caused, because these problems come from the heart of society, not from outside.[1] This became abundantly clear in the decade-long string of racist killings by the National Socialist Underground (NSU), along with how the public

---

1. *Migratism* describes the specific power relations produced by designating people as "migrants." Migratism is thus related, but not identical to racism, antisemitism, and Islamophobia. See Tudor, *From [al'mania] with Love*.

and officials treated the spree, from headlines dubbing the killings "kebab murders" to the destruction of evidence at the state level.

Nevertheless, racist violence is not taken seriously as a structural German (or European) problem; not recognized as terror(ism), violent acts are instead framed as instances of excess practiced by extremists and mentally disturbed lone wolves (see responses to the attempted murder of Cologne's mayor, Henriette Reker, in 2015). All this is in contrast to the *Charlie Hebdo* shooting, for example, which fit neatly into the discursive framework of "Islamist terrorism."[2] This kind of terrorism is considered both a fundamental threat to Europe and representative of Islam. The "Je suis Charlie" campaign following the attack on the French satire magazine was meant as a display of solidarity, but it was also a symbol of the collective threat to white Europe posed by Muslim terror. Conversely, there has not been a single expression of collective European responsibility for the racist terror against migrants or Europeans of color—which is not the same as collective distancing from the "xenophobic" riffraff said to be most active in the East or in the lower classes (in other words, far from those enlightened realms of the arts pages or academe). Racism as a structural problem that cannot be diagnosed as individual deviation from consensus values, but that runs through all of society, may

---

2. The social scientist Robin Schroeder describes the "core elements of scientific definitions of terrorism" as follows (Schroeder, "Rechtsextreme Anschläge"): First, an act is planned (i.e., committed with intent), thus pursuing a political goal or with the objective to effect political change. The term "political" here also means ideological and religious. . . . Second, the choice of target is based on the fact that these people—often in very broad terms—belong to a group that represents something the perpetrators reject for political reasons. Within the framework of this group, victims are usually targeted randomly. . . . Furthermore, recent discussions have concluded that victims of a terrorist attack must be civilians or "non-combatants." Third, terrorism is chiefly an act of communication, as suggested by the arbitrariness of those directly targeted, because its immediate victims are not the primary objective behind a terrorist attack. Instead, their suffering is a means to an end, a way to send an implicit or explicit message to the broader target group. Political communication achieved in this way amounts to an act of violent intimidation against the social group to which the victims of the attack belong; a demand made of the state (or states), with a threat, to alter a certain dynamic; as well as a call for political mobilization among sympathizers.

exist in the United States (so the thinking goes) but surely not in Germany.

Postmigrant and Postracist?

The problem is rooted in this line of thinking and is in fact one of the fundamental differences to the way the United States approaches migration and racism, which Europeans often perceive as excessively politically correct. Concealed behind the American approach is a difficult and unfinished process that touches every aspect of society. However popular the assertion that the United States became "postracial" when Barack Obama won the presidency in 2008, the country remains decidedly (and necessarily) in the realm of the racial—by which I do not mean its racist structures as such but rather their nameability and the ongoing conversations about what is "racial" in the US system. As Black Lives Matter and other movements have shown, this process is far from over.[3] It may even be in its infancy, though the steps taken since the 1960s *have* resulted in fundamental social change—change that remains a long way off for Germany, and not only because a majority of the population here doesn't see the need for it, which has always been the case in the United States as well.

If we view "postmigrant" and "postracial" as analogous ways of describing a condition, of claiming triumph or progress to the next stage in an ongoing process of social development and optimization, we discover that at best Germany has taken the first step toward confronting all things migrant; there can be no talk of "postmigrant." To be sure, migration has been a solid feature of German society for almost sixty years—meaning two generations—but the fervor in casting the "refugee crisis" and allegedly unprecedented deluge of "foreigners" as new phenomena indicates something else: the crisis is being used to undo the timid steps made toward

---

3. Black Lives Matter is a US American antiracist grassroots movement started by three queer Black women activists to mobilize against the routine shootings of young, unarmed Black men by police (see their website, http://blacklivesmatter.com).

migratizing society (or at least debating this possibility) since the 1980s. It's suddenly all so simple: here we have the white German helpers, who have earned their privilege and would never dream of giving it up but feel nothing but sympathy for those less fortunate, and there we have the brown (but not Black) legitimate victims of legitimate violence (usually US military force, not European economic exploitation, which typically affects the "economic migrants," regarded with far less sympathy, to the point of their representing a common enemy).

Also present, albeit currently eclipsed (at least in the popular imagination), is the counterpart to those shining lights, known as *Dunkeldeutsche* (dark Germans), in reference to the racist fringe—though their proven potential for violence still isn't perceived as a fundamental threat, or at least not one that can't be neutralized by welcome gifts for new arrivals. This works as well as it does because other dark Germans have vanished from the collective imagination: racialized people and migratized Germans are almost completely unseen in today's debates.[4] If individuals have a tale of escape in their immediate family history, they will sometimes be allowed to share their experiences of integration, but otherwise Germanness is again defined as white and (culturally) Christian. Whatever may have shifted or grown more complicated in recent years, this crisis has drawn it back into the familiar old categories.

---

4. It is symptomatic that in an article whose title translates to "Migrants and the Fall of the Wall," Daniel Bax—a white German expert on migration for the leftist daily newspaper *taz*, who undoubtedly sides with the marginalized—misjudged the founding year of Initiative Schwarze in Deutschland (Initiative for Black People in Germany; ISD) by a good decade; it was only a passing reference to the "angry descendants of migrants," anyway, and not about dialogue with the same. His gaffe is problematic because it reconfirms the prevailing belief among white leftists that the confrontation with German racism is a new phenomenon that has spilled over into the political realm from the United States, by way of the academy. The history of the founding of ISD and ADEFRA—Schwarze Frauen in Deutschland (Black Women in Germany) in the 1980s reveals a very different genealogy of antiracism in Germany, one that has gone mostly unnoticed, as it arose outside the white academic context. See Bax, "Debatte Mauerfall und Migranten" and Tsianos, "'Die deutsche Linke.'"

"Xenophobia" and Selective Racist Amnesia

The plight of today's refugees has had an alarmingly stabilizing effect on German identity. The wave of racist violence in response to the "asylum crisis" of the 1990s, the political shift to the right to accommodate "concerned citizens," the tightening of relatively generous asylum laws after they were put to the test for the first time—all that seems to have been forgotten, along with discussions about the need to name racism for what it is. Instead, *Ausländerfeindlichkeit* (xenophobia)[5] is back as the byword of the day, with a focus on the growing conflict between good Germans, who support refugees, and the xenophobic *Dunkeldeutsche* targeting them. At the same time, there is a remarkable lack of interest in the impact this conflict might have on nonmainstream Germans. The reason seems pretty clear: yet again, this group has been forgotten, as has the fact that a quotidian racism exists that was not ushered in by refugees and would continue to exist even in their absence. Racism has long affected racialized Germans because it is found at the heart of German society, not imported by "foreigners." The presence of foreigners is not a precondition for racism—racism produces them.

Broadening discussions of racism since the 1980s have also taken aim at mainstream German leftists, feminists, and queer folks. Among these progressive groups, the response to losing control over the discourse has ranged from uncertain to incensed—the debate about racism in children's books in 2013 showed how hard it still is for white Germans to accept that their positionality is neither neutral nor objective but rather subjective and limited, and that, because of their own positionality, racialized Germans have had different [other] experiences that cannot be ignored or subsumed under the dominant white point of view. Demonstrations of sympathy for refugees, on the other hand, are simpler, more uplifting:

---

5. The term *xenophobia*, which is the standard English translation for *Ausländerfeindlichkeit*, implies a fundamental fear (*phobos*) of the unfamiliar (*xenos*) underlying the hatred. Translated literally, the German term is rather more to the point and means hostility (*Feindlichkeit*) toward foreign people (*Ausländer*).—Trans.

refugees need help, which is generously provided by mainstream Germans (who understandably expect gratitude in return)—the roles of host and "guest" are unequivocal and necessarily unequal. Control over discourse and territory, which was under threat, is reestablished in the refugee debate (first by the separation between "real" war refugees and "fake" economic refugees). Refugees who are thankful—but more importantly who have no rights and are indisputably foreign, non-German—are far more pleasant to engage with than difficult, aggressive, demanding, and perennially offended migratized groups. Thus, the end of Germany's welcoming culture for this latest iteration of the foreigner is already on the horizon—as per usual, newcomers will be required to assimilate, which remains impossible because they are simultaneously expected to keep playing the part of the foreigner. When it comes to migratized people, nothing vexes the majority more than the Germanness they embody, but rather than changing this, Germany's welcoming culture does the very opposite: hidden behind the facade, the compulsive, never-ending repetition of the first encounter with the foreigner is a process I have dubbed "selective racist amnesia": the dogged dialectic of racist moral panic and the suppression of the historical presence of racialized populations.[6]

This active process of forgetting renders events and movements meaningless by classifying them as isolated phenomena without context, without cause and effect, without connection or reference point, leaving them without a spot in the collective memory. Recurrent cycles of verbal and physical racist violence can thus be ignored, as can resistance movements led by targets of that violence (from the Black community organizations ISD and ADEFRA to the refugee initiative The Voice, which has been active for twenty years), because two and two are never put together. For racism to be continuously portrayed as a response to the sudden appearance of a non-white group, any acknowledgment of the presence of people of color must be treated as if it were happening for the first time. This perpetually characterizes each encounter as constituting a state of exception and robs it of any sense of consistency: uprisings in French suburbs

---

6. See El-Tayeb, *European Others*.

sparked debates about the end of Europe but no strategic change. Instead, the next "state of exception" is met with the same astonishment as ever. We are seeing it now toward the supposed "stream of refugees," just as we have seen it in the past toward multicultural society. Yet again, the long (and long-suppressed) history of race and racism in Europe makes today's continental "multiculturalism," based on such markers of non-Europeanness as the headscarf or dark skin, appear unprecedented—a surprising and dramatic development that elicits societal adjustment at best and rejection at worst, and that can be declared a "failure" if necessary. *Multiculturalism* is thus not a descriptive term for a state of affairs (which cannot be undone by simply declaring it a failure) but a discursive strategy that manages and controls this state of affairs. The reasons for failure are of course to be found among the ever-alien representatives of minorities in the multiculti mix, as the culture of the majority tends to remain unquestioned.

Neoliberal Multiculturalism and Colonial Legacies

This brings me back to "postracial" and to aspects of the notion that are far from analogous to "postmigrant." If anything, the postmigrant is a very specific effect of the postracial. In the United States the latter term implies that, although racism has not been overcome, it is no longer systemic; that institutional discrimination against racialized groups is a thing of the past; and that a "colorblind" approach is the way to a future of equality. This means a distancing from the Jim Crow laws that remained in effect until the 1964 Civil Rights Act but also from the concerted challenges to white supremacy by the civil rights movement and the Black and Chicano Power movements that followed, which were inspired by this activism and the anticolonial liberation movements against Europe's racist domination of colonized populations. It was a domination formally tied up in a global system of exploitation that unilaterally benefited Western nations. This phase of (necessary) resistance is now considered successfully concluded; clinging to it is counterproductive or even indicative of "reverse racism," because these days we occupy the realm of colorblind liberal multiculturalism—according to the United States' postracial narrative, that is.

In Europe, on the other hand, most people figure that an American-style postwar transformation never occurred because there was no need for it. After all, there was no internal racist system of government here that needed changing. This assumption contains the belief that the long-term, fundamental consequences of colonialism (at least, those worth problematizing) only affect the colonized, not the colonizers, and that the Nazi racial state was an anomaly, not an expression of European deep structures (this is reflected in the growing popularity of totalitarianism theories that had fallen out of fashion before German reunification). Accordingly, comprehensive analyses of the global system of "racial capitalism," as Cedric Robinson and others term it, have been conducted primarily in the fields of postcolonial and critical race studies, including women-of-color feminism—which makes sense, since women of color around the world disproportionately face precarity in work and living conditions.[7]

Women-of-color feminism interprets the US ascent to global power under the auspices of neoliberal multiculturalism as part of racial capitalism and not as a phenomenon that vanquished this form of rule. Neoliberal multiculturalism promises to include previously excluded groups—provided they prove capable of inclusion. Not only are marginalized groups expected to self-police—the burden of proof that they are not pathological or dangerous lies with them—but they are also effectively played off against each other, while mainstream society adopts the role of mediator, custodian of basic rights, and uncontested arbiter of norms. The success of this strategy can be found in the exploitation of feminist arguments in favor of invading Afghanistan, as well as the pathologizing of Muslim communities in Germany as collectively homophobic, misogynistic, and antisemitic. Classifying such traits as representative means that, despite calls to "moderate Muslims" to distance themselves from extremists, exceptions continue to confirm the rule. In

---

7. See Robinson, *Black Marxism*.

fact, the two aspects of Western rule—US military power and European human rights management—have increasingly intersected since the early 1990s. At the heart of this development is the firm belief in the superiority of "Western values," which are supposedly diametrically opposed to those of the foreigner/foe. The enemy of neoliberal freedom, no longer to be found in the socialist East, is now back in the Global South, which has traditionally been seen as leagues removed from democratic ideals, if not outright antidemocratic. The same applies to the perception of those citizens whose "migrant background" is in the south, especially in the Islamic world. On both global and national stages, the crisis of (neo)liberal multiculturalism is thus blamed on population groups that are already marginalized economically and politically, while the lasting effects of (neo)colonial European rule go unexamined.

The Limits of Hegemonic Self-Critique

Continental European intellectuals have done little to examine the system of racialized capitalism and Europe's integral place in it. In fact, most have actively resisted the opening of European theoretical frameworks to the vital influences of postcolonial and critical race theories. Continental leftists have also neglected to challenge these structures effectively, or even to analyze them systematically. They remain entrenched in them, from a universalist Enlightenment humanism that casts the white European man as the paradigm of humanity to a continental Marxist theory that ignores race as a fundamental category of domination and views it instead as a particularist distraction from the universally relevant category of class—which is ironic, considering how racialized a category class is in Europe. But racism is supposedly always about something else, like fear of the future, economic insecurity, or socialist legacy, meaning an actual analysis of racism can always be put off until later. As a result, mainstream European debate has grown increasingly isolationist, stewing in its own juices, barely able to participate in a transnational dialogue in which Europe is no longer automatically granted dominance.

Civil rights movements in America forced a confrontation with societal racism, which led among other things to the establishment of Black and Ethnic Studies. Like Women's Studies and Queer Studies, these new academic disciplines, while still controversial today, represented the irreversible arrival of those previously excluded, in theory and practice, from the university and other bastions of influence and decision-making. This kind of opening never happened in Europe, Germany included, following the Holocaust and colonialism; instead, the practice of hegemonic self-critique was embraced, founded on the assumption that the European intellectual tradition offered enough of a foothold for correcting the system from the inside out, if need be. One of the issues here is that existing definitions of what is "outside" or "inside" Europe have been left unquestioned, such that criticism voiced by racialized Europeans, for instance, is perceived as coming from outside, because they have never been afforded a place within this tradition.

Rather than arriving at a pluralist model, Germany and Europe as a whole reproduced what Stuart Hall—writing in 1991, on the eve of the Maastricht treaty and the 500th anniversary of the "discovery" of America—called the continent's "internalist narrative": a narcissistic take on history that subordinates complex historical interactions to an insular model in which an essentialist notion of white Christian Europe is and must inevitably remain the norm.[8] In turn, only those who more or less conform to the norm may criticize it, conveniently ruling out the vast majority of postcolonial, decolonial, and intersectional approaches, which deconstruct racial capitalism and have long pegged it as a global (and thus also German) principle of dominance. The result of such isolationism is a whitewashing of theory, in part justified by asserting that the jumble of racialization and migratization in Germany is too complex to be addressed with concepts imported from the United States—as if the situation there were any less complicated. For decades, women-of-color feminism has worked with difference as an analytical category that can capture but does not aim to resolve these complexities and

---

8. Hall, "Europe's Other Self." See next chapter for a detailed discussion.

contradictions.[9] An approach like this was glaringly absent in the debate about the attacks in Cologne on New Year's Eve.[10]

---

9. Tellingly, intersectional approaches in Germany are largely associated with critical whiteness studies, a field dominated by white theorists, whereas in the United States, this work is led by scholars of critical race theory and women-of-color feminism. For more on the debate among German antiracist leftists, see Ibrahim et al., "Decolorise It!," published by members of the Netzwerk Kritische Migrations- und Grenzregimeforschung (Critical Migration and Border Regime Research Network), which rejects discussions of racialized difference as divisive identity politics. See also the critical response to this piece, primarily from people-of-color activists, who view naming different positionalities as a prerequisite for successful alliance policies (e.g., Accalmie, "Decolorize the Color Line?"). This fierce debate over the implications of such markers as "Black," but especially of "white," does a good job at outlining the different positions (and demonstrates, at least from where I stand, why a "color-blind" approach reliably reproduces existing structures of dominance).

10. Traditionally, on New Year's Eve, thousands meet in front of the Cologne central train station, next to the famous cathedral; in 2015, dozens or maybe even hundreds of drunk men targeted women in the crowd, stealing purses and phones but also sexually attacking them. A narrative quickly emerged of mass rapes committed by refugees (while the police accused "North African superpredators," or "Nafris" in police lingo). After extended investigations and a heated, often hysterical media and public debate, only one case of rape was confirmed, though there is no doubt that there was massive sexual harassment. Of those charged, one-third were refugees; the majority of the accused were Algerian and Moroccan nationals. Contrary to the obsessive investigation into the perpetrators' ethnic background, the victims were generically assumed to be white German women, which in turn allowed for the us-versus-them narrative that framed the event as a "civilizational break" and produced a plethora of racist images drawing on the large cultural arsenal of racist imagery going back to the colonial period. Public debates conflated demands for tightened consent laws and tightened immigration laws—successfully: before the attacks in Cologne, sexual harassment was not a criminal offense and rape was only considered as such if the victim resisted physically. While feminist groups had been calling for the law to change for decades, this only happened at that point, just as the deportation of migrants charged with criminal offenses (of all kinds) was made easier. This conflation confirmed what the majority already believed and affirmed its position as enforcer and disciplinarian. What did not happen was a larger debate about sexual violence in German society (white men could claim innocence and take on the role of protector merely by virtue of not being North African) or any attention to the massive sexual violence faced by female refugees. Instead, incidents like the one in Cologne seem to prove that the economic, social, and political marginalization of European communities of color is not a worthy subject of antiracism, since these communities fail to subscribe to the European project of liberal multiculturalism and are therefore not only responsible for their marginalized state but have in fact failed at Europeanness. See Weber, "German Refugee 'Crisis.'"

White Scholarship and Societal Racism

Excluding theories that advance subaltern and subversive rather than hegemonic critiques of dominance structures leads logically (if not always intentionally) to the exclusion of racialized scholars. Here is just one example to help illustrate this: In 2015, I was invited to present at a conference on the history of the concept of race in Germany, convened in preparation for an exhibit on the same topic.[11] The event felt timely, considering how much research on the topic has picked up in recent decades, though it remains on the margins of the academy. The stated objective of the conference—an interdisciplinary expert debate on the contemporary impact of racism in Germany—seemed of central sociopolitical significance given the NSU murder spree and the peak popularity of the Pegida (Patriotische Europäer gegen die Islamisierung des Abendlandes or Patriotic Europeans Against the Islamization of the Occident) movement at the time. However, my enthusiasm abruptly waned when I saw the slate of speakers, which resembled the roster for almost any other German academic gathering. Here, the fact that the invitees were almost exclusively white men seemed particularly counterproductive to the forum's stated goal and led me to issue the following response:

Dear XXX,

Thank you again for the invitation to the XXX Conference in XXX.... I was intrigued by the concept behind the conference, as described in the invitation.... For that reason, I must admit I was shocked when I received the program. First, I wish to make very clear that I am not questioning the participants' expertise in the slightest, nor do I presume to tell you how to plan your event. I must, however, be as clear in noting that one cannot have a productive session on race and racism with an almost all-white lineup. I am less concerned with who is represented than I am with who is *not* represented, namely the

---

11. See details of the exhibition, *Racism: The Invention of Human Races*, on the Deutsches Hygiene-Museum website at https://www.dhmd.de/en/exhibitions/archive/racism.

many researchers and activists from racialized groups doing important work on this topic, both in and outside of the academy. To name just a few: Peggy Piesche, Kien Nghi Ha, Maisha Eggers, Encarnación Gutiérrez Rodríguez, Nicola Lauré al-Samarai, Petra Rosenberg, Yara-Colette Lemke Muniz de Faria, Patrice Poutrus, Noa Ha, Nadja Ofuatey-Alazard . . . the list goes on. A "colorblind" approach, which ignores exclusions and hierarchies produced by racist structures, is methodically, pedagogically, and politically condemned to reproduce them. For one, racialized people remain the object of debate, rather than participating subjects—while white scholars are allowed to stay unmarked and "neutral." This happens even and especially when it is not white, but primarily marked, racialized academics and activists whose many years of work have finally forced mainstream society to confront this issue. Intersectionality—a theoretical concept developed by Black feminist writers, which is no coincidence—examines the blank spaces that emerge when theory is depositionalized and the dominant position is universalized, usually meaning the generalization of white male experience. In discussions of racism, this process should be challenged, not replicated. A productive debate must represent more than the dominant position and group. It requires a critical mass of "Others." This is particularly urgent because the exclusion of racialized academics from the debate on race, racism, colonialism, etc. is not an isolated case—far from it—and must therefore, in my opinion, be understood and addressed as systemic and systematic (which has been happening for some time on the part of those excluded, unfortunately without broader impact thus far. Please see https://blackstudiesgermany.files.wordpress.com/2015/02/communitystatement_blackstudiesbremen_dt_unterz815.pdf).

My intention is not to lecture or criticize anyone. It is precisely that kind of role I am not interested in assuming, but rather, I had hoped for a productive discussion. Based on my experience with similar events and similar speakers, that sadly seems an impossibility (from my perspective as a racialized scholar, a perspective that should be central in this context). I find this all extremely regrettable, particularly given how important I think the planned exhibition could be, as I've said. If racialized groups are already marginalized in the planning process, however, I have a hard time imagining how it could be possible to represent the positionality of these groups in the exhibition itself and thus make it relevant for a non-white/Christian audience. For this reason, I must unfortunately withdraw my participation.

I received a gracious response explaining that the conference was about an academic, not a political, reappraisal of the concept of race and that otherwise of course representatives of affected groups would have been invited.[12] The implied assumption that racialized people are incapable of producing analysis and can only register "concern" is actually less problematic here than the associated belief that white, heteronormative scholarship isn't political and subjective. Allow me to reiterate that this conference was not hosted by especially ignorant white people; the approach to and reasoning behind excluding racialized scholars—because this was an active process of exclusion, not an instance of passive neglect—are symptomatic of how scholarship treats (the history of) race and racism in Germany: what is missing here is a critique that recognizes that academic research is not always neutral and descriptive but has the power to define discourse. When it comes to their own positionality, white racialized scholars are incapable of self-criticism, even when "race" is the stated focus.

A Postmigrant Germany?

And so the unproductive monologue continues. People of color are occasionally invited, but this can never turn into real dialogue, as there is no shared base of knowledge.[13] Seminal works of contemporary research on racism—from Sylvia Wynter, Grace Hong, Lisa Lowe, Rod Ferguson, and so many others, reaching back to W. E. B. Du Bois, Eric Williams, Cedric Robinson, and Aimé Césaire—have yet to be translated into German. These thinkers' contributions must be incorporated into political and academic debates if there is any hope for "postmigrant" to not reinforce existing power structures as "postracial" already does. Instead, the work

---

12. The list of invitees was not expanded, nor did the billed debate on the criticism I had voiced take place.

13. This is comparable to what, decades ago, the American writer Katha Pollitt dubbed the "Smurfette principle": the (still widespread) practice in film and television of including a single woman in an otherwise all-male group, meaning she only interacts with men, not with other women. See Pollitt, "Hers; The Smurfette Principle" and Sarkeesian, "Tropes vs. Women."

of racialized scholars and activists, in and outside Germany, is often regarded as raw material to be whipped into shape by mainstream Germans. The faltering, overdue, and reluctant confrontation with racism (and research on it) that we are seeing today thus presents itself as voluntary and novel, while the actual engines behind it are barred entry: the hegemony of internalist history relies on stifling alternative worldviews, as these call into question the painstakingly normalized boundaries between Inside and Outside. And within this order, racialized groups always represent the Outside. Despite any seeming—or real—progress made, the continued inability, or rather unwillingness, to face up to the glaring whiteness underpinning Germany's self-image has terrible consequences for migrants and migratized communities, who are routinely ignored, marginalized, and cast as a threat to the very nation they call home. To move past the rhetorical plane, a postmigrant state must break this cycle by ending its dependence on migratization as representation of Otherness. The only way for a change that radical to occur, as necessary as it is, is for the long-established German identity to undergo real scrutiny.

In this work, I attempt to do just that by examining the identity that emerged in unified Germany, beginning right before the fall of the Wall and closing in the present moment of a *potentially* postmigrant society. After four decades of willful postwar normality, Germany was momentarily rattled by the collapse of the Soviet Union and its own reunification, and normalcy had to be reconstructed under altered global conditions. During this transitional period, the skeleton supporting the construct of normality became visible, though only briefly, before a new spatiotemporal model of European superiority covered it back up. This is where I start by outlining how Europe moved from an antagonistic East-West divide to a model of unified continental identity and collective memory. I focus on Germany's internal process of national reunification as well as its role in unifying Europe, assuming that one must begin by examining other states of posteriority relevant to the German nation—in particular Germany as a postfascist, postsocialist, and postcolonial society. Although we should question whether the triumph over some previous state implied by "post-" actually occurred, it is also critical to look at how important to national identity these previous states are thought to be. Broadly speaking, fascism is seen as a pan-German issue; the West views itself as solidly postfascist, whereas the East (especially in the eyes of the West) has not yet truly confronted, let alone overcome, its fascist legacy—in part because it is busy coming to terms with the legacy of socialism (here too with limited success). Despite the pre-1989 Federal Republic only making sense in relation to the existence of the socialist German Democratic Republic, the Western half of the united nation is rarely described as being postsocialist. Finally, colonialism and its repercussions in Germany play hardly any role in the collective consciousness. Although it lasted for centuries and extended into recent history, Europe's colonial past occupies the outermost margins of continental (and thus global) discourse on memory, meaning it cannot be leveraged in the search for solutions to current problems.[14]

Across three parts, I trace how these three "post-" threads dictate discussions about memory and the future in the public sphere. In reproducing and adapting the history of power, the public sphere remains one of the most important stages for debate on memory. It is here that popularized versions of the dominant narrative spread, and while they may seem less rigid or less serious, they are ultimately in line with the gist of so-called expert discourse. Given its relative openness, the public sphere (in both material and virtual forms) *can* offer marginalized groups the possibility of intervention. This shows up in the discursive treatment of memory and in physical manifestations of these discourses in the shape of museums, monuments, or memorials. Institutionalized memory in the public sphere makes tangible whose histories have become part of mainstream discourse and whose perspectives remain excluded; by contrast, alternative spaces of memory are often fleeting, rarely institutionalized, and manifest in temporal disruptions of dominant discourses. The latter's reproduction of particular versions of the past is usually in the

---

14. As Andreas Huyssen has demonstrated, there has been an explosion of (global) discourses on memory since the 1980s. Paradoxically, this has not led to a greater plurality of what is remembered but to the globalization of certain topics that inevitably draw on Western narratives of the past. Huyssen, "Present Pasts."

interest of mobilizing particular discourses in the present. I illustrate this point with a series of concrete examples, from Roma activists' failed attempt to appeal to Germany's postfascist conscience by occupying the former Neuengamme concentration camp in 1989 and thus preventing their deportation to Yugoslavia, which was on the brink of civil war, to the transformation of Berlin's center, from a postsocialist space to a postcolonial yet simultaneously forward-looking showplace, through the Humboldt Forum and Museum Island. These are vertices of the discourse on German normalization that quickly gained importance in unified Germany, which also included an end to the "sense of guilt" for Nazi tyranny and genocide. Embracing a future unburdened by the past resulted in a projection of this past onto marginalized groups, from racist ostracism of Roma refugees to debates on Islamofascism and anti-German sentiment in which mainstream Germans are styled as victims of a new fascism and Islamophobia is cast as an antifascist stance.

Other attempts to draw neglected topics and groups into German history demonstrate the degree to which questions of language are ultimately questions of dominance: Who is allowed to compare what (or whom) to aspects of the Nazi regime? Who decides what to call marginalized groups? Does political correctness enrich or stifle social dialogue? We see this play out in two very different exhibitions, *Besondere Kennzeichen: Neger. Schwarze im NS-Staat* (Special features: Negro. Blacks in the Nazi state) and *Die Dritte Welt im Zweiten Weltkrieg* (*The Third World in World War II*), both controversial, though for unlike reasons. Discourses intersected, as did groups that claimed control over their own histories, which repeatedly underscored the fact that one's own history is always that of the Other(ed) as well. "Integration" into established hegemonic structures that does not entail submission to existing structures of dominance (structures necessarily based on exclusion) is therefore impossible; it is the structures themselves that must be questioned.

There is a causal connection between the declared failure of Europe's multicultural present and the continent's selective racist amnesia, the insistent externalization of racism and racialized groups from European history. This externalization enforces an unexamined normative white, (culturally) Christian identity that positions migratized groups as the greatest threat to a Europe they have in truth long been part of. Accordingly, their presence is primarily perceived in connection to crises and is quickly forgotten when it comes to constructing European identity, which remains trapped in internalist principles—the ideal state thus remains a Europe in which migratized people are either invisible (i.e., "assimilated") or absent. A fundamental reassessment of the concept of Europe, in which neither "white" nor "Christian" acts as privileged membership criteria, remains unfathomable (except in the nightmare scenarios presented by Pegida or in Bat Ye'or's *Eurabia*).[15]

Instead of endless navel-gazing punctuated by acute and haphazard crisis management, Germany (and Europe) must acknowledge its involvement in global happenings and shared responsibility for present and past crises. This is especially (but not solely) in the interest of those whose lives have never counted much in the Eurocentric hierarchy and whose daily deaths at Europe's borders number in the hundreds, yet go ignored with alarming ease, but "colonial history teaches us that violence always 'comes home.'"[16] This book explains how hegemonic memory is reproduced but also describes activist strategies that resist this process by transgressing, in the broadest sense of the word, crossing boundaries between nations, identities, genders, communities, politics, and art, and between yesterday and today—all in service of arriving at an alternative model of German identity that does not hinge on exclusion and othering but adopts the perspective of the excluded and othered in a

---

15. *Eurabia: The Euro-Arab Axis* (2005) is probably the best-known title by Gisèle Littman, who publishes as Bat Ye'or. Like her other pop-historical works, the book posits a conspiracy between the European Union and Arab states with the aim of destroying Israel and the United States by indirect means, namely Europe's Islamization. It assumes an innate antagonism between Enlightened, tolerant Judeo-Christian Europe and fanatic, antisemitic Islam (which explains the supposedly natural alliance between Islam and European fascism). Ironically, her academically discredited writings are immensely popular among European fascists (the Norwegian mass murderer Anders Breivik cited her as an inspiration), but she has also received attention in the mainstream and among Islamophobic leftists.

16. Kundnani, "Violence Comes Home."

practice of critical remembrance that opens new possibilities for the future.

A brief note on terminology: I use a number of terms throughout the book that may not be familiar to all readers, such as *racialized* or *migratized*. These will be defined as they come up.

When identifying groups, particularly those whose right to self-naming is challenged by the majority, I endeavor to use the names preferred by those groups or community activists. I recognize that these names are sometimes controversial within the communities themselves (an unavoidable consequence of the role language plays in processes of social hierarchy). I do not see this as a reason not to use them, but I acknowledge that terminologies are constantly evolving.

I use the term *Holocaust* when discussing the Nazi genocide of Jews and of Roma and Sinti but *Shoah* and *Porajmos* when differentiating between the two.

Part 1

Post/Colonial Capitalism

1

A Few Basics

Internalist History and Evolutionary Time

New German Reality: Crisis as a Permanent Condition?

> Identity is always an open, complex and unfinished game—
> always "under construction" (in Europe as much as in the
> Middle East, Africa or the Caribbean). It always moves into the
> future by a symbolic detour through the past.
> —Stuart Hall, "Europe's Other Self"

This book approaches contemporary conflicts surrounding German identity by examining their historical contextualization, or more precisely, by addressing the gaps therein. Individual and collective memory alike depend on where we find ourselves today and what we hope for ourselves tomorrow. Discourse on memory allows us to decipher the past and to put it to use. It defines what history is and what it will remain, what constitutes the present, and what kind of future might be imaginable. Historical concepts will always be mooted and mutable, at once shaped by and actively shaping our understanding of what is now. This process typically seems automatic and inevitable: the present necessarily follows a past that must lead logically to this particular present. Fractures in this process and the fact that it is a construct come to light when our understanding of the here and now changes dramatically, that is, when the dominant logic of historical development fails and no one can say what might replace it.

The collapse of the Soviet Union and reunification of Germany represent this kind of rupture in the supposed continuum of historical development: German and European visions of the future and memories of the past had to be reconfigured to account for these newly altered constellations. This posed fundamental challenges to individual and collective memory structures: the view of history that now dominated saw Germany (and Europe) as a whole whose division had been unnatural and therefore necessarily temporary. Constructing a unified neoliberal European body out of decades of East-West antagonism was a tremendous strain, as was reunified Germany's swift ascent, given that much of Europe had long seen the country's historical hunger for power as the primary antecedent of two world wars. For the next twenty-five years, however, most tensions seemed under control. Despite enduring economic disparities between East and West, the 2008 financial crisis (the brunt of which was borne by southern European Union [EU] member states), and the resulting austerity measures Germany pushed, which aggravated disagreements within the bloc, no alternative has presented itself to the continental union under the aegis of capitalism. Though old grudges may linger, the Federal Republic's position at the heart of Europe is as undisputed as its role as economic engine and political voice of the EU, which views itself as a guarantor of global stability, a more prudent, human rights–oriented partner of the United States, the remaining superpower. I argue, however, that this process has never been as smooth as it might seem, and that the opportunity for real reorganization was missed at all levels during the transition from Cold War logic to the current world order, with consequences that are manifest now and will be so even more in the future.[1]

Germany is currently rebuilding its identity, as is Europe. The fact that this reorganizing is perceived as a series of crises seems to suggest that the continent is barreling toward yet another fissure. News media and countless roundtables have fixated on how global events (the Greek debt crisis, rising refugee movement, or ISIS-directed attacks in European cities) will affect the future of the nation, though few have asked, Why now? or Why these events but not others? Differences aside, a common denominator emerges: these events are read as crises, each disturbing a system that otherwise works, more or less. Furthermore, they are seen as external forces, the root causes for which lie elsewhere. Germany appears as a hermetic island of stability, quite possibly the last remaining refuge in an otherwise chaotic world. This is a hard-won status imperiled by the nation forever having to solve problems others have created. There is an atmosphere of overextension, whether by the EU's financial crisis, the Muslim minority, or the masses of migrants who want nothing more than to come to Germany.

This putative moment of crisis has been the normal state of affairs, though, at least since reunification. Even the particulars are mostly constant, from the asylum crisis to the refugee crisis, from dual citizenship to multiculturalism, from the *Türkenproblem* to problems with Muslims, from Roma gangs to North African criminal clans, and so on and so forth. If every snapshot of reunified Germany conveys this sense of crisis, one has to wonder where these images—once their moment has passed—fit into a historical period otherwise conceived as stable and crisis-free. At the same time, it is unclear what would remain of Germany's identity, were it stripped of these supposedly external crises. Does this identity actually rely on producing crises? And what does the continual *reproduction* of crises, always presented as novel, force us to forget?

---

1. I wrote this before the 2015 "refugee crisis," since then, the consequences have become evident.

Un/German as a Category of Normalization

> As Europe consolidates and converges, so a similar exercise in boundary maintenance is in progress with respect to its Third World "Others." Currently, the two favourite discursive markers in this discourse are "refugees" and "fundamentalism."
>
> —STUART HALL, "EUROPE'S OTHER SELF"

This book explores the question of German identity by adopting a marginalized perspective, namely that of people categorized to this day as "un/German." Not only are these groups not perceived as belonging to the national collective, their very presence is assumed to endanger and destabilize it. I will examine this dynamic by connecting the major historical fissures—German reunification and the end of the Cold War—to various "minor" rifts, assuming that the latter herald another rupture challenging today's dominant understanding of the past and present: the steady and irreversible growth of a European population that is neither white nor culturally Christian, the descendants of those who traditionally represented the Other within white Christian European society. Recognizing these groups as part of the continental collective requires that Europe as a whole redefine itself and exchange its internalist understanding of the present, future, and past for a more inclusive framework. The alternative—the sustained exclusion of those who do not conform to a restrictive and ultimately racist image of Europe—is certain to have disastrous consequences, as is becoming increasingly clear.

The process of racializing German and European identity is key here and warrants explanation: *racialization* is the act of attributing collective quasi-biological and/or cultural characteristics to certain groups, allowing for their perception as not belonging, even though they may be an established part of society. These characteristics, supposedly inherent in racialized subjects, are defined as both opposed to and incompatible with the dominant identity. This renders impossible the assimilation or integration often demanded of them, unless the dominant group changes the criteria of compatibility, as it alone can do.[2] Western societies rely on this superficially paradoxical process in order to function.[3] I contend that racialization and constructing the un/German are mutually dependent; the relationship between racism and national identity is thus more intimate than often admitted. Furthermore, I argue that racism is action, not reaction. It cannot be disregarded or projected to the margins of society, nor is it merely a form of *gruppenspezifische Menschenfeindlichkeit* (group-focused enmity);[4] in its German version too, racism is a fundamental component of the global capitalist system.

The big question in this process is not how and why the "integration" of certain groups fails but rather how and why certain groups within the nation are cast as outsiders. I am concerned with the normalized or even naturalized condition of not belonging to the national collective, a feature in German history since the state's founding in the late nineteenth century. My study focuses on the last four decades, from the years directly preceding the fall of the Wall to today, and on the way in which the new normal is defined by its distinction from the old normal, now deemed aberrant. Racialization, I contend, is one constant within this process that helps stabilize German identity in its distinction from the many iterations of the un/German. Memories of Nazism and state socialism

---

2. We are therefore not talking about qualities that a marginalized group may display that objectively distinguishes it from the dominant group. Instead, this is a flexible system in which traits may gain or lose significance. The headscarf, for example, functioned as a marker of alterity in Germany as early as the 1970s. Then, it signaled the wearer's status as a "guest worker," with strong connotations of class and provincial background. Over the course of the 1980s, however, the hijab became a symbol of a hierarchical gender order diametrically opposed to Western values and supposedly characteristic of Islam. Both interpretations allowed categorical judgments about the wearer without having to consider individual motivations.

3. See Balibar and Wallerstein, *Race, Nation, Class*; Chow, *Protestant Ethnic*.

4. *Gruppenspezifische Menschenfeindlichkeit* is an analytical category, frequently used in German academia and policy, that is meant to cover all forms of discrimination against specific groups, from ableism to transphobia. Due to its extreme broadness, this category is unable to address structural differences between, for example, fatphobia and anti-Black racism and therefore contributes to the lack of analytical language around structural racism. For a definition of the term, see Küpper and Zick, "Gruppenbezogene Menschenfeindlichkeit."

play a central role, of course, but it is equally important to unpack the (in)visible effects of a colonial past and present; to identify how these effects manifest in post/colonial cities; and to understand how they have influenced the widespread perception of racialized Europeans as being excessively peripatetic, perpetual new arrivals without roots in the (European) nation-state. These questions are rarely posed, especially in Germany, which considers itself largely untouched by Europe's colonial past. However, this temporal and geographical distancing from Europe's shared history fits right into the (lack of) continental accounting for its colonial legacy. Uncovering the roots and ramifications of this process, looking into the monuments and gaps in German colonial memory, can provide insights relevant to the continent as a whole. It also opens up the bigger question of how racialized subsets of the population could possibly "integrate" into a dominant society that denies them their place in its history.[5]

An adequate analysis of racism's enduring social function requires addressing its European roots. Without this, the call for the "integration" of groups, on whose exclusion German identity still hinges, appears naive, if not downright cynical, especially when they are also assigned an involuntary role in processing the nation's past: Integrating a reunited Germany into the heart of Europe—itself undergoing the process of unification—required that recent European history be rewritten and a new version of the shared past created,

---

5. The assumption that colonialism is a thing of the distant past, without any lingering effects on former colonies (let alone on former colonizers), is utterly untenable. Take, for example, the process of European unification in the 1950s, which envisioned a postnational Europe, though not a postcolonial one. This model—in which European territories like Algeria were considered part of the European economic zone (without, however, granting equal rights to the non-European citizens of these countries)—was revised following the Treaty of Rome in response to successful anticolonial independence movements. Nevertheless, vestiges of this system remain, such as the French and Dutch Caribbean territories. In line with Europe's self-image as a bastion of human rights and progress, the EU today frames the advent of European unification in 1957 as a *precondition* for Africa's subsequent independence. Not only does this preening narrative recast the protracted, bloody battle against European colonization as some kind of service Europe provided, it denies the entrenched neocolonial structures in the relationship between the EU and Africa. See Hansen and Jönsson, "EU Migration Policy towards Africa."

one in which former adversaries of East and West might be reconciled. On the one hand, Germany functioned as a microcosm of this (extremely lopsided) reassessment of the postwar period. On the other, integrating the new German nation presented Europe with a singular conundrum, as the continent's twentieth-century history had hitherto been defined as the conflict between a democratic Europe and German aggressor. The issue was solved in part by simply recasting European Muslims in the role of the undemocratic foe that Europe is united in fighting.

Post/Fascist, Post/Socialist, and Post/Colonial Germany

> The problem is . . . the "barbarians" are already inside the gate; and face-to-face with them, European cosmopolitanism does not stand up well to the test.
> —STUART HALL, "EUROPE'S OTHER SELF"

Unified Germany's newfound position at the physical, political, and economic center of Europe meant it had to prove it had truly left behind its Nazi and antisemitic past. This assurance was partly found in public and political focus on an antisemitism supposedly endemic to the so-called third generation (of migrants), largely equated with Muslim youths. Discourse surrounding the country's education crisis, urban violence, and honor killings had already classified these young people as thuggish, intolerant, and "unintegrated." In the antisemitism debate, Jewish and Muslim Germans are cast as adversaries, while the white Christian majority assumes the role of mediator. The discursive juxtaposition of (Jewish and Christian) "Germans" on one side and "Muslims" on the other both implies a connection between Islam and antisemitism and suggests that neither belongs in Germany.

This strategy erases the connections between historical European antisemitism and contemporary Islamophobia through the racializing of religion, a tactic throughout European history that by no means ended in 1945. As ever, the vast majority of antisemitic offenses are committed by white Germans (as is "xenophobic"—i.e., racist and Islamophobic—violence).[6] It would make sense then to examine the link between antisemitism, racism, and Islamophobia, all on the rise across Europe, rather than pinning the crisis of (neo) liberal multiculturalism on a population that is already economically marginalized and politically disenfranchised.[7] The fact that this rarely happens—and that it is still so easy to categorize Muslim Germans as retrograde, violent, and intolerant, ergo not (yet) truly German, or that Islam and antisemitism seem a natural pairing in today's discourse—has as much to do with repressed colonial history as it does with an insufficient reckoning with European antisemitism and the collapse of the socialist state. The latter brought with it the end of the social market economy and gradual exclusion of Muslims as well as the sustained marginalization of East German history and culture of remembrance.

East Germans' Germanness, however, was never called into question. Meanwhile, the descendants of postwar "guest workers" are still denied that status and have for decades represented the primary target for eastern German aggression. Public discourse treats this endemic "xenophobia" (a term that perpetuates the exclusion of the targeted group from the national collective, not unlike referring to people as "second- or third-generation immigrants") as further proof of eastern Germans' backwardness after forty years of socialist dictatorship. In keeping with the internalist narrative, western Germany is upheld as the norm, a society (relatively) free of the evils plaguing the rest of the world, like racism, poverty, or homophobia—unless, of course, such ills are introduced by those grappling with the aftereffects of a backward, intolerant system (i.e., East Germans and eastern Europeans), or those whose very culture embodies this backwardness, namely people from outside Europe and their descendants. Progress—which, along with prosperity, is considered the West's natural state—is hampered by the presence of those who lag behind, those who have not fully landed in this western German reality. They live in

---

6. The Left Party in the German parliament requests quarterly police records of antisemitic crimes, with the perpetrators differentiated according to "right-wing extremist", "left-wing extremist", or "immigrant background."

7. See Shooman, "Zur Debatte" for a survey of comparative studies on the topic.

anachronistic enclaves, whether in *Dunkeldeutschland* (lit. "dark Germany," a pejorative term for eastern Germany) or in Muslim parallel societies and force mainstream society to slacken the pace of progress in order to give them a chance to catch up.

My study recognizes Germany as post/fascist, of course, but asserts its function as a post/colonial and post/socialist space as well. This framework allows us to challenge the almost reflexive acceptance of northwestern Europe as the neutral standard, against which sundry deviant Others are defined, including the socialist East and colonial subjects. I examine this constellation and its effect on contemporary German discourse on memory from a perspective that not only assumes that the post/fascist, post/socialist, and post/colonial past and present are necessary to comprehend such discourse but considers them an inextricable part of it. Using local but interconnected case studies, I illustrate the interaction of normative space-time models in this process, and rather than stick to obvious patterns, I point out unseen or suppressed historical connections. I pose the following questions: How do post/fascism, post/socialism, and post/colonialism manifest spatially in German cities? And how are spatiotemporal representations of the fascist/socialist/colonial past projected onto racialized bodies (a practice that then allows for their exclusion from the German present)?

The most effective ideologies are invisible. We do not hunt for deep structures that constitute these ideologies' internal and external logic. We assume their absence. Meaning is found on the surface: it's obvious. (Of course white people are more German than Black people. Of course Western and Islamic values are diametrically opposed.) If effective structures of dominance are so thoroughly integrated in our understanding of the world that we take them for granted, then the first order of business is to distance ourselves from this pseudo-natural situation. This text endeavors to bring deep structures to light by deconstructing their obviousness. I question why certain constellations, processes, or assertions are accepted without hesitation, even when they are oxymoronic (as in a term like "third-generation immigrant"). Individual constructs, presented as obvious or natural, are neither coincidental nor isolated; rather, they join to form a system of logic. These elements are mutually referential, meaning selective interventions alone are insufficient for producing long-term changes.

An Analysis of European Racism

> Living with, rather than simply forgetting, "difference."
> This is preferable to the endless forgetting—the historical
> amnesia—coupled with a vapid postmodern nostalgia
> which is globalisation's stock-in-trade.
> —STUART HALL, "EUROPE'S OTHER SELF"

As long as the superordinate ideology remains intact, selective interventions (candlelight vigils, "We can do it!" rhetoric[8]) will come up short in effecting structural change. What is needed instead is an analysis of racism that accounts specifically for European realities, from neocolonialism and racialized religion to the Roma as a continental, stateless minority. I will model the approach in this book and demonstrate how such analysis can build on existing antiracist activism and people-of-color theoretical practice. This includes interrogating why these existing theorizations have not found their way into academic and public debates, save when they are presented as the work of mainstream German thinkers. A comparative perspective—which challenges interrelated concepts of racism around the world—also allows us to scrutinize Europe's supposed eminence as a global ground zero, a neutral benchmark, at once singular and universal, against which all other regions are measured. This status pertains to debates on racism in particular: as Europe is home to white people, they do not need to be qualified as white there—it is obvious that European = human = white. Here at home, they were never colonial settlers, which leads to the widespread fallacy that the colonial and racist regimes established elsewhere by Europeans or their descendants had no impact on the continent itself. Critical theories of European racialization processes can poke holes in this European exceptionalism. For instance, one

---

8. Karnitschnig, "Merkel's Three Little Words."

could apply analytical approaches developed in settler colonialism research to craft urgently needed theories on antiziganism. After all, structures of dominance rarely bend to the constraints of national historiography.

Whereas the introduction to this book presented an admittedly polemical summary of my view of conditions in Germany, this chapter is dedicated to a number of theoretical concepts indispensable to my analysis. Comprising the core are Stuart Hall's definition of an "internalist" European history and Johannes Fabian's concept of "evolutionary time." I will first expand on European definitions of self and other, then return to Germany and its specific role in this constellation. Taken together, the various sections constitute an analysis of the space-time model of knowledge production that necessarily regards racialized populations as spatially and temporally out of place—out of place within the discourse that establishes norms regarding nation, gender, sexuality, and religion and that consigns these groups to a position outside Germany as well as outside modernity. This prevailing notion is especially pronounced in current debates about German Muslims and the archaic, antimodern parallel society they allegedly occupy. As I will show in the following chapters, however, it has been part of German thinking for much longer, with wider-ranging consequences.

Overlapping histories of migration, colonialism, and racism create connections between racialized groups in Europe—particularly Black, Roma, and Muslim communities—that result in shared spaces, cultures, and positionalities. Dominant discourse largely fails to recognize these connections and intersections. Instead, each group serves a set symbolic function: Muslims are cast as an internal menace, the Other in our midst that nevertheless remains alien, whereas "Africans" (which includes Black Europeans) represent the masses that aren't here yet but are already straining the borders, a demographic and racial Goliath threatening to overrun Europe's David. (These are the metaphors that have normalized the deaths of thousands of African refugees at Europe's outer limits for decades.) Roma, the racialized European minority par excellence, though afflicted by extreme violence, poverty, and marginalization, are almost absent as a legitimate presence in Europe today. At the same time,

Roma feature prominently as "Gypsies" in romanticized European folklore that bears little resemblance to a five-hundred-year history involving genocide and enslavement; such tales contribute all the more to a whitewashing of European history that depicts a fictive Judeo-Christian harmony coupled with "gypsy" romantics. The discursive separation of racialized groups is symptomatic of the negation of commonalities among communities of color (and between these communities and white Europe) in an internalist discourse that cannot accept permeable boundaries and must instead produce strictly delineated, hermetically homogeneous groups.

Europe's Internalist Crisis

> The story of European identity is often told as if it had no exterior. But this tells us more about how cultural identities are constructed—as "imagined communities," through the marking of difference with others—than it does about the actual relations of unequal exchange and uneven development through which a common European identity was forged.
> —Stuart Hall, "Europe's Other Self"

After decades of apparent stability, Europe has recently been stumbling from one crisis to the next. The EU, long regarded as a guarantor of economic stability and model for a postnational future, now routinely finds itself on the brink of collapse. No sooner was Grexit averted than Brexit gained traction, and now rumblings of withdrawal can be heard from some eastern European member states, whose eagerness to belong to the union was always considered a given. The Greek austerity crisis, which cast doubt on the survival of the euro, created the first failed state within the (western) European collective.[9] Greece's economic collapse thus provided

---

9. As Achille Mbembe has shown, the *failed state*—heavily indebted and increasingly dependent on private creditors or vulture funds yet authorized to implement austerity measures led by the International Monetary Fund and the World Bank—is becoming a regular part of the neoliberal world order, though so far

the first indication that the EU, including its northwestern core, is not shielded from growing forces of destabilization around the world. The island of prosperity is starting to crumble, which has been obvious at its edges for some time. Destitution in the eastern and southern borderlands has worsened, causing greater instability in these regions. Thousands of people, often Roma, have fled systematic discrimination, violence, and poverty in eastern Europe only to be deported back to their "safe" countries of origin.

The situation on Europe's southern border is no better. A good ten years ago, the German media was already circulating images of desperate people on overcrowded boats adrift in the Mediterranean or attempting to cross the barbed wire fence between Morocco and the Spanish enclave of Ceuta. That fence was a bulwark against the tens of thousands of West Africans trying to reach Europe by this overland route, though more and more were going by sea. This set off intense debates about a "migration crisis," whose actors were soon classified as "economic migrants" with no claim to refuge in Europe. As is standard in cycles of racialized panic and forgetting, interest in the crisis dissipated as quickly as it had emerged. In the decade since, although more than twenty thousand people have drowned in their attempt to reach Europe, their deaths have barely registered a response[10] —after all, most of these people were Africans, and Europe has a long tradition of normalizing death and disaster in Africa.[11] Survivors landed in increasingly overwhelmed border regions like Malta and Lampedusa. In the wealthy northwest of the continent, the stable core of the union, all this was largely ignored—that is, until it could be ignored no longer, as tens and then hundreds of thousands of refugees made their way here, "suddenly"

---

mostly outside the West, primarily in Africa. The government debt crises in Greece and in Puerto Rico, an unincorporated US territory, demonstrate that this new normal has reached the West now, too, established by such multilateral agreements as the (now defunct) Trans-Pacific Partnership and the Transatlantic Trade and Investment Partnership, which furthered the practice of placing multinational corporations outside the reach of state authority. See Mbembe, "Necropolitics."

10. For information on the Missing Migrants Project, run by the International Organisation for Migration, founded in 1951, see their website, http://missingmigrants.iom.int.

11. See Nederveen Pieterse, *White on Black*.

throwing Europe into crisis. Unexpectedly swept up in global misery, the continent had to respond quickly—as it so often does—to solve problems started outside its borders, whether in extremist Muslim states to the southeast, perennially underdeveloped and war-torn Africa to the south, or an aggressive, undemocratic Russia to the east. This narrative implies that all would be well in Europe if it weren't for these external pressures. Not only does it discount Europe's active role in the chaos that supposedly hems in the continent, it also fails to consider the fundamentally illusory quality of an internalist conception of Europe as clearly separable from its neighbors. According to this model, "Europe is [always] able to produce from within her own borders and resources, both material and spiritual, the conditions for the next phase of social development. This has been the dominant narrative of modernity for some time—an 'internalist' story, with capitalism growing from the womb of feudalism and Europe's self-generating capacity to produce, like a silk-worm, the circumstances of her own evolution from within her own body."[12] Stuart Hall wrote these words some twenty-five years ago, in the run-up to the Maastricht treaty, which ushered in the final phase of European unification. He analyzed Europe's chances at reorienting itself outward, in acknowledgment of its own connectedness and complex shared history with the rest of the world. He also examined the dangers of its defending internalist tendencies regarding the integration of Eastern Europe and minorities in Western Europe. Hall's conclusions are alarmingly prescient, as relevant today as in 1991. The inward-looking narrative of progress is a key component of European identity, and it's a difficult one to shake, as the outward-looking alternative challenges European models for the future while demanding a reassessment of the past. Taking this step is unavoidable, though, as the internalist worldview fails to move the needle in understanding global and continental affairs today. Hall argues that the internalist model is similarly unhelpful in describing European history, because it presents continental identity as a given, a driving force, when in fact this identity is being constantly retooled, with the lines demarcating it from an

---

12. Hall, "Europe's Other Self," 18.

equally mutable outside world continually redrawn. As a result, the hegemony of internalist history requires the suppression of plural positions, be they about Europe's borders, which cultures belong there, or what constitutes a "real" European.

European history did not occur in a vacuum any more than the present does. The austerity policies mentioned earlier—practically unheard-of until recently but now part of the basic continental lexicon—illustrate how internalist historiography works: Europe used the resources of the Global South to attain prosperity, meaning Western growth has never occurred free of austerity being enforced in other parts of the world. This exploitative dynamic has enabled economically and ecologically untenable policies to prevail well past the colonial period. One fairly mundane but structurally illuminating example can be found in the fishing industry: In recent decades, commercial overfishing has decimated European fish populations. The EU introduced total allowable catches to protect the local stock. Germany and other European fishing nations did not adopt sustainable models to meet the new fishing quotas; they simply started overfishing elsewhere. There was no fundamental shift in thinking. Instead, the consequences of unsustainable European practices were just passed on to African countries. Over the last ten years, West and East African coastal areas—which are sovereign, protected by international treaties, and teeming with fish—have been overrun by illegal European and Asian fishing fleets. As a result, what remains of the African fish population is on the brink of destruction; local fishing economies are dying; and a traditional staple food, the primary source of animal protein for much of the population, is becoming unattainable.[13]

This practice continues unimpeded to this day, despite appeals from impacted African nations to the international community. Meanwhile, European fleets fishing unlawfully in Somali waters—which they have been doing since the collapse of the Somali state in the early 1990s—do not fall under the umbrella term of *piracy*, whereas the label is applied to various Somali groups, including fishermen taking a stand

---

13. See Vidal, "Is the EU Taking Its Over-Fishing Habits to West African Waters?" and Fioretti, "European Commission Cuts Fish Quotas."

against illegal European activity, who are regarded and prosecuted as pirates.[14] There are many other examples of modern pillaging, whether it be coltan mining in the Democratic Republic of the Congo or lithium extraction in Chile. Achille Mbembe, one of today's leading postcolonial theorists, has written about the role of "failed," often African, nations in the global neoliberal economy: "Correlated to the new geography of resource extraction is the emergence of an unprecedented form of governmentality that consists in the *management of the multitudes*. The extraction and looting of natural resources by war machines goes hand in hand with brutal attempts to immobilize and spatially fix whole categories of people or, paradoxically, to unleash them, to force them to scatter over broad areas no longer contained by the boundaries of a territorial state."[15] European overfishing in African waters is one element contributing to this forced scattering. This and other forms of economic and ecological force will further escalate the process in the future, creating more economic migrants as well as more violent conflicts, whether over oil, as in Iraq and Iran, or over water, as in Yemen.[16] All that Europe takes note of, however, are the ultimate consequences of what it itself has set in motion, like northward migration from Africa, a deadly pursuit for thousands each year, the cause of which is presented as some vague blend of poverty and underdevelopment that the internalist narrative ascribes to Africa as its normal condition. Meanwhile, for decades the International Monetary Fund and World Bank have imposed harsh austerity policies on African nations. Among other things, these structural adjustment plans, as the policies are known, have dismantled state health systems and forced the sale of resources, including fishing rights.[17]

This imbalance and its roots in colonial structures are repressed in current European discourse and overshadowed in the collective consciousness by seemingly generous aid packages that discount centuries of colonial exploitation and its role in European growth.

---

14. See Samatar, Lindberg, and Mahayni, "Dialectics of Piracy."
15. Mbembe, "Necropolitics," 34. This description is particularly applicable to such states as Iraq, Afghanistan, and Syria.
16. Endres, "Der Wassermangel."
17. See Ziegler, "Europas Gier."

The same goes for exploitative practices today—one need look no further than the Transatlantic Trade and Investment Partnership, which threatens to cement African nations' role as suppliers of raw materials.[18] Repression does not resolve the contradictions it hides, however. Unresolved conflicts, which remain unnamable in the dominant logic, reemerge and engender erratic, grave crises. This in turn threatens the coherence of the dominant discourse, which gives rise to new mechanisms of repression that secure the hegemony of the prevailing ideology. The Haitian anthropologist Michel-Rolph Trouillot suggests the term "unthinkable history" for these objects of repression: "When reality does not coincide with deeply held beliefs, human beings tend to phrase interpretations that force reality within the scope of these beliefs. They devise formulas to repress the unthinkable and to bring it back within the realm of accepted discourse."[19] In order to do that properly, in order to process events that seem not to make sense within an existing logic, simply reinterpreting the present is not enough. We must integrate this interpretation into the overarching story that we—individually and collectively—tell about ourselves and the world. For instance, if we view colonialism as mostly a thing of the past, there must be a different explanation for the instability that endures in formerly colonized

---

18. See Fischer, "TTIP Talks." This is not about pointing fingers, about whether "Europe is to blame for all the injustice on Earth," or whether "it's high time Africa learned to look after itself," etc. It goes without saying that development processes are complex. Such debates, however, do not contribute much to the anemic analysis of causality between European wealth and "development" and African poverty and "underdevelopment."

19. Trouillot, *Silencing the Past*, 72. In his seminal study, Trouillot uses the Haitian Revolution to illustrate this process. The revolution was one of the most radical wars of independence in history and the only successful slave uprising ever recorded. It occurred during the so-called Age of Revolutions that began with the American and French Revolutions, so why is Haiti—a nation in the Western Hemisphere, like the others—largely ignored? Trouillot posits that this is because Haiti's revolution was and remains unimaginable. To be more precise, what was unimaginable was that humans deemed less-than-human in two regards—their being both African *and* enslaved—were capable not only of planning and executing a revolution but of establishing a republic (the third in the world) that was more democratic than any other Western system of government. Meanwhile, and perhaps most unthinkably, the Republic of Haiti was able to defend itself successfully against the world's two most powerful nations, France and England.

parts of the world, such as deficiencies in development—a position that underlies the astoundingly paternalistic demand for the Global South to "finally" take responsibility for itself, rather than expecting handouts from the West. Demands like that will only make sense once the West stops passing its problems on to the Global South.

Evolutionary Time

> Once Time is recognized as a dimension, not just a measure, of human activity, any attempt to eliminate it from interpretive discourse can only result in distorted and largely meaningless representations.
> —Johannes Fabian, *Time and the Other*

We humans generally aren't great at gauging the consequences of our actions or taking them seriously, especially when the negative outcomes of certain acts won't become evident until some unspecified future. Though we know it probably isn't a good idea to pour another glass of wine or eat another piece of chocolate, and though we truly had every intention of working out, more likely than not we'll reach for the bottle, have the chocolate, and skip the gym, because that's what feels better in the moment, and whatever happens, we'll deal with it then (the point at which we curse our past self for being so shortsighted). Part of this has to do with how we experience time: in some ways, the self that exists in the future, fated to deal with the effects of today's actions, is a different person, one for whom our empathy is conditional. This limited capacity to grasp the long-term consequences of our actions plays an important role collectively and individually; at the collective level, it may be even more important, because the consequences truly are borne by others. We know that climate change is real and requires drastic countermeasures, but we don't truly grasp it, because it's easy for us—the prime perpetrators in the "developed" West—to ignore its effects. We tell ourselves that minor individual interventions (driving a hybrid, installing greywater systems) can replace sweeping collective change. Evidence from across the planet suggests the opposite is true, but spatial distance between those who caused the problem and those who suffer its consequences works as effectively as the temporal divide between now and everything to come. Ironically, according to the space-time model used to define Western superiority, it is actually the other way round: What supposedly distinguishes people and societies in the West (and Europe, in particular) is their ability to favor forward-looking models over instant gratification. This is allegedly why the West has seen progress, while development elsewhere has stagnated or at least trailed behind.

There is a centuries-old tradition, as Hall demonstrates, of depicting human development as linear, inevitably emerging and driven from the heart of Europe. In fact, it is only when the West is able to project its reactionary mirror image outside its borders that it can see itself as progressive—though, depending on the focus, these borders are fluid (as will become clear in the following sections). In the early 1980s, anthropologist Johannes Fabian studied the process that yielded the normalization (if not naturalization) of this hierarchical worldview. He identified our perception of time and the interplay of space and time—the temporalization of space, the spatialization of time—as key factors: evolutionary time, a "scheme in terms of which not only past cultures, but all living societies were irrevocably placed on a temporal slope, a stream of time—some upstream, others downstream," is tied to a spatial world order in which Europe forms the center of universal time/space.[20] The rest of the world is viewed and judged relative to that center, then fixed in the time and place assigned to it: "As soon as culture is no longer primarily conceived as a set of rules to be enacted by individual members of distinct groups, but as the specific way in which actors create and produce beliefs, values, and other means of social life, it has to be recognized that time is a constitutive dimension of social reality."[21] It's hard for us to grasp that our understanding of time is cultural and not simply a reflection of reality, but Fabian shows that time is a fundamental aspect of our social existence. The ostensibly

---

20. Fabian, *Time and the Other*, 17.
21. Fabian, *Time and the Other*, 24.

neutral model of objective or universal time, which capitalism made global, is a construct specific to a particular history and geography. Universal time was linked directly to the secularization of Judeo-Christian notions of time; that is, a concept in which linear time followed one particular monotheistic redemption narrative was replaced by a model centered on humans, of the European variety, with time measured according to distinct successive phases, from birth, childhood, and adolescence to adulthood and death. Fabian follows the gradual rise of the latter model during the Enlightenment and the transition from cyclical, "pagan" time to linear, Judeo-Christian and later secular time. Its global implementation was consolidated in the late nineteenth century, coinciding with the Berlin Conference of 1884–85 and the advent of European imperialism as the continent's nations began to aggressively develop and exploit colonized territories. One must not underestimate the role such nascent scientific disciplines as ethnology and anthropology played in legitimizing and powering this process (the newfangled medium of film was also significant).[22] In her study of gender, race, and nationalism, Anne McClintock observes, "In the nineteenth century, the social evolutionists secularized time and placed it at the disposal of the national, imperial project. . . . In the image of the family tree, evolutionary progress was represented as a series of anatomically distinct family types, organized into a linear procession, from the 'childhood' of 'primitive' races to the enlightened 'adulthood' of European imperial nationalism."[23] The image of the human family—civilized European father, strict but fair, watching over the childlike (or worse, pubescent) "natives"—was a hallmark of the colonial imagination and has yet to be purged fully from the Western psyche. Movement between (time-)spaces became more common and less regulated with the end of European colonial rule and the start of organized labor migration, yet the model of evolutionary time remained intact. The temporal (dis)placement of the Global

---

22. See Shohat and Stam, *Unthinking Eurocentrism*.
23. McClintock and Mufti, *Dangerous Liaisons*, 94. One convenient side effect of this imagery was that the delayed founding of the German nation-state, often considered a flaw, could now be read as a sign of progress.

South in Europe's past (as in routine references to "Medieval Islam" or to "prehistoric" conditions in Africa) is how "developing countries" are arranged within the Western space-time model. This means that in Europe migrants from the Global South were perceived as coming not only from a different place but from a different time. As far as dominant perception was concerned, they were forever stuck in the wrong place at the wrong time.

A logic is thus constructed by which unremitting Western progress is measured against a laggard racialized outside, an outside that by definition can never be the engine of global historical development but must remain in the margins, today as in the past.[24] While Fabian focuses on the discipline of anthropology and its "Others," he reminds us that "our theories of their societies are our praxis—the way in which we produce and reproduce knowledge of the Other for our societies."[25] There is no dialogue, then, but a monologue in which "we" explain to ourselves what the Other is. What does this mean for discourse about internal Others within a society? Does the notion of parallel societies involve one of parallel times? How does this construct influence analysis of societal processes? Together, internalist history and evolutionary time provide the foundation for the myth of European civilization's superiority. The myth presents

---

24. In other words, this outside does not exist at the same time or developmental phase as Europe, nor does it occupy its own, alternative process of development; instead, it is positioned on the very same developmental track, the only conceivable one, which is measured exclusively in terms of European history. Thilo Sarrazin's 2010 anti-immigrant bestseller *Deutschland schafft sich ab* (Germany abolishes itself) adopts this line of argumentation, which demonstrates its ongoing relevance (see Ash, "Germans, More or Less"). The only global movement the South can conceivably initiate is backward movement. For instance, casting Islamic fundamentalism as the greatest threat to world peace is primarily justified with the assertion that it would lead back to the (European) Middle Ages (or fascism). Needless to say, other theoretical and practical models of development do exist. See Chakrabarty, *Provincializing Europe* and Mignolo, *Darker Side of Western Modernity* on the concept of "other modern subjects"; Halberstam, *In a Queer Time and Place* and Muñoz, *Cruising Utopia* on "queer temporality"; and Battiste, *Reclaiming Indigenous Voice* on indigenous concepts of time. The issue is that the dominant space-time understanding provides the foundation of our worldview, so even if we are critical of its most glaring faults (like its model of development), it is almost impossible to divorce our thinking from the logic of evolutionary time.

25. Fabian, *Time and the Other*, 165.

Europe as a discrete spatial and temporal unit, but this seeming clarity comes at the cost of a brutal hierarchy of value that is directly determined by postulated proximity to this very Europe but that also courses through Europe itself.

In addition to the fact that cyclical conceptions of time often encourage more sustainable use of resources than the evolutionary model, Western societies rarely stick to their ostensibly future-oriented approach. Instead, they adopt an "out of sight, out of mind" attitude, which allows them to remove the immediate negative consequences of their actions to a spatial elsewhere, usually the Global South (often portrayed, of course, as existing in the past, compared to Europe, which adds to the space-time tangle). Radical countermeasures could halt climate change caused by the West, and what could possibly benefit the planet more? Such measures, however, would hamper short-term Western economic interests, rendering them a nonstarter.[26] The ability to forfeit the comfort of the status quo—which is known to be unsustainable and trained toward a catastrophic, if not yet fully palpable, future—is entirely lacking, particularly in the West. Still, the superiority of Western civilization goes unquestioned at the very moment when the results of its actions refuse to be ignored any longer: Structural adjustment plans pushed by the World Bank and the International Monetary Fund in the Global South focus on opening markets and dismantling social benefits, even though such measures have long been known to exacerbate mass poverty. Mounting economic inequality, repeatedly identified as the root of political and social instability, is nevertheless cemented in such global treaties as the Transatlantic Trade and Investment Partnership and the Trans-Pacific Partnership. Military interventions in the "war on terror" result in more terrorism and burgeoning numbers of refugees. It is a vicious cycle, and an obvious one at that, yet the same failed strategies are doggedly implemented, with progressively disastrous outcomes. However foreseeable these outcomes, Europe is always caught unawares. (I live in the United States now, and as people here like to say, "The definition of insanity is doing the same thing over and over again and expecting

---

26. See Nelson, "EU Dropped Climate Policies" for more on the oil lobby's sway over EU climate policies.

different results.") What might seem like a bizarre inability to learn from history makes a lot more sense when one acknowledges what Europe would have to surrender to clear the way for real change: its understanding of itself, its future, and its past. This means rejecting internalist history and engaging in an honest confrontation with everything this history has obscured for centuries, even—and especially—when Europe looks at itself in the mirror.

Not Here, Not Now: Exterminable Lives

> Moreover, coevalness is a mode of temporal relations. It cannot be defined as a thing or state with certain properties. It is not "there" and cannot be put there; it must be created or at least approached.
> — JOHANNES FABIAN, *TIME AND THE OTHER*

What has become known as "the greatest refugee crisis since the end of World War II" proves that the current model is untenable. At the same time, the crisis cannot be explained within this model: How can the image of Europe as cradle of universal human rights, a region that has surpassed all others in practicing these ideals, albeit not always perfectly, coexist with that of Europe's southern border being the deadliest worldwide? More people perish needlessly in the attempt to reach Europe than anywhere else on earth. For the better part of a decade, though, the deaths of thousands, most of them African refugees, by drowning in the Mediterranean were roundly ignored, particularly by the wealthy northwestern nations, which instead put the onus on "frontline" countries like Italy, Spain, and Greece to "stem the tide" and rescue the shipwrecked. In no way did the refugee crisis take the EU by surprise in the summer of 2015—the EU was instrumental in creating it.[27] Two assumptions

---

27. Take, for instance, Italy's Operation Mare Nostrum, which rescued around 150,000 people in the Mediterranean Sea between October 2013 and October 2014. The EU denied the Italian government's repeated pleas for support and instead blamed the effort for driving up refugee counts. In October 2014, Thomas de

underlie the disregard for these mass casualties: (1) the lives lost are of lesser value than those of Europeans, and (2) those who perished don't belong in Europe, and fending them off is a top priority, even if it means thousands must die.

This assertion may appear exaggerated, but let's review the facts: Every year since 2004, for more than a decade, at least two thousand people lost their lives unnecessarily, without anything being done about it—on the contrary, the EU squashed the Italian government's search and rescue operation. When the European community did get involved, it favored repressive measures, beefing up border security and deporting refugees from Ceuta and Melilla before they could apply for asylum, an illegal tactic tolerated (if not encouraged) by the EU. "Reception centers" for refugees were established in transit countries like Morocco and Libya, and military support went to some sending countries, like Senegal, to stop migration before it started.[28] In other words, what was most important was controlling and curtailing people's freedom of movement, while international law took a back seat. The rescue of human lives, if even included in the hierarchy, was tertiary. What could possibly explain this, other than a callous indifference justified by the notion that these deaths aren't that big a deal? "These people," whether in the Global South or in Europe, simply count less.

A third factor has been missing from the concerted reformulation of European past and present that links post/fascist and post/socialist narratives to tell a Western capitalist success story. That other aspect—Europe's colonial past—is equally in urgent need of reappraisal: it manifests both in a steadily growing, post/colonial continental population that nevertheless remains "un-European" and in

---

Maizière, Germany's federal minister of the interior, went so far as to say, "Mare Nostrum was intended as a search and rescue operation, but has proven to be a bridge to Europe." The EU ultimately replaced Operation Mare Nostrum with Triton, an initiative carried out by the European Border and Coast Guard Agency, or Frontex. Frontex sought more to deter than to rescue and monitored a much smaller area than the Italian navy had. Renewed warnings about the inevitable rise in deaths at sea were again ignored. (See "Flüchtlinge—Italien beendet Rettungsaktion.") In other words, the spike in the number of fatalities in the early summer of 2016 (up to one thousand per day) was foreseeable—and avoidable.

28. See Jakob, "Europas blutige Außengrenze."

the futile attempts to define Europe's geographic, political, and identitarian borders, once and for all. Religion and race play a key role here: although never named outright, it's obvious that the groups classified as fundamentally foreign and incapable of integrating are also those who—by means of racialization and religious affiliation—embody the Other vis-à-vis white Christian Europe, namely Afro-Europeans, Roma, and Muslims. The permanent presence of this branded Other in contemporary Europe represents the crisis of the dominant space-time order and activates mechanisms of control, old and new. This state of exception—being branded as permanently in the wrong place at the wrong time—is not only characteristic of refugees but of the post/colonial population in general. Immobilization, whether in prisons, refugee camps, or ghettos, is thus on its way to becoming the normalized response to the presence of such "mobile" groups as refugees, migrants, or diasporic minorities. Racialized populations within Europe are increasingly identified in this manner, while their alleged lack of roots justifies restricting their movement to segregated neighborhoods and prisons.[29]

Refugee policy is another area in which failed models are endlessly replicated: most of the "solutions" currently [in 2016—Trans.] up for debate on how to manage refugees from the Middle East already proved unsuccessful ten or twenty years ago when they were first implemented to address similar "refugee crises," yet barely any reference is made to those (ongoing) crises. Instead, a clear distinction was made early on in German debates between "real" refugees, displaced by war and persecution (especially from Syria), and "phony" economic refugees, primarily West and North Africans and Roma. The latter group is blamed for abusing asylum law and overburdening the system, keeping assistance from getting to those in actual need. Although differentiating between real and economic refugees makes sense at first, to the point of seeming almost inevitable, closer examination reveals holes in the reasoning: Life-threatening poverty

---

29. Neocolonial studies in Africa and neoslavery studies in the United States point out the fuzzy lines between incarcerated and not-yet-incarcerated members of groups branded as criminal, useless, and dangerous, regardless of whether an individual is in an actual prison or not. See Mbembe, "Necropolitics" and Childs, *Slaves of the State*.

appears as a regrettable but unalterable part of life for certain (backward) groups in certain (backward) regions. Racialized mass poverty is never mentioned as the by-product of a global economic system that disproportionately benefits the West, nor is economic violence recognized as a form of violence at all, let alone a legitimate reason for fleeing. For decades, nations of the Global South have petitioned for food security and shelter to be recognized as human rights on par with the freedom of expression or assembly, but Western states have shown no interest in expanding the list of global fundamental rights, which they would have to commit to protecting. Ultimately, it does not matter much if Europe declares itself unable to accommodate millions of refugees if the reasons for their flight, including economic ones, persist. Whether you look at the consequences of European overfishing for West African communities or Facebook reactions to terrorist attacks in Paris and Beirut, the underlying hierarchy of human life remains the same.

The anthropologist Ghassan Hage has created this visual shorthand:

> Look at the swamps created by the differential of exterminability and mournability between Muslims and non-Muslims.
>
> NEWYORKbaghdadLONDON
> TELAVIVgazaMADRID
> BOSTONkabulOSLO
> PARISaleppoBRUSSELS
>
> It is in those and similar dips in the affective tectonic plates in which we are all embedded where some of the emotional propellors of Islamic terrorism grows.

Hage does not claim that the sole root of terrorism lies in the difference between exterminability and mournability, but he illustrates how preposterous and willfully dishonest it is to assume that it would not have an emotional effect on people to be treated collectively as more expendable than others. He continues,

> If you cannot see those affective swamps and what is allowed to fester in them, if you cannot see how it is drowning *all of us* in a destructive

culture of exterminability, a culture of selective indifference to the killing and death of some, you are not seeing much at all.

Yet it is a collective responsibility, particularly for those of us living in the West, to see and discuss and understand those swamps and their effects. If for nothing other than the fact that it is not the Muslims who have created them, it is the West. It is years of colonial impunity.[30]

Internalist explanatory models, meanwhile, assume either that underdevelopment, overpopulation, and despotism will keep the Global South mired in crisis, making it incumbent on Europe to seal itself off (this is the conservative take), or that refugees' flight is linked to Western intervention policies, especially if the focus is on the Middle East. The second instance, which is the progressive stance, identifies US militarism as the main culprit and calls for Europe to quit tagging along and move to hobble American imperialism. Both approaches ignore the central role European colonialism plays in creating the current crisis. The internalist narrative not only allows for but requires belief in the superiority of European civilization, a superiority not based on subjugation and exploitation (as Europe's progress always comes from within) but on a superior value system founded on equality, fairness, and democracy that allows individuals, groups, and nations to live up to their full potential.

To legitimize a world order in which Europe serves as a role model for global progress, Western superiority must be upheld as a simple fact (and a generally good thing). Furthermore, it must be agreed that the West bears no structural responsibility for the conditions that force it to intervene outside its borders—whether that intervention be political, economic, or military—in efforts to establish a system that corresponds to its model of development. The Hungarian sociologist Josef Böröcz, in considering Western Europe's function as a model for the post/socialist Eastern bloc, notes,

> In order to think of any contemporary social form as the desirable "already" for the desirous reformers of the "not yet," it is necessary to assume, as liberal thought does invariably, that the "backwardness" of those that are "not-yet" advanced has no causal connection to the previous advancement

---

30. Hage, "Terrorism, Brussels, etc." Emphasis in original.

of the more "developed" role model. If the achievement of the "advanced" social forms is acknowledged to be due to benefits derived from somebody else's wretchedness, or if the suffering of the wretched is recognized as having been caused by the "advancement" of the developed, the teleological blueprint becomes morally unacceptable and even nonsensical.[31]

In order to prevent the collapse of the "teleological blueprint," blatant contradictions—like the real differentials of exterminability and mournability—are not challenged but externalized. In other words, the problem is projected outward, with nothing amiss in a Europe that applauds itself as the inventor and champion of human rights (after all, the EU *was* awarded a Nobel Peace Prize in 2012 for these very achievements). Instead, the incongruity is found among those still denied full human rights, who keep botching their chances at joining the civilized world because of their fanaticism, barbarism, poverty, and dogged resolve to belong, to be more than extras in the success story of the West, at best, or collateral damage, at worst.

During the "refugee crisis," though the situation seemed to change daily, it soon became clear that supposedly surprising (unprecedented, unforeseeable, etc.) developments were in fact part of a familiar pattern, one of mulish refusal to face the consequences of disastrous European models of identity and development. Crises are coming in quicker succession and are becoming less governable, because their causes have never been addressed. Current crises are an expression of escalating global inequality and the sustained dismantling of political rights. They will not be the last, either. It is increasingly naive to believe that Europe (and the United States) will continue to profit from this system without ever suffering the negative consequences. One necessary first step is to dispel the notion that a democratic Europe provides aid to its southern neighbors for purely humanitarian reasons and to engage instead with the more complicated relationship between Europe's prosperity and its colonial and neocolonial deeds. Germany exemplifies this process, however removed it considers itself from the colonial context. Whereas the country's colonial past has vanished almost completely from public consciousness, it has left unmistakable traces in the public space.

---

31. Böröcz, "Goodness Is Elsewhere," 17.

2

Internalism and Universalism

Where Are Europe's Borders?

"Europe and the Wider Mediterranean Region"

For centuries, European economic stability was linked causally to (neo)colonial structures of dominance, meaning instability could always be shunted outward (as in the case of European fishing fleets in West Africa), while time and again the European model of success seemed to prove its superiority. Such instability—which could never be externalized completely, despite all structural efforts—is now advancing on the center. Part of the Greek crisis was the country's humiliation caused by austerity measures imposed by the European Union (EU) that are otherwise reserved for the Global South. The financial plan's harsh material consequences were reinforced by a steadfast perception of Europe as the center of civilization and progress, naturally endowed with the highest standard of living—poverty as the quasi-natural state of the "Third World" goes hand in hand with prosperity as the West's natural state. The "West" is not monolithic, though, and the economic crisis revealed fractures within Europe, shining a light on the long-standing hierarchy between the Northwest, on the one hand, and the South and East on the other. The latter areas cannot claim European status with any real confidence, both because of their peripheral location and, more importantly, because of associated cultural ascriptions—just look at the accusations of laziness, disarray, and corruption lobbed at Greeks during debates on austerity measures; the same discursive strategies and tropes had been used in the 1970s against *Gastarbeiter* ("guest workers") from these regions.[1] This hierarchy within Europe is based on a much older dispute over the essence of European identity and belonging. It is a dispute that never has and never will yield consensus but one that nevertheless keeps reproducing certain stereotypes—including that of lazy "Mediterranean types"—as empirical truths. The northwestern corner of the continent, where EU founding members are clustered, bills itself as "'core' Europe," made up of countries readily associated with such European values as freedom, equality, democracy, secularism, and above all, economic stability. Compared to suspect border states in the Balkans or the Mediterranean, no one would ever think to question the European status of places like Germany, France, or the Netherlands.

Accordingly, Germany's moral authority and dominance within the EU is most effectively challenged with reference to the repercussions of Nazi rule, the most "un-European" phase in German history. This came out in discussions on Greek reparations, sparked in turn by the debate over self-inflicted or "cultural" aspects of the Greek economic crisis.[2] Greece's call for Germany to repay a massive

---

1. That said, the racialization of Southern Europeans—known by the blanket term *Südländer*, or those from "southern lands"—has been pushed from the collective consciousness since the 1990s and replaced with a focus on European Muslims and the notion that their failure to integrate is because of religious or cultural characteristics that set them leagues apart from Christian/secular Europeans, including Southern Europeans. See Terkessidis, *Interkultur*.

2. Greek claims extend beyond compensation for the massacres and destruction the country suffered under Nazi occupation to include a loan of 476 million reichsmarks Greece was forced to lay out in 1942, which was never repaid. It is disputed whether repayment—about 11 billion euros—would be considered reparations or the fulfillment of a civil loan. Like its predecessors, the German government

forced loan from World War II was a deliberate attempt to shift the moral balance of the Grexit debate by reversing the seemingly clear roles of debtor and donor. The conflict was nothing new: for decades, the nations had argued over who bore moral and material responsibility for the Nazis' exploitation of the occupied land. As it had in the past, Germany refused to respond to Greek demands. It was a refusal based less on international law than on material advantage: Greece lacked leverage beyond the moral argument (which was no more useful for Greece than it is for African states requesting that international courts uphold their claims against violations of maritime sovereignty by European ships). Germany, by contrast, led the EU in imposing an austerity package on the Greek government. The parallels to discourse surrounding Africa's cultural "underdevelopment" and European responsibility seem clear; indeed, the demand for reparations for genocide, slavery, and colonialism gained new prominence in 2013 when a union of Caribbean nations, the Caribbean Community (CARICOM), brought a suit against France, the Netherlands, and Britain, among others.[3]

It might seem as though Germany would be exempt from this debate or occupy a unique position, as claims for reparations from the German state tend to relate to the Nazi era and not to colonial rule. I will demonstrate, however, that the internalist repression of European colonial rule and its aftermath has shaped Germany profoundly. Conversations about the German colonial legacy, especially in Namibia, are slowly reaching a wider public; the debates usually maintain the perspective of the white German perpetrator and focus

---

insists on the first interpretation, arguing that all claims were adequately addressed in the Reparations Treaty of 1960 and the Two Plus Four Treaty of 1990 (Greece never signed the latter). See Caspari, "Muss Deutschland?" and Deutscher Bundestag, "Aus dem Zweiten Weltkrieg."

3. In December 2013, the Caribbean Community (CARICOM)—an intergovernmental alliance of fifteen Caribbean nations—requested a "reparatory dialogue with beneficiary slave-owning European states" (Britain, France, Spain, Portugal, the Netherlands, Norway, Sweden, and Denmark, in particular) about the enduring effects of these countries' crimes against humanity. See CARICOM Reparations Commission, "Press Statement." Ten years later, CARICOM combined forces with the African Union in the fight for European reparations. See CARICOM, "Remarks by Dr. Carla N. Barnett."

on parsing the relationship between colonialism and Nazism, especially with regard to the Herero genocide (even questioning whether it counts as genocide at all). Less attention is paid to the lasting impact these structures of dominance have ("the living legacy of these crimes," as the CARICOM statement puts it)[4] —the impact on formerly colonized nations, certainly, but also that on former colonizers, who not only passively repress their history but actively employ internalist historiography and models of evolutionary time to integrate their past into the notion of European civilization's superiority. When disparate discourses on memory collide, as is happening more and more these days, a further identity crisis arises. An especially fraught element in this crisis, which I will expand upon later, is the perception of the Israeli-Palestinian conflict and the relationship between antisemitism and anti-Zionism, which is often strongly influenced by one's own relationship to colonial history. Explicitly Eurocentric and nominally universalist approaches share in denying the survival of colonial logic, which should not come as a surprise: internalism and universalism are two sides of the same coin. In both, Europe appears at once wholly independent of the rest of the world and uniquely representative of humanity in its most perfect (or at least most progressive) form, bound together with others in a chain of development that invariably leads back to Europe. I would like to illustrate this dynamic using two examples that couldn't seem more different.

---

4. The CARICOM Reparations Commission identifies six primary areas in which this legacy is borne out: (1) public health (the Caribbean population has the highest rates of hypertension and type 2 diabetes globally, both caused in part by chronic stress); (2) education (at the end of colonial rule, more than 70 percent of the Caribbean population was illiterate, a gap the region is still struggling to close); (3) cultural institutions (while museums and research centers in Europe outline the imperial past, there are no comparable outlets for telling the story from the victims' perspective); (4) cultural estrangement (African slaves were systematically stripped of their cultures and languages); (5) psychological trauma (for more than four centuries, Africans were deemed nonhuman); and (6) "scientific and technological backwardness" (colonizers mandated that the Caribbean produce raw materials, thus hindering any form of industrialization).

Colonial Aftershocks 1: How Did the *Kanake* Get to Germany?

Our first example is one of the most visible *and* invisible vestiges of German colonial rule: the term *Kanake* (plural *Kanaken*). *Kanake* is used broadly to demean those people who "don't belong here." It is a common word that every German knows and understands, but people are less familiar with its origins, which is astounding considering that, in some ways, the word encapsulates precisely what it means to be un/German. One could argue that *Kanake* represents the intersection of racialization and migratization: the moniker refers to the unacceptable state of being deemed "not (really) German"; this can but does not necessarily mean "non-white" or "non-Christian."[5] And why is the only word that exists for members of this group so aggressively pejorative and exclusionary? Perhaps it is in response to the threat they pose to the line drawn by such accepted, seemingly neutral terms as *foreigner* or *migrant*: *Kanaken* imperil the ostensibly clear distinction between Germans and "foreigners." They are neither one nor the other but instead contradict the internalist model by challenging the overall structure of what can be considered German and what cannot. People targeted by the epithet have used this interpretation to assert a radical stance in everything from hip-hop to activism, as in the case of Kanak Attak:

---

5. Non-white and/or non-Christian *Kanaken* are racialized in additional ways. As a Black person who was born and raised in Germany, I am intimately familiar with the friendliest form of *Kanak*ization, namely the question, "So, where are you *actually* from?" It is something I have been asked more times than I can count, in spite of my German passport and total command of the German language. In this instance, being racialized as Black is the one and only requirement to be perceived as a *Kanake*, or non-German. There are other factors that resist being subsumed under the banner of racism: a person's language or religion can invite *Kanak*ization, even if they are racialized as white. Refer to the preface for the definition of *racialization*, but see also Alyosxa Tudor's important distinction between racism and "migratism." The latter term describes the specific power relations produced by designating people as "migrants." Migratism is thus related but not identical to racism, antisemitism, and Islamophobia. See Tudor, *From [al'mania] with Love*.

"Our lowest common denominator is to attack the *Kanak*ization of certain groups of people by means of racist ascriptions with all the social, legal, and political consequences associated with the act. Kanak Attak is anti-nationalist, anti-racist, and rejects any form of identity politics, such as those that feed on ethnological ascriptions."[6] The activists, too, were less interested in the etymology of *Kanake* than they were in appropriating the term to express resistance, so the question of when and how *Kanake* found its way into the lexicon was left unanswered. It is pretty easy to find out, however, that *Kanaka* means "human being" in Polynesian and serves as a proper name for various Polynesian peoples, such as Kanaka Maoli for Indigenous Hawaiians.[7] Germany's colonial holdings were located mainly in Africa but also included the Pacific islands of Samoa and Papua New Guinea, both of which are inhabited by speakers of Polynesian dialects.

German colonizers wanted more than to simply rule over and exploit these populations; they were keen to study them. They believed it would grant them a better understanding of earlier stages of human development; the European perspective, informed by evolutionary time, held that colonized "primitive peoples" still occupied this past. Scientific studies of language, customs, and the "nature" of the "natives" were part of the colonial system, be it through colonial authorities granting researchers access to "objects of study" stripped of their rights or through the colonial officials themselves

---

6. This is part of the Kanak Attak manifesto, published in 1997, which begins, "Kanak Attak is a self-selecting union of different people that extends beyond the boundaries of the ascribed 'identities' practically foisted on them from birth. Kanak Attak doesn't ask to see a person's passport or where they come from; it opposes these questions." See their website, http://www.kanak-attak.de. The group was active from the late 1990s to the mid-2000s.

7. See Kehaulani, *Hawaiian Blood*. This origin story can be found online and even on *Planet Wissen*, a show on Germany's public service broadcaster ARD: "German sailors referred to their mates from Polynesia and Oceania as 'Kannakermänner' ['*Kannaker* men'—Trans.]. This was by no means an insult. On the contrary, 'Kannakermann' was a positive label, as the seamen from these regions were known for their tremendous skills and loyalty." The source of this claim was a Wikipedia entry (2016 version) on "Kanake (Schimpfwort)" [*Kanake* (Slur)—Trans.], which did not provide a single reference. This does not come as much of a surprise, as there is scanty documentation of this genealogy. See Trost, "Woher stammt das Wort."

undertaking the research.[8] One such official was Joachim Friedrich von Pfeil, who in the early 1880s was instrumental in the German colonization of East and South West Africa. Later he served in the German New Guinea Company, part of the colonial apparatus in the Pacific, and from 1887 to 1889 he was an administrative official in the Bismarck Archipelago, still known by that name today. In his *Studien und Beobachtungen aus der Südsee* (Studies and observations from the South Seas), published in 1899, von Pfeil presented a comprehensive and authoritative analysis of the island inhabitants he had studied, from property rights and agriculture to their "character." He called them by the name they used themselves, *Kanaken*. To help orient his readers, the blue-blooded colonizer made it clear from the start that "the *Kanake* truly is far inferior to other colored peoples"[9] (it went without saying that any "colored peoples" were, in turn, far inferior to white people). He then substantiated this assertion with countless anecdotes about lazy, superstitious, misogynistic *Kanaken*. (Von Pfeil was as vexed by the misogyny as he was by the fact that the *Kanaken* failed to hit their children. Worst for him, though, was the persistent aversion the *Kanaken* showed toward white settlers.)

The Germans' primary interest may have lain in the African protectorates, but studies in the South Sea colonies were certainly not limited to von Pfeil's work. These representations of the colonies spread across the German Empire during a period of "colonial enthusiasm," as it was known. The craze brought together the government—represented by the Colonial Department, initially a division of the Foreign Office, and from 1907 by the Imperial Colonial Office—and nationalist associations that advocated for the interests of the bourgeoisie, which had no direct influence in parliament. Often in competition with conservative governing parties, these associations were quick to adopt new forms of mass media on the rise in

---

8. See, for instance, the work of Eugen Fischer, whose lifelong career as an expert on "miscegenation" started in German South West Africa (present-day Namibia), where he conducted forced medical experiments on a group of people known as the Rehoboth Bastards. Fischer's success spanned the years of the Weimar Republic, the Third Reich, and into the postwar era. See El-Tayeb, *Schwarze Deutsche*.

9. Pfeil, *Studien und Beobachtungen*, 25.

the late nineteenth century. Picture postcards, photographs, sound recordings, and the budding film industry enabled previously unseen levels of public involvement in politics. Propaganda flourished. One early pinnacle was the First German Colonial Exhibition in 1896. More than two million people visited the six-month exhibit in Berlin, which among other things put 103 "natives" from the German colonies on display. Around that time, propelled by the fervor around the exhibition, the German Colonial Museum was founded in Berlin; propaganda materials were distributed to schools nationwide; colonial science lectures were introduced at nearly all universities; various companies began producing trading cards with colonial images, which were hugely popular; and the new, immensely successful genre of the colonial novel emerged.[10]

"Colonial enthusiasm" propaganda assured the German people of their own superiority, demonstrated the benefits of imperialist government policy, put oppositional factions on the defensive, and, last but not least, allowed nationalist associations to become important social forces. It does not seem unreasonable to assume that the term *Kanake* became a derogatory designation for racialized groups in this context. Similarly, "Hottentots" became a fixture in the German collective consciousness over the course of the colonial war in Namibia. Popular perception was informed greatly by the persistent resistance of the Nama people, dubbed Hottentots, who, like the populace of the Bismarck Archipelago, were unwilling to accept German rule. The pejorative lives on today in such colloquial sayings as "Hier geht's ja zu wie bei den Hottentotten" (It's like life among the Hottentots), which amounts to exclaiming, "It's a zoo in here!" A sense of these terms' negative connotation remains, even when the memory of the original colonial context is lost, because what has not changed is the implicit hierarchy of value and spatialization of nonbelonging.

---

10. See El-Tayeb, *Schwarze Deutsche*. Beginning a few years later, in 1899, streets in the Berlin neighborhood of Wedding (and in many other German cities) were renamed after German colonies and colonizers. Despite decades of protest by the Black community in Germany, most of the names remain. See Kopp and Krohn, "Blues in Schwarzweiss."

Colonial Aftershocks 2: Berlin Is on the Mediterranean

At first glance, the Berlin-based Multaka project seems as far as possible from this unacknowledged racist history. Initiated by the Museum of Islamic Art in conjunction with the Museum of the Ancient Near East, the Museum of Byzantine Art, and the German Historical Museum, and with support from the federal government, the project aspires to integration, not exclusion. Its full name hints at this mission. "Multaka: Museums as Meeting Point—Refugees as Guides in Berlin Museums" places Syrian and Iraqi refugees in partner institutions, where they serve as Arabic-speaking tour guides, leading groups of fellow refugees through the collections. The initiative outlines three interconnected goals: "to strengthen [refugees'] self-esteem and promote the confident and constructive introduction of the refugees into our society" by allowing them to see just how much each museum values its Syrian and Iraqi artifacts as "outstanding testaments to the history of humanity"; to foster understanding of the shared roots between Islam, Judaism, and Christianity and to explore the potential for a pluralistic society; and finally, in the German Historical Museum, to "become more intimate with German culture and history, with all of its crises and renewals."[11] Here, German reconstruction following World War II is meant to serve as an encouraging example for the visitors from war-torn regions. According to Multaka's 2015 website, most of the guides (of which there were nineteen total—eighteen from Syria, one from Iraq) named the German Historical Museum as their museum of choice.

Multaka launched in November 2015, with the free weekly tours initially funded for one year.[12] The project has been well received; national and international media outlets have praised Multaka as a heartening example of how culture can unite what politics divides. Newspaper articles about the initiative tend to follow the same

---

11. Museum for Islamic Art, "Multaka: Museum as Meeting Point."
12. As of April 2016 (when this book was written), the project had turned to Facebook for donations to keep the tours running. By August 2024 the project has secured long-term funding and won multiple awards. See https://multaka.de/en/startsite-en.

template, introducing one or two of the guides, telling their personal stories of escape and integration into life in Germany, and sharing a few takeaways from the tours they lead. Only a few journalists have reported on visitors' responses to exhibits at the German Historical Museum; usually, a few examples are given to describe the effect of Middle Eastern artworks on the refugees—memories of home, the time before the war began, and the destruction that followed.

Four of the five articles I examined more closely paint that scene,[13] but all cite another common response described by the guides—it would seem that the refugees home in on an issue the project pitch failed to consider: "A lot of people have asked why all these things are in Berlin, and since when," the guide profiled for *Berliner Zeitung* said.[14] The Syrian tour guide interviewed for the *Guardian* shared something similar: "The first question we usually get asked is: how did all this end up in Germany?"[15] The *Süddeutsche Zeitung* stated succinctly, "Within two minutes, Radwan Hamed, who is from Damascus, voices the question every Arab here must ask: What is the Ishtar Gate doing in Berlin, and why isn't it in Babylon?"[16] The *New York Times* was most blunt: "Sometimes people say: 'The Germans have all our heritage! They stole it!'"[17] None of the articles dig deeper into this question or try to answer it (and only the *Times* and *Guardian* make any reference, however chary, to the greater controversy surrounding looted art), and nor do the tour guides. Instead, readers are presented with the guides' identical responses to the question of how Middle Eastern artworks wound up in Germany:

---

13. My sources were two local dailies—*Berliner Zeitung*, which is read more widely in east Berlin, and *Tagesspiegel*, whose readership tends to live in the western part of the city—as well as the national *Süddeutsche Zeitung* and two international papers, the *Guardian* and the *New York Times*. All described tours in the Pergamon Museum, save the *Tagesspiegel*. Sonja Zekri of the *Süddeutsche Zeitung* is the only writer among the five who speaks Arabic and could fully participate in the tour. (Regarding his guide in the German Historical Museum, meanwhile, the writer for the *Tagesspiegel* commented unselfconsciously, "There's no following what he's saying, because the tour he leads through the German Historical Museum is in Arabic.")

14. Fritz, "Projekt 'Multaka' in Berlin."
15. Oltermann, "Berlin Museums' Refugee Guides Scheme."
16. Zekri, "Wiedersehen."
17. Donadio, "Berlin's Museum Tours."

"'I don't think that's important. It's good,' [Gaith] Konjoue explains, 'that the monuments are safe. So much in Syria has already been destroyed'";[18] and "Often, the visitors say the art is probably better off in Berlin because so much in Syria has been destroyed by the war and the Islamic State, [Razan] Nassreddine said."[19] The *Guardian* turned to the director of the Museum of Islamic Art for a statement: "'Some objects have a complicated history,' said [Stefan] Weber." And that's that. The limits and challenges of "[promoting] the confident and constructive introduction of the refugees into our society" quickly become apparent, because in so doing, questions arise that the dominant society does not necessarily want to answer. Instead, the questions are dismissed as irrelevant. The final outcome is positive, after all, and to confirm this, the refugees are allowed to chime in again. Even the *Süddeutsche* article—which benefits from the writer's linguistic access and ability to present more nuanced depictions of visitor responses—favors a young man who expresses gratitude "to Germany for 'taking such good care' of the treasures of his homeland." A cynic might suggest that the internalization of this line to justify Germany's behavior is proof of successful integration.

The point here is not to denigrate the Multaka initiative but to ask how the project fits into a greater "complicated history," and why the details of this history are so often downplayed or withheld rather than explored. The reason these details are concealed, one can assume, is largely because the answer to the visitors' question is less complicated than it is awkward: these precious artworks are here because they were stolen. When Ghassan Hage references "years of colonial impunity," that is exactly what he means.[20] True acknowledgment of that fact would mean an end to impunity, which in this case, at least, would take the form of art repatriation, if that is what the formerly colonized nations wanted. It would also require an open examination of historical and contemporary justifications for hoarding such treasures in Western museums. Silence about the origins of Europe's premier collections of non-European art, meanwhile, feeds

---

18. Fritz, "Projekt 'Multaka.'"
19. Donadio, "Berlin's Museum Tours."
20. Hage, "Terrorism, Brussels, etc."

a culture of remembrance in which colonial structures maintain sway over the present, among other things by shielding Europe from the consequences of its past and current actions. Museums deliberately obscure this connection, evoking an apolitical educational tradition based on presenting and safeguarding a common global cultural heritage.[21]

Berlin's Museum Island is a prime example, itself a United Nations Educational, Scientific and Cultural Organization World Heritage Site and home to all Multaka partner institutions, save the German Historical Museum.[22] As such, it is worth taking a closer look at its self-presentation. Its website's home page wastes no time in telling us that the "initial plans for the construction of the Museumsinsel Berlin were driven by the humanistic ideals of the Enlightenment that prevailed in the early 19th century." The account of the island's history opens with Friedrich Wilhelm II founding the Altes Museum as a "sanctuary of art and science" in 1830 and carries on through the completion of the Pergamon Museum in 1930. No mention is made of the ensuing fifteen years, save a terse depiction of the complex as a casualty of war: "After the Second World War, the ... collections belonging to the state of Prussia were either strewn over countless sites ... or had been destroyed; the buildings themselves were severely damaged." The reason for the destruction goes unspoken, as does the fact that the island was part of the German Democratic Republic until the Wall came down. Instead, the line about World War II is followed directly by reunification and the "[merging of] the collections of former East and West Berlin."

It comes as no surprise that colonialism is omitted from this account, sketchy as it is. What is remarkable, though, is how the

---

21. This practice is coming under fire by a growing number of artists, and it is no coincidence that most belong to racialized groups (e.g., Fred Wilson, Carrie Mae Weems, and Sasha Huber). Christian Kravagna points to early German critics of this institutional practice, like Hannah Höch. Kravagna, "Konserven des Kolonialismus."

22. Five museums are located on the Museum Island: the collection at the Altes Museum (Old Museum) represents classical antiquity; the Neues Museum (New Museum) houses mostly Egyptian treasures; the Pergamon Museum contains both the Museum of the Ancient Near East and the Museum for Islamic Art; the Museum of Byzantine Art is located in the Bode Museum; and the Alte Nationalgalerie (Old National Gallery) exhibits nineteenth-century European painting and sculpture.

Museum Island is introduced instead: "Situated in the very heart of the city, the Museumsinsel Berlin is one of the country's major sights, attracting hundreds of thousands of guests from all over the world each year. This unparalleled museum ensemble was the cradle of today's Staatliche Museen zu Berlin and is where it showcases its magnificent collections of art and cultural artefacts spanning several millennia from Europe and the wider Mediterranean region."[23] An institutional group that presents German audiences with looted art from North Africa and the Middle East—a good four-fifths of annual visitors to the Museum Island seek out exhibitions from these regions[24] —casts itself as a project that exposes people "from all over the world" to examples of European art and culture. Oh, right, and to artifacts from the "wider Mediterranean region," too—Iraq, Syria, and Egypt, in particular, exactly those parts of the Mediterranean unequivocally distinguished from Europe and defined as the Middle East or North Africa when it comes to the thousands of people fleeing the area. What, then, is this designation, "Europe and the wider Mediterranean region," all about? If anything, shouldn't it just be called "the Mediterranean region"? When people make casual reference to the Mediterranean, the image does not usually exclude those coastal countries that belong to Europe, like Italy or Spain. Besides, with the exception of the Old National Gallery, the Museum Island's five institutions all focus primarily on the Mediterranean region, European and non-European alike; Europe is primarily represented by ancient Rome and Greece, a share that scarcely justifies the prominent positioning the non-Mediterranean part of the continent enjoys. "Europe and the Middle East" would be more accurate but less hierarchical. "Europe and the wider Mediterranean region," by contrast, positions the latter as a kind of natural appendage to the former—they were collecting European art anyway, so they figured they might as well toss in this free-floating region too.

This is the message: Our common culture is on display in these museums, so there's no need to question why treasured artifacts from

---

23. Staatliche Museen zu Berlin, "Museumsinsel—Profil."
24. Stiftung Preußischer Kulturbesitz, "Jahrespressekonferenz."

the Middle East are held by German institutions, as we all have the same claim to this art. Sure, little common ground is found in the Mediterranean these days—many Europeans instead see it as a clear dividing line between a civilized Western world and a totalitarian Islamic realm—but this does not weaken the message. On the contrary. One of the Multaka guides is quoted favorably in the *Berliner Zeitung* piece as saying that "it was also nice that visitors could learn about the rich culture of the Middle East—his culture. 'We're not just a war-torn country. The museum makes that very clear.'"[25] However obvious it may be that the "wider Mediterranean region" memo hasn't reached him yet, the guide is affirming the role of Europe as the protector and keeper of world culture. In the same spirit, the *Guardian* quotes a member of the group who, while touring the Pergamon Museum, is reminded that "Syria hasn't always been the way it is now. We used to be tolerant." This provides the author with a segue to report on plans for the guides, once their German skills have improved, to lead groups of German visitors and "tell [them] about the hidden connections between their cultures."[26] The notion that newly arrived Iraqis and Syrians would have to spell out these connections, despite the Germans' having held these cultural artifacts for more than a hundred years, does not give the reporter pause or cast any doubt on the civilizational value of the whole undertaking.

Berlin Babylon: Art Is Universal

Imagine how different the response would be if plans were announced to ship the *Mona Lisa* or the Brandenburg Gate off to Quito to expose the world to European culture. But, of course, that would never happen. Meanwhile the Pergamon Museum—the most popular institution on Berlin's Museum Island, with around one million visitors annually, followed closely by the Egyptian Museum—houses the Ishtar Gate, built in 575 BCE in Babylon, in present-day Iraq. The German archaeological excavations that led a few years later to the

---

25. Fritz, "Projekt 'Multaka' in Berlin."
26. Oltermann, "Berlin Museums' Refugee Guides Scheme."

gate's relocation to Berlin began in 1899, the same year Friedrich von Pfeil published his studies on *Kanaken* and Germany laid claim to another Polynesian colony, Samoa. As the Pergamon Museum's visitor figures attest, the Ishtar Gate is breathtaking. Nevertheless, it is utterly devoid of context—the context in which it was constructed is as opaque as that in which it was brought to Berlin. There is nothing here to help uncover the "hidden connections" that made it possible for Germany to gain priceless works of art or, in some cases, to acquire them from other colonial powers. Appeals for repatriation—from calls for the Ishtar Gate to be returned to Iraq to requests for the bust of Nefertiti, "discovered" in 1912 by Ludwig Borchardt and housed in the Egyptian Museum, to go back to Egypt—have been denied time and again. The same reasoning is always furnished, namely that Germany's actions were legal at the time and, more importantly, that the "artworks are part of the world heritage of humankind, which regardless of their location should be made accessible to as many people as possible."[27] And making things accessible just happens to be easier in Germany than in Iraq. This isn't a specifically German argument, of course. "The power and promise of encyclopedic museums" has also been championed by James Cuno, who [from 2011 to 2022] oversaw the wealthiest museum on earth, the Getty Museum in Los Angeles (built with oil money),[28] as CEO of the J. Paul Getty Trust. He argues that "[by] preserving and presenting examples of the world's cultures, they offer visitors the world in all its rich diversity. And in doing so, they protect and advance the idea of openness and integration in a changing world."[29] Accordingly, he

---

27. Minister of State for Culture Bernd Neumann issued this statement in 2011, the last time the German government refused to return the bust of Nefertiti, which Egypt has been demanding since 1925. Presse- und Informationsamt der Bundesregierung, "Kulturstaatsminister Bernd Neumann."

28. J. Paul Getty made his fortune in part by acquiring oil production rights in Saudi Arabia, which in turn contributed directly to the kingdom's rise to first regional and then global power. Despite the Getty Museum's pretense to universality, its collection is limited to "Western art." As for Western art from the Mediterranean region, the museum's ongoing conflicts with Italy and Greece demonstrate that these artifacts were not always acquired legally either. See Fontevecchia, "The Getty Family."

29. Cuno, "Culture War." See also his books *Who Owns Antiquity?* and *Museums Matter*.

opposes the repatriation of cultural objects that were acquired "legally" (or simply stolen) during colonial occupation and, in the name of enlightened humanism, decries the notion as damaging to the "legacy of humankind." Cuno deems demands for restitution selfish, small-minded, and ignorant of art's belonging to the "world's cultural heritage," whereas a handful of wealthy nations hoarding this heritage is in the common interest.

Apart from the fact that rejecting myopic nationalist interests in favor of enlightened cosmopolitanism applies to cultural objects from crisis zones but does not extend to the human beings fleeing those places, Cuno's position neglects to acknowledge that the concentration of world heritage in the West is not accidental, nor is it based on some innately superior artistic sensibility but rather on the extreme power hierarchy of colonialism. A project like this, aimed ostensibly at edification, is possible only because it started as a colonial project: Germans and other Europeans were the ones in control, not those native to the place, for whom such projects were possible only under colonial rule. This also meant that cultural treasures became the colonizers' property, and without having paid a cent, colonizers shipped these objects off to the metropole (and sold them among themselves). Beyond the cultural devastation, the economic damage to colonial regions is valued in the trillions.[30] At the same time, without their looted artworks, many of the world's most famous museums would have to shutter, as the stream of visitors (and thus revenue) would dry up.[31] This focus on the material foundations of Western museum practices leads back to the question of reparations that old colonial powers never paid. On the contrary, just as it was plantation owners—not the formerly enslaved—who were compensated after the abolition of slavery in the United States (with the result that Black Americans today own a whopping 1 percent of the nation's private wealth),[32] European colonial powers demanded a

---

30. The bust of Nefertiti alone is estimated to be worth 300 million euros. See "Das zweite geheime Gesicht."

31. This would certainly be the case for Berlin's Museum Island, whose biggest attractions fall into this category. If these collections closed, Berlin's tourist industry and the city's status as a cultural hub would suffer.

32. See Bruenig, "Racial Wealth Gap."

hefty fee for their territories' independence.[33] In their call for "reparatory dialogue," the CARICOM nations outlined six areas in which the long-term consequences of colonialism and slavery are most glaring. Cultural institutions came in at number three: whereas Europe has invested in such institutions as museums and cultural centers to provide its people with an understanding of a colonial past in which they function as the rulers and beneficiaries of slavery, the group argues, there are no equivalent institutions in the Caribbean. It is here that these crimes were committed, where victims were left disenfranchised, cut off from their institutional and cultural experiences and

---

33. The Republic of Haiti, for instance, was founded in 1804 after the Haitian Revolution, the only known successful slave revolt in history. France, itself a young republic at the time, thus lost its most profitable colony, where, on average, enslaved Africans did not survive beyond seven years working the sugarcane fields. England and its slaveholding former colony the United States subsequently joined France in doing whatever they could to restore control over the Black republic. After France threatened another invasion in 1825, the nations ultimately agreed on reparations—that is, payments from Haiti to France for the loss of (human) property totaling 90 million francs, or 15 billion euros in today's money. For more than a century, until the late 1940s, France—that enlightened state, birthplace of universal human rights—accepted repayment for that debt, damning Haiti to perpetual poverty. Haiti has petitioned for reimbursement, a call France has vehemently rejected. In 2015, French president François Hollande traveled to Haiti. His rationale for refusing recompense—underpinned by Haitian president Michel Martelly's remark, "No negotiation, no compensation can repair the wounds of history that still mark us today"—denies the current material consequences of this historical violence. Tharoor, "Is It Time for France to Pay?" See also Trouillot, *Silencing the Past* and Hay, "Why France Should Pay." The practice of forcing former colonies to compensate colonizers for lost "investments" (as though these had benefited the colonial population and had not, in fact, served exclusively the easier exploitation of the colonies) was not limited to France and continued well into the twentieth century. The Netherlands, for instance, charged Indonesia 4 billion guilder as a fee for ending its "police actions" and for "releasing" the extremely lucrative colony in 1949. (Colonial powers often referred to wars of independence as "police actions," which did not fall under the Geneva Convention, meaning colonizers could not be punished for breaching it. As a result, it took nearly seventy years for the Dutch government to be held accountable and forced to indemnify Indonesian survivors for the massacres it committed.) The fact that Indonesia "only" managed to pay off 600 million guilder is often presented as a loss for the Dutch. See van Zanden, *Economic History of the Netherlands* and Penders, *West New Guinea Debacle*. These sums—and these are just two examples of many—cast petitions for reparations from formerly colonized states and European "development aid" in a different light: contrary to popular belief, the Global South has always been responsible for financing Western growth.

memories. This crisis, the CARICOM Reparations Commission concludes, must be addressed.[34]

Babylon's Burning

History is not the sole concern here. Another is the material value of art, an increasingly important market, whether among the super wealthy or multinational corporations looking to invest strategically.[35] As per the logic of the evolutionary space-time model, the most highly traded contemporary art is almost exclusively the work of Western artists (predominantly male, with a handful of women),[36] whereas the metric for non-European artworks is age—the more ancient, the more valuable. As we know, most of these investment pieces are already "safe" in the West. Moreover, Western governments, corporations, and museums invest in rescuing endangered cultural objects in crisis zones, often with the help of nongovernmental organizations. Iraq, for instance, has seen countless artifacts looted over the course of its colonial period, and then again during the First and Second Gulf Wars. After invading Iraq in 2003, the US government was excoriated (by museums and others) for having failed to include the protection of these goods in its invasion plans, which international law requires of warring parties. Protecting cultural objects has now become part of the fight against the Islamic State, whose wanton destruction of pre-Islamic art lends new moral weight to the Western commitment to defend world heritage. What remains unmentioned is that this destruction did not start with ISIS. In September 2014, Secretary of State John Kerry delivered a speech at the Metropolitan Museum of Art in New York, a location chosen deliberately for announcing the next phase in the fight against ISIS. In response, the Iraqi artist and curator Rijin Sahakian commented, "Standing in front of Egyptian and Assyrian reliefs, he spoke about

---

34. CARICOM Reparations Commission, "Press Statement."
35. See Horowitz, *Art of the Deal*.
36. See Guerrilla Girls, *Guerrilla Girls' Bedside Companion* for a feminist analysis of the role of racism, sexism, and homophobia in the art market.

the cultural destruction wrought by ISIS (which is of course a very real issue, the destruction of artifacts and of life), and tied it to the announcement that the US would be embarking on a bombing campaign. Nowhere was there any discussion of the parts of Babylon that had already been destroyed by the US Military building a base on its ruins, the exact kind of works that he was standing in front of and making the case for the war on ISIS."[37] Sahakian is a vocal critic of investments made in "disaster art" in Iraq and elsewhere, often by the very parties profiting most from said disasters. Considering that outside of "safe zones" the basic infrastructure for a halfway normal life is still missing, she sees less humanism than whitewashing at play when the United States, Europe, and the Gulf States move to protect monuments or construct cultural centers inside heavily guarded green zones that are inaccessible to most of the population. In her statement (well worth reading) on the end of Sada, a project she founded to support young Iraqi artists, Sahakian outlines the ongoing exploitation and destruction of Iraq and names its profiteers, among them proponents of "encyclopedic" or "universal" museums; these institutions always need funding, and that increasingly comes from multinationals.[38] She counterposes their Enlightenment humanism with a radically different vision of world heritage and our shared responsibility for its preservation:

> Sada's intention was never to re-create an art "scene" or "market" in Baghdad, nor to privilege nationalist endeavors, which rely on the pretense of loyalty to artificial boundaries, armies and the notion that histories belong solely to particular territories or peoples. History is, in fact, shared. If we, as a community of artists, educators and citizens of the world hope to understand what is taking place in our education systems, governments and the mechanics of the arts and accessibility, then we must take this global site into consideration and look at what our information—or

---

37. Kim and Khoshgozaran, "Politics as Currency."
38. Meanwhile, a robust and extremely lucrative black market exists for stolen artworks from Iraq and Syria, with clients primarily located in the United States, Europe, and the Gulf States. It goes without saying that the same museums that refuse to return art stolen during the colonial period condemn today's illegal art trade, which follows much the same pattern. See Maak, "Die Tempel der Isis," and "Antiken-Schmuggel."

lack thereof—says not simply about Iraq but ourselves and the systems we take part in every day.[39]

When presented within a real material context in this way, the ostensibly apolitical, progressive cosmopolitanism of Western museums and curators proves neither apolitical nor altruistic. Instead, it plays just as important a role in justifying and implementing the dominant system as "*Kanake!*"-shrieking Alternative für Deutschland (Alternative for Germany) voters or German arms exports (some of which have gone to Saudi Arabia, which is busy creating the next humanitarian crisis with its bombing campaigns in Yemen). The appreciation shown for cultural objects stolen during the colonial period cannot be divorced from the ongoing pillage of "failed states" and apathy toward what Hage calls the "differential of exterminability and mournability" of human lives.[40] Perhaps one of the Multaka project's main accomplishments, whether desired or not, is that it highlights this connection. One can only hope that "our society" meets the very well-intended "confident and constructive introduction of the refugees" with the same constructive spirit.

Humboldt Forum: Postcolonial Is Preferable to Postsocialist

As notions of Germanness grow more diverse, they can no longer be couched in a single universalist-internalist narrative. This has been made clear in the public debate surrounding the Humboldt Forum, located adjacent to Berlin's Museum Island [which opened to visitors in mid-2021—Trans.]. Together with the Museum Island, the Forum is part of a master plan to cast "the center of Berlin as a place of universal enlightenment, a place of world art and expertise, facilitated by the Staatliche Museen zu Berlin (SMB, Berlin State Museums) as the largest universal museum in existence," as Peter-Klaus

---

39. Sahakian, "On the Closing of Sada."
40. Hage, "Terrorism, Brussels, etc."

Schuster, then SMB director, wrote back in 2005.[41] There are any number of reasons why disputes about the timing and legitimacy of such a project should focus on the Humboldt Forum. For one, it will house "non-European" objects that were relegated after reunification to the collections in Dahlem, a neighborhood far from central Berlin. One hundred years earlier, Berlin's ethnological collection was the largest in the world; the African division alone grew from 3,500 pieces to 47,000 between 1880 and 1914.[42] The eager ethnologists who made these contributions often did their collecting on the side, employed primarily as colonial administrators, like our old acquaintance Joachim Friedrich von Pfeil, who simultaneously researched and ruled over German protectorates and their inhabitants (his findings conveniently justified such an arrangement).

Ethnological collections often failed to distinguish between art, culture, nature, and "natives"—figurines and furniture might be displayed alongside a skull or the corpse of a Namibian anticolonial resistance fighter slain by German troops.[43] It is easier to see here than on the Museum Island that these are stolen artworks. The colonial practice of exhibiting human beings—dead or alive—in museums and zoos is also far more striking than the sight of ancient Egyptian mummies.[44] In short, the motley quality and presentation of non-European collections alone demonstrate that the exhibition pieces did not represent a reflection of self but of what was perceived—then and now—as Other. Not impressive precursors to our own civilization but a look back at the earliest chapters of human history.

---

41. Schuster, "Das universale Museum."
42. See Zimmerman, *Anthropology and Antihumanism* and Förster, "Nichts gewagt, nichts gewonnen."
43. See Zimmerer, "Humboldt-Forum."
44. In praise of the universal museum in Berlin, SMB director Schuster once again emphasized that colonial transactions "[observed the strict] division of finds," but as Kwame Opoku points out (using the Benin Bronzes as an example), the only thing being observed there were regulations founded on the legitimacy of colonial theft of land, culture, and human life. In 1897 the Berlin Ethnological Museum acquired the bronzes in a legal transaction from England, just months after the British had conquered Benin and begun the plunder of thousands of artworks. Not only was the museum director and anthropologist Felix von Luschan aware of this but he openly endorsed the robbery. See Opoku, "Looted/Stolen Artifacts."

Paradoxically, from this perspective, millennia-old Assyrian reliefs seemed closer developmentally to the present—that is, Europe's here and now—than contemporary "primitive art" from West Africa, which was considered representative of that prehistoric epoch; this, too, is a product of the evolutionary time model, in which non-European provenance necessarily implies positioning in the past.

The concept behind the universal museum in Berlin shows that this hierarchical worldview still reigns. Former SMB director Schuster explicitly says so in his vision for the completed Humboldt Forum: "European collections on the Museum Island and non-European collections on [Berlin] Palace grounds will have the means, unlike anywhere else, to enter into a uniquely close dialogue in the heart of Berlin."[45] Ignoring, for a moment, the question of why Berlin, of all places, should be preordained for such dialogue, let's remember that most artworks on the Museum Island *are* non-European. Syrian, Iraqi, and Egyptian art is absorbed into Europe here; not allowed to stand on its own, it acquires a sort of proto-European aspect, while at the same time people from those regions are defined today as the greatest threat to European identity—including (at times especially) those who have actually been Europeans for a long time but who never really *can* be, because of their Middle Eastern roots. The same does not apply to their cultural heritage, without which Europe seems unable to define (and delimit) itself. This shows that Europe's borders are indeed fuzzy and flexible—first a decades-long debate will question whether Turkey can ever become part of Europe, then it will go without saying that Egypt belongs to it; after all, who wants to see Nefertiti in a museum of African art?

This flexibility is not accidental, though, nor does it result from Europeans' confusion about their identity. Instead, it aligns logically with the perception of self and Other covered in this chapter, which—informed by the nexus between internalism and an evolutionary notion of time—considers Europe to be independent of the rest of the world, which in turn is understood solely in relation to Europe, namely as the supplier of raw materials for European development, both material and cultural. This view is grounded in the

---

45. Schuster, "Das universale Museum."

same Enlightenment tradition invoked by proponents of the universal museum, but really it does not differ much from colonial attitudes that convinced Europeans that *they*—and certainly not "degenerate" present-day members of a given culture—were the true descendants of those who had crafted such masterworks as the Ishtar Gate or the bust of Nefertiti. (Incidentally, in the nineteenth century, when the narrative of ancient Greece as the cradle of European civilization crystallized, northwestern Europeans viewed modern Greeks in the same light, so the current response to the Greek crisis is nothing new.)[46] Art theft thus became a means of "rescuing" the world's cultural heritage and remains so to this day, though now it is crises, war, and poverty outside Europe providing the justification and no longer the "racial inferiority" of those who made the art. The outcome is the same: the supposedly shared world heritage in the Pergamon Museum, which Europeans played no part in creating, isn't shared—instead, the fortress of Europe is expanded.

Should museum directors in Berlin care how many Nigerians or Egyptians are able to view the stolen art, or does it not matter, since we're all just humans (though some significantly more so than others)? Lest we forget, a systematic destruction of history accompanied the cultural and economic plunder of the colonies. In state-run and mission schools, it was drummed into colonized children that European civilization was superior to their own and that they had no real culture to speak of, all while exemplars of the same were carted off to European museums and art collections. And today? It seems more important to ensure the survival of these cultural goods by means of universal museums than to ensure the survival of "non-European" refugees by means of open borders.

There is at least one other reason the Humboldt Forum is so controversial: in order to build it, the Palace of the Republic had to be

---

46. As Edward Said established, it was the interplay of all sectors of society that made this message so effective—at some level it reached everyone. Ethnology might not pique our interest, and there are plenty of folks who haven't visited Berlin's Museum Island, but we have probably all read at least one Agatha Christie novel (in my case, it's closer to fifty), and it's this very image of the world that Christie—who was married to an archaeologist—created in her books.

razed. That structure was a glaring reminder of an unpopular fact in a forward-looking German discourse on memory: the forty-year history of the German Democratic Republic (GDR). The political decision against leaving the palace intact as a memorial to that history, in one form or another, and in favor of tearing it down and latching onto an older, seemingly less fraught version of Germany instead is symptomatic of the unified nation's approach to its divided past. The complexities and complications of hegemonic discourses on memory were particularly evident in postwar West Germany. The West German example is unique in that it represented an attempt to recreate a national memory based on common history, shared values, triumph over external challenges, and the struggle for freedom and unity (all standard features of national myths), but one that also included Germans as perpetrators who destroyed these values. This endeavor was always tense, and attempts were made to resolve the tension and to land on a traditional, heroic model of national memory—by differentiating strictly between "Nazis" and "Germans," for example, claiming that most Germans "had no idea what was going on," or by tracing the origins of fascism back to the Soviet Union under Stalin.

This attempt at normalization seems to have concluded, with some success, after the Soviet collapse and German reunification. East German postwar history now serves as an example of German victimization under external, totalitarian powers.[47] This eased the unified country's integration into a collective European memory, one reconstructed after the end of the Cold War, in which the experience of occupation by totalitarian regimes (Nazi Germany and the

---

47. Discourse around the victimization of Europe by "un-European" totalitarian regimes, in which fascism and Stalinism are largely interchangeable, is particularly problematic in Germany's case. It bears mentioning, though, that the transnationalization of European discourse on memory snuffed out what had already been a delayed and faltering debate about widespread collaboration in occupied nations during World War II (especially France and the Netherlands) and its roots in endemic European antisemitism. Instead, as I will explain in greater detail in Part 3, European Muslims were designated heirs to the antisemitism so popular in prewar Europe. White Christian Europe is thus able to externalize the prime element of its past that disrupts the narrative of a traditional Judeo-Christian bond—a bond that supposedly now manifests in the joint battle against Muslim intolerance.

USSR) was central. (The victimization of colonized populations by these same European powers, meanwhile, was ignored, despite the fact that Europe's postwar history was, and still is, profoundly shaped by the resulting wars of independence.)[48] At the same time, conflating GDR history with Soviet Stalinism and totalitarianism allowed for the categorical exclusion of forty years of East German experiences from the new, all-German culture. This rendered reunification a de facto annexation and upheld a linear, internalist historical narrative, in which East and West German memory could not stand side by side, let alone on an equal footing. West German identity and memory remained dominant, while alternative (in this case East German) positions were suppressed, as usual—with terrible consequences, as usual. As East Germany vanished with hardly a trace, East Germans' inability to adapt immediately to the new, Western standard was interpreted as misplaced nostalgia for the socialist past and as indicative of East German backwardness, political apathy, and basic incapacity to succeed under capitalism.

This was the backdrop to conversations about the Palace of the Republic. The question of whether one should encounter the past or future in central Berlin took on moral weight and seemed key to Germany's future role on the world stage. Had the Palace of the Republic been restored, it would have served as a reminder that more than one Germany existed, that different, even contradictory visions of Germanness existed that were nevertheless connected; it would have occasioned more of an inward, skeptical gaze.[49] Some who wished to preserve the palace accused West Germany of victor's justice and the blanket condemnation of the GDR that went along with it. Palace opponents dismissed the accusation as an expression

---

48. France's brutal war in Algeria (yet another "police action"), in which more than a million people were killed, is just one example. The fighting reached beyond Algeria's borders into France. The bloodiest postwar massacre in France was not the Paris attacks in 2015, as many argue, but the murder of several hundred Algerians by Paris police in October 1961. See El-Tayeb, *European Others*, 36–41.

49. The Norwegian artist Lars Ramberg may have illustrated this point best. Between 2002 and 2005, the building was rebranded the "People's Palace" and became a venue for art and cultural events. For several months in early 2005, Ramberg's piece—twenty-foot-tall glowing letters that spelled out the word *Zweifel* (doubt)—was installed on the palace roof. See Bravo, "'Volkspalast.'"

of *Ostalgie*,[50] a melancholy, unconstructive clinging to the past that serves no use in the present. Those in favor of demolition oriented themselves toward the future and a broader world. The reconceived center of Berlin was meant to represent Germany's new role. It was a symbolic prestige project, which makes its point of departure all the more relevant: Berlin Palace, constructed in the fifteenth century, served first as the royal Prussian residence and then as the imperial residence. It was badly damaged in World War II and leveled in 1950 by the GDR government. Its reconstruction to house the Humboldt Forum is extremely loaded and stands for a German course correction after the missteps of the twentieth century; it signals a return to the tradition of poets and thinkers,[51] which—unlike National Socialism and communism—has endured for centuries, not decades. Between the old palace facade and the "encyclopedic" collection contained within, the structure is a reminder not of what vanished after reunification but of what was rediscovered: German normalcy, casting off the memory of Nazism, the Holocaust, and war, and embracing an untroubled future in the tradition of enlightened Prussianism.[52]

The reorientation worked pretty well: In a 2014 poll, when asked to name the defining event in their country's history, 49 percent of German citizens responded with reunification. Sixteen percent pointed to Nazism and World War II, while only 0.5 percent mentioned the Holocaust, which came up even less than Prussia and the

---

50. The colloquial term *Ostalgie* is a portmanteau of *Ost* (East) and *Nostalgie* (nostalgia). It describes an idealization of or yearning for aspects of life in socialist *Ostdeutschland*, or East Germany.—Trans.

51. The alliterative cliché *Dichter und Denker* (poets and philosophers), originally a nod to the "Great Men" of Weimar classicism and Romanticism, has been used to describe the German people for hundreds of years. Germany is often referred to (with varying levels of reverence) as the *Land der Dichter und Denker* (nation of poets and thinkers).—Trans.

52. *Die Leere Mitte* (*The Empty Center*), a 1998 film by Japanese German artist and theoretician Hito Steyerl, proves that it's possible to tell the story of this place, the symbolically laden center of Berlin, in a way that connects these historical periods. She accomplishes this in part by engaging the perspective of people who have been excluded, from Jews turned away at toll gates to the city center in the nineteenth century to Polish laborers rebuilding Potsdamer Platz in the 1990s for a pittance. See Gerhardt, "Transnational Germany."

German Empire, cited by 3 percent of pollees.[53] Its undeniable success aside, this normalization process was highly contentious, as the scale of the controversy surrounding the Palace of the Republic's demolition demonstrates.[54] It should come as no surprise, then, that the conflict over what defined Germanness in the united republic would hinge on symbolic decisions. Nevertheless, curators and administrators seemed blindsided by pushback to the Humboldt Forum's content and approach.[55] The primary cause for the Forum's clumsiness in confronting an increasingly critical public is that, rather than considering other positionalities, its representatives uphold the internalist German perspective not merely as the norm but as the only possibility.[56] Irritation follows confusion in response to critical positions that share no common ground with internalism: the only appropriate response—granting that one's personal stance is just that, and that its superiority or even legitimacy cannot be

---

53. Foroutan, Canan, and Arnold, "Deutschland Postmigrantisch I."
54. See Feldmann, "Denkmalwert oder Denkmalsturz" and Boddien and Engel, *Die Berliner Schlossdebatte*.
55. Starting in 2013, critical voices from around the world joined to form No Humboldt 21! In its founding resolution, the association declared,
As already was the case during those times when "exotic curiosities" were displayed in the "cabinets of wonders" belonging to the Princes of Brandenburg and the Prussian Kings, the Berlin Palace—Humboldt Forum will apparently serve the purpose of developing a Prussian-German-European identity. This concern is actually directly opposed to the aim of promoting a culture of equality in the migration society and is being pursued to the detriment of others. The supposed "stranger" and "other" will be constructed with the help of the often centuries old objects from all over the world, and the extensive collection of European art on Berlin's Museum Island will be put to one side. In this way, Europe will be constructed as the superior norm.
See No Humboldt 21!, "Stop the Planned Construction."
56. See, for instance, the idea to name the square outside the Humboldt Forum after Nelson Mandela. Meant to quell criticism, it was not well received in Africa or Berlin. The South African embassy responded politely, but in no uncertain terms: "Although the decision to name public places like squares, streets, official buildings and the like rests entirely with the municipal authorities of Berlin, the Embassy of South Africa would expect that careful consideration be given to the integrity and legacy of Mr Mandela in their decision-making processes—particularly to his unequivocal standpoint on matters like colonialism, racism, slavery, cultural and material exploitation as well as respect for the cultural heritage of the people and nations of Africa." Bristow, "South Africa Lukewarm."

stated as fact but must be substantiated by means of argumentation among equals—is yet unthinkable.

If one reads the demolition of the Palace of the Republic as a move to encourage a positive German discourse on memory—one in which referencing the past no longer arouses ignominy but invokes a proud enlightened tradition, as embodied by the Humboldt brothers, and which slots seamlessly into wider European discourse—then it must also be seen as a decision in favor of a single, linear history with no allowance for divergent narratives. Not only did the reality of German normality go unacknowledged, the radically varied backgrounds and experiences among those who define themselves as the *Volk* (the people) were repressed entirely. This is all the more problematic because the new German reality is defined not only by the conflict between East and West German memory but also by disparities between hegemonic and migratized Germans. The plural experience of Germanness that results cannot be contained within an internalist, reactionary narrative that clings to a worldview that relied on the exclusion of the Other to function. Part 2 of this book explores concrete examples of this construct, as well as alternatives to it.

Part 2

Post/Socialist Reckoning with the (Nazi) Past

3

Roma, Sinti, and the Question of German Guilt

The Others Were Always Here

The narrative of Europe as a "colorblind" continent, where racism is as alien a reality as non-white inhabitants, warrants far more scrutiny than it receives. It is soon exposed as a convenient construct when read with an eye on the history of European Roma and Sinti populations. This racialized group has been persecuted and marginalized across Europe for centuries, a fact not reflected in the continental self-image. On the rare occasions that it is acknowledged, racism targeting Roma and Sinti is mostly shrugged off as anachronistic: either eastern Europe's democratic deficit after decades of communist rule is to blame or it's the minority group's own retrograde culture arousing resentment in western Europeans. There are clear parallels between the latter construct in particular and the representative function Indigenous groups perform in settler-colonial discourses found in non-European Western nations like the United States, Canada, and

Australia. "Natives" there are ascribed a kind of mystical affinity to the land, while their systematic exclusion is simultaneously justified by claiming that they are unable to adapt to the modern world: at the end of the day, the issue is that they have not evolved, that they literally embody the past and have no place in the present. This makes them victims of civilization, damaged by the march of progress, a process that is as natural as the innate connection to Mother Earth that their colonizers' descendants grant them, for which no one can therefore be held responsible. Despite clear differences, this is reminiscent of the temporal relegation of Roma and Sinti to a romanticized European past in which "Gypsies" function as noble savages—proud, seductive, enigmatic, and dangerous, the incarnation of a doomed world. This aligns with their exclusion from contemporary Europe, and here, too, we see parallels in the disciplining of racialized communities whose internal structures are deemed incompatible with modern societies: segregated schools, stolen generations, and forced sterilization, to name just a few methods.[1] This makes sense when one bears in mind that these practices of representation and control do not arise from actual qualities of Aboriginal and Torres Strait Islander peoples, Native Americans, or Roma but from the evolutionary model of time Europe employed in restructuring the world. Racism was not invented in the colonies or the American South. It comes from Europe. Evolutionary time has shaped intracontinental developments since long before the advent of post/colonial migration; it has existed since modern Europe set about inventing itself.

Jews and Roma, who were part of the continental population of modern Europe, were cast as the "stranger" within. The new norm was defined against the counterpoint they provided, a practice that continues to this day. This process of racialization is specific to Europe, and examining it allows us to poke holes in European colorblind exceptionalism. However, this requires a methodology that goes beyond hegemonic self-critique and engages seriously with decades of transnational interdisciplinary research on racism outside of continental

---

1. See Roma Union Frankfurt am Main, Leidgeb, and Horn, *Opre Roma! Erhebt Euch!*; Pusca, *Eastern European Roma in the EU*; Smith, *Everything You Know*; and Byrd, *Transit of Empire*.

Europe. For instance, analytical strategies developed in settler colonialism studies could be applied to the pernicious racism targeting Roma and Sinti populations, which the academy largely ignores. A comparative analysis of racism, one that encompasses European antisemitism as well, could draw from the intellectual traditions of such thinkers as Hannah Arendt, Aimé Césaire, and W. E. B. Du Bois; Du Bois's work spans much of the twentieth century, and he was far better known in Germany a century ago than he is today.[2]

Whereas the aforementioned authors focused more on colonialism and the Holocaust,[3] European antisemitism and racism toward Roma and Sinti are similarly well suited for comparative study. There are myriad reasons this rarely happens, among them white German scholars' reluctance to touch European racism, the rampant anti-Roma racism that pervades academia, and last but not least, the role of the Holocaust in stabilizing European identity. All too often, this allows for retrospective self-exoneration that precludes confrontation with other forms of European racism as well as the longer history of European antisemitism. That history, meanwhile, is inextricable from the German response to migration. After the Berlin Wall fell, perception of Eastern European immigrants shifted. Once viewed as victims of communism with special privileges, they were now seen as not-(yet-)quite-European. This resulted in two tiers of European Union membership, an indication that even unified Europe does not occupy the same time-space, with eastern Europe still a "Second World" bloc nestled between the capitalist West and Global South. What primarily separates it from the latter is its affiliation with Europeanness, to be proven among other things through an identification with whiteness and Christianity. The implied racialization was made explicit when it

---

2. See Chandler, "Possible Form of an Interlocution." Max Weber set about having Du Bois's *The Souls of Black Folk* translated in 1905, but ultimately it took until 2003 before a German version appeared. This seems symptomatic of Germans' stance toward the study of racism, especially when it comes to racialized writers. It is fairly glaring that, on the rare occasion that research from the United States is cited, it tends to be pieces by David Theo Goldberg, Howard Winant, or other white authors. Though they have undeniably produced important work, that work originates from a much broader corpus in which Stuart Hall, Paul Gilroy, Sylvia Wynter, Cheryl Harris, and W. E. B. Du Bois himself are the real heavy hitters.
3. See Rothberg, *Multidirectional Memory*.

came to the Roma, yet again the target for aggression against the putative Other. This was not only true for (re)emerging eastern European nations, whose ethnonational understanding of statehood essentially necessitated the exclusion of minorities, but also for western European nations, including Germany, the destination for many Roma fleeing this exclusion. Politicians and pundits exploited their presence using familiar patterns racializing social and economic fears that shaped German debates about migration throughout the twentieth century.

Majority opinion still clings to the image of a formerly culturally diverse but ethnically and religiously monolithic Germany (and Europe), thrown off-kilter by the unforeseen implications of the labor migration that began in the 1950s and has resulted in the nation finding itself confronted for the first time with a population that is fundamentally (religiously, culturally, "racially") different and whose ability to integrate remains uncertain. This before-and-after binary fails to capture the reality in Germany on multiple levels; what is more, it presents a perspective that makes it impossible to overcome the assumed division between German and un/German. Not only is the increased presence of nontraditional Germans almost inevitably presented as an invasion—discussions about migrants pretty reliably ask if there aren't already "too many" of them—but a distorted image of the past also emerges. Considering the Holocaust's centrality in Europe's culture of remembrance, there is surprisingly little interest in reconstructing everyday European Jewish life beyond the context of the Shoah (and with it, everyday European antisemitism) and of the role of migration within it. Instead, a certain German and European "homogeneity" is remembered as the natural state of things, while in fact it resulted from the Nazi genocide of Jews, Roma, and Sinti as well as massive "ethnic cleansing" during the interwar period. As it turns out, migration and migration management (and debates about both) have influenced German reality for centuries.

The Greatest Migrant Crisis since the End of World War I

All of Europe experienced huge waves of migration (voluntary, involuntary, or a mix) during the interwar period. In the years prior, Europe's multiethnic empires—Austro-Hungarian, Russian, Ottoman—had routinely channeled tensions into pogroms against minoritized populations. These empires' partial collapse after World War I led to the sweeping redrawing of borders (as the Berlin Conference of 1884–85 had done for European colonial holdings in Africa), followed by expulsions and mass exodus.[4] At greatest risk were minorities who had no homeland where they were the majority to theoretically shield or receive them (of course, the exclusion and forced categorization of groups on the basis of race and religion were also hugely problematic for those who could thus be deported to an unfamiliar "homeland"). This affected mostly Roma and Jews, who attempted to migrate to parts of Europe that had not closed their borders to migrants, often in the hopes of continuing from there to the United States or other countries in the Americas.

The Weimar Republic became a prime destination, especially for Jewish migrants, both because of its relatively liberal immigration laws and the major ports in Hamburg and Bremen. There were already networks in place, too: from 1915, the German Empire had heavily recruited (some might say conscripted) eastern European workers for the arms industry, among them many Jews.[5] Despite the Weimar Republic's relative willingness to accept them, Jews from eastern Europe were perceived less as victims of racial persecution in their countries of origin than as people fleeing poverty. Accordingly, public and political discussions revolved around the question of how great a financial and cultural burden Jewish asylum seekers would place on Germany; how to ensure their quick migration onward; and how to distinguish the small fraction of "real" refugees from the bulk of "social parasites" and petty criminals. The Imperial Immigration Bureau, established in 1918, declared that "[despite] privations in Germany, the cost of living was much lower and quality of life far better than in the peripheral states to the east. Furthermore, Jewish elements engaged in illicit enterprises there were not nearly as restricted as they were in Poland, for instance, where skulduggery was punished less by authorities than by the population taking the law

---

4. See Aly, *Rasse und Klasse*.
5. See Oltmer, "Verbotswidrige Einwanderung nach Deutschland."

into its own hands."⁶ Further fodder for propaganda was the fact that most asylum seekers were young unmarried men. They were increasingly portrayed as criminals and a threat to German women. Prussia set up temporary internment camps for Jewish refugees in the mid-1920s, and in 1923, thousands of young white German men descended on Berlin's Scheunenviertel, a Jewish neighborhood. They attacked residents and looted stores, killing one and injuring 175.⁷

The criminalization of refugees undoubtedly contributed to burgeoning antisemitism in Weimar. Eastern European Jews—often poor and Orthodox—were cast as fundamentally different and dangerous (i.e., as representatives of a supposed "real" Jewishness that included assimilated German Jews) and as an intolerable burden on Germany, which was still suffering from the impact of the war. One result of the hate campaign against Jewish refugees was a thorny relationship between the German Jewish minority and the migrants, which manifested in both solidarity and ostracism. An example of the former is an open letter by Albert Einstein published by the Berlin daily *Tageblatt* in December 1919. I present it here in full, as his criticism of Weimar society's treatment of refugees shows that what we are witnessing today is one instance in a broader pattern representing German normalcy, not some unprecedented exception to the rule. Einstein's appeal sounds scarily relevant, though it was written more than one hundred years ago (the same could be said for the *Tageblatt* editorial staff's tepid liberal stance):

Immigration from the East
BY PROFESSOR DR. ALBERT EINSTEIN

We are pleased to provide space for the following remarks by the preeminent scholar and wish to add that we share his view on the expulsion of poor Eastern European Jews who have already immigrated. Whether a cap on immigration will be set in the future remains to be seen—however, any such legal recommendation would have to be general and not directed solely at certain religious communities and circles.
—The Editors

---

6. Oltmer, "Verbotswidrige Einwanderung nach Deutschland," 116.
7. See Oltmer, "Verbotswidrige Einwanderung nach Deutschland."

Among the German public voices are increasingly heard that demand legal measures against Eastern European Jews. It is claimed there are 70,000 Russian, i.e., Eastern European Jews, in Berlin alone; and these Eastern European Jews are alleged to be profiteers, black marketers, Bolsheviks, or elements that are averse to work. All these arguments call for the most sweeping measures, i.e., herding all immigrants into concentration camps or expelling them.

Measures that devastate so many individuals must not be triggered by slogan-like assertions, even less so as objective reexamination has shown that we have here a case of agitation by demagogues that does not reflect the actual situation and is not a suitable means for counteracting existing wrongs. Agitation against Eastern European Jews especially raises suspicion that calm judgment is being dimmed by strong anti-Semitic instincts and, simultaneously, that a *specific* method is chosen which, by influencing the mood of the people, diverts from the true problems and from the real causes of the general calamity.

As far as is known, an official inquiry by the authorities that would undoubtedly reveal the baselessness of the accusations has not been conducted. It may very well be true that 70,000 Russians live in Berlin; but according to competent observers, only a small fraction of them are Jews, while the overwhelming majority are of *German descent*. According to authoritative estimates, not more than 15,000 Jews have immigrated from the East since the signing of the peace treaty. Almost without exception they were forced to flee by the horrible conditions in Poland and to seek refuge here *until they are given an opportunity to emigrate elsewhere*. Hopefully, many of them will find a true homeland as free sons of the Jewish people in the newly established Jewish Palestine.

It is quite likely that there are Bolshevist agents in Germany, but they undoubtedly hold foreign passports, have at their disposal ample funds and cannot be seized by any administrative measures. The big profiteers among the Eastern European Jews have certainly, long ago, taken precautions to elude arrest by officials. The only ones affected would be *those poor and unfortunate ones*, who in recent months made this way to Germany under inhumane privations, in order to look for work here. Only these elements, certainly harmless to the German national economy, would fill the concentration camps, and there perish physically and spiritually. Then one will complain about the self-made "parasitic existences" who no longer know how to take their place in a normally functioning economy. The misguided policy of suddenly laying off thousands of Eastern European Jewish laborers—who were coerced into coming to Germany during the war—and thus depriving them of their means of livelihood, leaving them with nothing to eat and systematically denying them job opportunities, has indeed forced people into the black market to keep themselves and their families from starving. The German economy, too, is certainly best served if the public supports the efforts of those who try to channel Eastern European Jewish immigrants into productive work (as, e.g., the often mentioned "Jewish Labor Office" does). Any "order of expulsion"—now so vigorously demanded—would only have the effect that the worst and most harmful elements remain in the country, while those willing to work would be driven into bitter misery and despair.

The public conscience is so dulled toward appeals for humanity that it no longer even senses the horrible injustice which is here being contemplated. I refrain from going into details. But it is disturbing when even leading politicians do not consider how much their proposed treatment of Eastern European Jews will damage Germany's *political and economic position*. Has it already been forgotten how much the deportation of Belgian laborers undermined the moral credibility of Germany? And today, Germany's situation is incomparably more critical. Despite all efforts, it is extremely difficult to reestablish the disrupted international relations; in all nations only a few intellectuals among the peoples of the world are initiating some first attempts; the hope for new economic connections (e.g., the material help of America) is still very weak today. The expulsion of the Eastern European Jews—resulting in unspeakable misery—would only appear to the whole world as new evidence of "German barbarism," and provide it with a pretext, in the name of humanity, to hamper Germany's reconstruction.

The recuperation of Germany can truly not be accomplished by the use of force against a small and defenseless fraction of the population.[8]

European "Unmixing" and Racialized Religion

The intermingling of culture, race, and religion that defined Weimar-era discourse on Jewish migrants and their menacing Otherness was a familiar feature in antisemitic tropes but also reflected a broader understanding of the relationship between aspects of identity that fed into visions of national identity sought by the modern state. This manifested in international negotiations following World War I that replaced Europe's crumbling multiethnic empires with "homogeneous" nation-states in an effort to reorder the continent and ensure its long-term pacification. The most extreme consequence was the population exchange authorized by the Treaty of Lausanne, intended to put a formal end to border disputes between Greece and

---

8. *Berliner Tageblatt*, December 30, 1919, in Janssen et al., *Collected Papers of Albert Einstein*. (English translation supplement),110. Emphasis in original.

Turkey. In this instance, religion was the deciding factor in determining ethnonational affiliation: around 1.5 million Christians from Turkey were forcibly relocated to Greece, and almost 500,000 Muslims from Greece were expelled to Turkey.[9] The treaty between the two nations, administered by the League of Nations and signed in 1923, sanctioned the wartime expulsions and provided for the "unmixing" of European border zones—in other words, it defined Europe as Christian and banished Muslim Europeans to their religious "homelands." Jewish Europeans, meanwhile, were rendered perennially homeless and un/European.[10]

The calculation was that this forced "ethnic homogenization" of Europe would put an end to old conflicts. Rather than rooting out the cause of these conflicts in despotism, racism, antisemitism, or economic exploitation, policymakers homed in on the existence of a multiethnic, multireligious European population. Ironically, the United States was the only League of Nations member to vote against the policy, despite the Jim Crow laws and ongoing violent resettlement of Native Americans back home. After World War II, the United States came around and approved a massive population exchange in Europe, referring explicitly to the "success" of Lausanne. The twentieth century saw upward of forty million Europeans forcibly relocated.[11] The actual heterogeneity of the European population—religious

---

9. The term *race*, which the League of Nations initially used to distinguish between resettled groups (and those awaiting resettlement), was changed to *people*, per Turkey's request. See Aly, *Rasse und Klasse*, 35.

10. So much for Europe's Judeo-Christian tradition: this tradition is very real, of course—as real as its Muslim-Christian counterpart—but ideologically the Christian majority has denied it fervently until the recent past. In an act symbolic of this recent change, in 2014 the Spanish government moved to grant citizenship to descendants of the Jewish Moriscos, who were expelled from Spain in the fifteenth century. There are no plans to offer the same to descendants of Spanish Muslims, expelled in the seventeenth century, most of whom now live in Morocco. This in turn reveals more about current relations than about these groups' place in European history. See Aidi, "Interference of Al-Andalus" and Stavans, "Repatriating Spain's Jews."

11. See Aly, *Rasse und Klasse*. In a seminal study, Götz Aly describes the mass resettlement sanctioned in the Treaty of Lausanne as a "novelty of international law," defined as a human rights violation in the 1948 Universal Declaration of Human Rights. He fails to mention the earlier systematic forced relocation of populations in the European colonies, which was also sanctioned by international agreements (see,

and otherwise—was muscled into conformity with a nation-state ideology that over the course of the twentieth century was increasingly presented as "just the way it is," despite the fact that further expulsions were necessary to maintain these "natural" ethnonational borders. It is important to note that this process (as with racism and antisemitism in general) was not about some innate fear of foreigners, an explanation still popular today for racist (a.k.a. "xenophobic") attitudes and acts. Instead, it was about the systematic regrouping of a heterogeneous population into those who have a claim to the "homeland" and those who—despite centuries of living there—are reduced to foreigners without any rights.

This regularly affected the Roma, who live all over Europe but have no state, which makes them particularly vulnerable under the model of (manufactured) ethnonational homogeneity. In virtually every instance of expulsion or forced resettlement in service of an ethnonational concept of the state, Roma were deemed fundamentally foreign, which not only justified their exclusion but made it imperative. To this day, the perception of Roma and Sinti as "foreign bodies" has barely changed. This is especially evident in the way mainstream discourse treats the history of their persecution under the Nazis. The process of acknowledging the genocide of this group was halting, delayed, and dictated by "experts" rather than victims—from the early postwar era, during which *Zigeunerforscher* (lit. Gypsy researchers) freely continued the studies they began under Nazism, to the contentious Memorial to Europe's Sinti and Roma Murdered under National Socialism unveiled in Berlin in 2012. The ongoing exclusion of racialized groups from councils and expert committees also means that the public sphere has become the only point of intervention available to Sinti and Roma. A nominally open arena, accessible to all, it at least provides an opportunity to disrupt dominant discourses. This is especially true when prevailing

---

for example, the Berlin Conference of 1884–85). It is one thing for European powers to separate colonial matters from international law on the basis of an alleged civilizational deficit in the people slated to be colonized; it is quite another for that policy to remain a blind spot in research today rather than providing a critical lens for studies of European politics.

views are changing, as was the case around the time of German reunification. Still, Roma and Sinti attempts to steer the discourse by means of public interventions—such as their occupation of the Neuengamme Concentration Camp Memorial in Hamburg in 1989[12]—have been largely unsuccessful. Instead, this particular period of upheaval was officially concluded with its discursive integration into hegemonic historiography, with Roma and Sinti perspectives as absent as ever. The experiential parameters of the majority (or in this case, the perpetrators) defined the assessment of a past in which the historical experiences of majority and minority overlap, thus allowing the perpetrators to remain the norm in a process that necessarily yields results friendly to the status quo.

German reunification symbolizes the nation's successful normalization, which acknowledges the Nazi past but no longer considers it meaningful for the present. Material expressions generally accompany such instances of symbolic closure. In Germany's case, those were the monuments for the victims of National Socialism erected in Berlin, including the disputed memorial honoring Sinti and Roma. The controversies surrounding this site, the last of three to be built, illustrate the second piece that led subaltern interventions to fail: mainstream Germans' refusal, even among those sympathetic to the cause, to relinquish their discursive hegemony and recognize the authority of racialized communities. When Roma activists tried to point out historical patterns as a problem that required intervention, for instance, the attempt was self-righteously dismissed. At the same time, these patterns continued, more or less unchecked, as illustrated in the Rostock pogrom of 1992, whose first target was Roma refugees. By occupying highly symbolic public spaces (discursive and physical), the activists aimed to decry the treatment of refugees as well as highlight the historical persecution of Roma and Sinti and modern-day Germany's attendant responsibility to them. I will use my hometown of Hamburg to illustrate this conflict.

---

12. See Schmemann, "Gypsy Protesters."

1939–1989: Exterminated—Persecuted—Expelled[13]

Unlike most other German states prior to 1933, "Red Hamburg," a labor movement stronghold since the late nineteenth century, did not have any special "Gypsy ordinances" to regulate or limit Roma and Sinti immigration or employment. After the Nazis came to power, however, the Hanseatic city-state quickly adapted. In 1938 the Reich Central Office for the Suppression of the Gypsy Nuisance was established in Berlin, at which point the persecution of Roma and Sinti intensified around the country. That fall, authorities in Hamburg adopted plans for a "Central Gypsy Collection Camp" to intern the city's roughly 850 Roma and Sinti residents. The German invasion of Poland rendered the plans redundant, as approximately 1,000 Sinti and Roma were deported from northern Germany to the Belzec forced labor camp in Poland. In addition, just a few months after the city had approved the Central Gypsy Collection Camp, the SS converted a disused Hamburg brickyard into the concentration camp Neuengamme, a new subcamp of the Sachsenhausen concentration camp. In 1940 it was expanded to become a stand-alone camp with upward of eighty-six subcamps. Initially political prisoners from other German camps represented the bulk of Neuengamme inmates, but over time they were joined by prisoners from occupied territories. Starting in 1941 the prison population was comprised mostly of Soviet and Polish prisoners of war, resistance fighters from northern and western Europe, and Jews from the East.

Prisoners at Neuengamme were subject to forced hard labor; in addition to manufacturing bricks for pompous fascist buildings on the banks of the Elbe River, they were tasked with harbor expansion and river-regulation projects on the Elbe. From 1942 inmates also worked in arms factories at Neuengamme's many subcamps. On top of forced labor and deplorable conditions in the camp, which cost many prisoners their lives, experiments were conducted by SS physician Kurt Heissmeyer, who infected inmates with tuberculosis and

---

13. The title of this section is a translation of *1939–1989: Vergast—Verfolgt—Vertrieben*, the title of a 1989 photo exhibition on Roma in Hamburg.

typhoid. (In order to destroy the evidence of these experiments, the SS murdered twenty interned Jewish children at a school located on Bullenhuser Damm in Hamburg-Rothenburgsort shortly before the end of the war.) In 1942 and 1943, 448 Soviet prisoners of war were gassed and at least 1,000 enfeebled inmates were injected with deadly poison. As US and British troops advanced in early April 1945, the camp was evacuated, and thousands died on the forced march northward. The remaining 10,000 prisoners were moved onto three ships in Lübeck harbor in mid-April. On May 3, British bombers mistakenly hit two of the ships, killing 7,000. Of the 100,000 people imprisoned between 1938 and 1945—about 10,000 of them women—not even half survived. After the war ended, Neuengamme was used as a transit camp for displaced persons, then as a prison for former Nazi functionaries, until the site became the permanent home of a juvenile detention center and the Vierlande correctional facility in 1948. A plaque commemorating the concentration camp victims was installed in 1965, but it took until 2006 for the prisons to finally be moved elsewhere and the whole site to be established as a memorial.[14]

Sinti and Roma were among those detained in the concentration camp. Along with Jewish and Soviet prisoners, they occupied the lowest rung of the camp hierarchy, suffering some of the worst abuses and receiving the smallest rations. They were assigned the hardest tasks and were some of the primary victims of medical experimentation. It is likely that around five hundred Roma and Sinti were interned at Neuengamme, though it is impossible to say for sure, as the SS destroyed all documentation before ceding the camp. Some stories have survived, like that of Suleika Klein, who was born in 1928 and died of tuberculosis at the Hamburg-Sasel subcamp in 1945. Before being transferred to Neuengamme, Klein had been imprisoned at Auschwitz and Ravensbrück. While at Auschwitz, she was raped by a *Kapo*, fell pregnant, and later delivered a stillborn baby at the camp.[15] Johann Wilhelm "Rukeli" Trollmann, a Sinto

---

14. See Garbe, *Konzentrationslager Neuengamme* and Wrochem, *Das KZ Neuengamme*.
15. See Wünsche, "Die nationalsozialistische Verfolgung."

from Hannover born in 1907, was arrested in 1942 and sent to Neuengamme, where he died in 1944. Eleven years earlier, Trollmann had become the German light heavyweight boxing champion; just a week later, he was stripped of the title, which was not restored until 2003, after extensive organizing. At his final competition in July 1933, before his boxing license was revoked because of his "un/German" and "Gypsy-like" fighting style, Trollmann appeared with dyed blond hair and a white powdered body. His brother Heinrich was murdered at Auschwitz in 1943.[16]

In 1956, the Federal Court of Justice issued a landmark ruling on "Gypsy persecution" in the Third Reich that denied survivors the right to reparations. According to the ruling, racially motivated persecution did not begin until 1943, with deportations to Auschwitz-Birkenau; everything prior to that was classified as a regulatory policing response to "antisocial" perpetrators. The ruling was revised in 1965, but even so, victims of Nazi persecution often had to fight for decades for the reparations they were due. Sinti and Roma survivors—perennially defamed as liars, cheats, and social parasites—experienced special challenges in asserting their claims. For those who *were* successful, stories like that of Giovanna Steinbach, a Sintiza from Hamburg, were sadly common: she finally received 60,000 deutsche marks as redress for her time at Auschwitz, which had left her with grave health issues, only to have Hamburg's social security office seize two-thirds of the sum as repayment for welfare benefits she had received in the 1950s.[17] However cynical, the episode did not

---

16. See Herold and Robel, "Zwischen Boxring und Stolperstein" and Repplinger, *Leg dich, Zigeuner*.

17. See Behrens, "Nur geduldet, nicht respektiert." Most German Roma and Sinti were stripped of German citizenship under National Socialism. When they demanded it be restored after the war, many were instead issued alien passports—it would seem "Gypsies" were as un/German in the Federal Republic of Germany as they had been in the Third Reich. Black Germans had similar experiences, given their automatic classification as "obviously" not German. West Germany and Nazi Germany embraced the same logic: "I applied for German citizenship again in '47. And 1963 is when it was finally granted. I was even asked if I had a receipt for having lost it. Utter madness! I had to write an essay in German, to prove that I could write flawlessly. My baptism record and other documents didn't count; I was treated like a foreigner." Oguntoye and Ayim, *Farbe bekennen*, 82–83.

conflict with dominant logic, as "regulatory responses" to "antisocial Gypsies" continued seamlessly after the war. Such responses were an expression not (only) of Nazi racial policy but of deep-seated racism, evident in the way authorities dealt with this group.[18] From 1951 to 1970, for instance, Hamburg police maintained *Landfahrerakten* ("vagrant files") first compiled by the Nazis. These were not made available to the public until 1980, when they were turned over to the Hamburg State Archive (which initially denied access to individuals who might have a personal stake in the files). A year later, it came to light that the police had continued their "Gypsy files," meticulous genealogies of the city's Sinti and Roma families. In other words, blanket accusations and collective punishment, based on the presumption of an inherent criminal and antisocial disposition, persisted in former West Germany.[19]

"We Will Occupy This Building Until Further Notice. The Victims Hold the Domiciliary Rights."[20]

Resistance to this ongoing persecution by authorities in Hamburg came primarily from the Rom und Cinti Union (Roma and Sinti Union; RCU), an association formally founded in 1983, though it had been active since the mid-1970s. From its inception, RCU pursued a different strategy to the Central Council of German Sinti and Roma, an older advocacy group that had been active since the 1950s and was officially established in 1982. This was in part related to tensions between migrants and Germans: the former did not feel adequately represented by existing organizations, whereas the RCU

---

18. This was also true in the German Democratic Republic (GDR). Although Sinti in the GDR were officially recognized as targets of the Nazi regime, they were the only group of victims required to prove their "antifascist, democratic stance" to receive individual recognition, which was often unsuccessful. See Winckel, *Antiziganismus*, 42.

19. See Wiedemann, "Angeblich von der Mauer gefallen."

20. The title of this section is a quote from a statement issued by Sinti and Roma activists occupying the former site of Neuengamme concentration camp in 1989. See "Erben der Opfer," *Der Spiegel*, November 11, 1989. www.spiegel.de/politik/erben-der-opfer-a-ec767983-0003-0001-0000-000013497181.

explicitly focused on migrants and rejected older associations for being overly assimilationist. The Central Council of German Sinti and Roma had been conceived as a civil rights organization. Its primary focus was creating awareness about the history of Nazi persecution and advocating for recognition of Sinti and Roma as a national minority, which would entitle them to protection against discrimination. Sinti and Roma were recognized as victims of the Nazi regime in 1982, partly in response to a 1980 hunger strike at Dachau concentration camp, where activists protested vagrant laws and registers still maintained in Bavaria. Acknowledgment as a national minority came in 1995 but in the form of a regulatory exception, as the government's rigid interpretation of the Council of Europe's Framework Convention for the Protection of National Minorities only allowed for this status to be granted to "traditional ethnic groups," that is, groups to which the following applies: "They are German nationals; they differ from the majority population in having their own language, culture and history and thus their own distinct identity; they wish to maintain this identity; they have traditionally been resident in Germany (usually for centuries); [and] they live in Germany within traditional settlement areas."[21] Danes, Sorbs, and Frisians tick all the boxes, but German Sinti and Roma fall short, as they do not meet the fifth and final criterion.[22] Minority status was therefore withheld from Roma and Sinti who were from families that had not verifiably "traditionally been resident in Germany," namely migrants and stateless people as well as those who were born in Germany but who could not prove that their families were "traditionally ... resident." The protection afforded by this understanding of minority status is cultural, intended primarily

---

21. Federal Ministry of the Interior and Community, "National Minorities."
22. See the "National and International Minority Rights" page on the website of the Federal Ministry of the Interior and Community, from 2014 (German language only): "Since 1993, Council of Europe member states have been working on a Framework Convention for the Protection of National Minorities, which was presented for signing on February 1, 1995. The Convention, implemented in Germany in 1998, prohibits any discrimination against a person on the grounds of belonging to a national minority and any assimilation against his or her will. Furthermore, it obliges member states to protect the right to freedom and to take extensive measures to promote national minorities."

to preserve aspects of German traditions, be it the Frisian language or Sorbian garb; the aim is not to guard against persistent discrimination, which would explain why neither Black nor Turkish Germans are defined as minority groups.

The RCU, meanwhile, operated transnationally, viewed Sinti and Roma as a *European* minority, and framed discrimination as a continental problem that had to be addressed across borders. (The RCU was a driving force behind the Roma National Congress, an organization acting throughout Europe to defend the community, especially those with stateless status.) Its founder, Rudko Kawczynski, was born in Poland and grew up as a stateless person in Hamburg. In 1983 he organized the group's first major action, a hunger strike at the decommissioned Neuengamme concentration camp, clearly inspired by the earlier protest at Dachau mentioned earlier. The RCU's demands were far less radical than either the act itself or public responses suggested: all the group asked for was access to the police department's "vagrant files," which had been housed in the Hamburg State Archive for several years. The archive refused permission until an administrative court ruling and an intervention by Mayor Klaus von Dohnanyi compelled it to grant the activists access. The files ultimately confirmed that mere identification as Roma or Sinti was sufficient grounds for inclusion in the records— in other words, this was blatant racial profiling. At the same time, both city and state denied having any information on Roma and Sinti populations residing in Germany, claiming that group-based statistics of that sort were not kept.[23]

The files also revealed other historical patterns. For instance, they showed that Ruth Kellermann, who had made a name for herself as a "Gypsy expert" in Nazi Germany, continued to be used as a court-appointed expert after the war. (She was also a popular guest lecturer in women's studies at the University of Hamburg, until Giovanna Steinbach and other RCU activists crashed one of her events.) After the RCU filed a complaint against her in 1984, the Hamburg public prosecutor's office finally brought proceedings against Kellermann for aiding and abetting plans of mass murder.

---

23. See Behrens, "Nur geduldet, nicht respektiert."

Kellermann countersued, asking for the charges to be dropped, but the court concluded there was sufficient evidence "that the claimant was active during the period from 1938 to the end of the war in a field in which her work at least contributed to enabling the persecution and extermination of the Gypsies."[24] Nonetheless, the case was dropped in 1989 due to a supposed lack of evidence. Frustrated by such rulings, lack of cooperation by local authorities, and a worsening racist atmosphere, the activist group around Kawczynski increasingly turned to confrontation, media offensives, and civil disobedience. The RCU's subsequent actions aimed at securing the right of residence for Roma from eastern Europe living in Hamburg, but recognition of both Nazi persecution and contemporary racism were wrapped up in this objective.

Beginning in the early 1980s, around 1,500 Roma had come to Hamburg from Yugoslavia and Poland and applied for asylum. Nearly all their applications were rejected, because political persecution was not detected in the countries of origin, or so German authorities alleged. The systematic racism that Roma and Sinti people endured did not fall under any official category of persecution, a fact that holds today, even though the situation worsened after the end of state socialism. This community's aggressive exclusion from eastern European society—ghettos, walls, segregated schools, forced sterilization—is partly a response to economic transformations, partly an affirmation of Europe's shared racial identity. While on the one hand, western European nations condemn such policies as inhumane vestiges of socialist rule, on the other, similarities can be found in western Europe's response to Roma fleeing conditions in eastern and central Europe, from pogroms to forced registration to mass deportations. Germany is no exception, despite the Porajmos. The difficult circumstances facing the migrants in Hamburg—poverty, marginalization, a precarious legal status that made it illegal for them to work—were not viewed as a problem Germany bore particular responsibility for solving, given the Nazi genocide perpetrated against Roma and Sinti. Instead, the Roma themselves, however few in number, were seen as the problem; after

---

24. See Kompisch, *Täterinnen* and Behrens, "Nur geduldet, nicht respektiert."

all, the authorities and the general public alike already perceived and treated them as inherently criminal. Accordingly, the solution the city senate pushed for was their removal—deportation, that is.

Deportations from Hamburg were scheduled to begin in early 1989, and in response, the RCU organized another hunger strike in Neuengamme. The protest ended two weeks later, after Senator of the Interior Werner Hackmann approved a six-month ban on deportations, during which individual cases were supposed to be reviewed. In August, shortly before the ban was due to expire, several hundred Roma occupied the memorial, as it had become apparent that the city would not grant more than 150 of them the right of residence. The senate rejected the possibility of conferring a general right of residence, as they argued it would violate the principle of equal treatment for asylum seekers. Special treatment for Roma based on Germany's historical obligation was never on the table.[25] An exhibition titled *Krieg Gegen Polen* (War against Poland) that had been set to open the day the occupation began was relocated from Neuengamme to Bergedorf Castle. In his opening address, Second Mayor Ingo von Münch stated, "Issues with Roma and Sinti should not be mixed up with the commemoration of the many victims in Poland and other European countries." He also described the protest as "inappropriate toward the memory of the victims at Neuengamme."[26]

---

25. As Senator of the Interior Hackmann later explained to Kawczynski, "You are demanding we grant these 1,200 people the right of residence. To that I say: We can't do that in Hamburg. I don't want to, either. I acknowledge my historical responsibility, and I'm not leaning on the 'mercy of late birth.' I acknowledge Nazi atrocities, but we cannot use asylum law and the right of residence to solve Yugoslavia's economic woes, which is really the main reason these people came here." Kawczynski and Hackmann, "Sie haben mich reingelegt." All that is to say, granting 1,200 people the right of residence was not only more than a city of nearly two million people could handle but also pushed the limits of historical responsibility for genocide.

26. Hassel, "Durchhalten bis zur Abschiebung."

4

"We Are the *Volk*"

From Racist Terror to Terrorized Germans

"The More People Sort of Melted Together, the More We Fell Behind"

As far as Rudko Kawczynski was concerned, if anyone's behavior toward Neuengamme concentration camp victims was inappropriate, it was the city of Hamburg's. The protest organizer disputed accusations of politicizing a "neutral" memorial site and pointed out that the occupiers were resisting mass deportations back to the sites of their persecution (especially as ethnic tensions in Yugoslavia were escalating at the time)—a concern that surely bore parallels to the memorial's mission. Whereas the charitable aid organization Arbeiter-Samariter-Bund (ASB) initially provided the activists with basic services and supplies, the Red Cross adopted the view that the occupation was politically driven and therefore lay outside their ambit. ASB withdrew after a few days, and in early October, citing trespassing, the city dispatched police to forcibly remove the occupiers.

There were several shows of solidarity: the Jewish community of Hamburg demanded an apology from the city for ordering a police operation at a former concentration camp; the Arbeitsgemeinschaft für Arbeitnehmerfragen (Association for Labor Issues) of the Social Democratic Party condemned the senate decision and declared, "It is irreconcilable with the social democratic tradition that the heirs of Nazi victims should still be expelled today";[1] the Social Democratic Party's parliamentary group in Schleswig-Holstein offered to shelter Roma from Hamburg; and, as in months prior, some churches offered temporary asylum. Overall, though, the situation did not attract much attention, let alone outrage over state violence against one of the primary victims of National Socialist extermination policies—and at a site of this extermination, no less.

The Roma activists' strategy, in Hamburg and nationwide, relied on the protection afforded by publicity, the assumption that the state would not carry out violent mass deportations while in the international spotlight. For a brief spell, such acts as the occupation of Neuengamme, the hunger strike in Cologne Cathedral, or *Bettelmärsche* ("begging marches")[2] through Germany to the Dutch and Swiss borders were successful in drawing attention. Public interest soon turned elsewhere, however, and political pressure waned: there was the failed attempt by Hamburg's senator of the interior to persuade other federal states to establish minimum numbers of Roma refugees they would admit, and in North Rhine-Westphalia, concessions initially made after the protests were retracted. Other events had come to command public interest: The head of the German Democratic Republic (GDR) Erich Honecker had just resigned when the occupied concentration camp was cleared in October 1989, and a few weeks later, on November 9, an antideportation demonstration followed by a symbolic occupation of the brickworks at Neuengamme were utterly eclipsed by the excitement surrounding the opening of the inner German border. Looking back, Kawczynski

---

1. "Zigeuner: Die Erben der Opfer."
2. The term *Bettelmarsch* ("begging march") references the fact that people marched without supplies, relying on communities along the way to provide them with food and shelter.

reflected in 1991, "At that time, analogous to what we were doing there, this German reunification began to pass us by, and it's actually quite significant that the more the border to the East opened up, the more people sort of melted together, the more we fell behind, and people turned to open brutality, lost all shame."[3] Leading up to the fall of the Berlin Wall, the West German media was dominated by reports on the East German "refugee wave" crossing the Czech border and filling reception centers in Bavaria. Although there are of course significant differences between what happened then and debates surrounding the migrant crisis of 2015, the general mood in 1989 was also one of overextension. Despite whatever sympathy West Germans expressed at the plight of those fleeing, what they really seemed to want was for them to stop coming. Fittingly, on the day the Wall fell, West German Chancellor Helmut Kohl vowed to improve conditions in the East so that people could stay there—or go back. And, subtle as ever, Minister of the Interior Wolfgang Schäuble stressed that West Germany was experiencing a housing shortage.[4] One could argue that a consequence of the (actual or imagined) burden of accommodating the mass arrival of a large and growing group of refugees—in this case, East Germans—was the hardening toward another, much smaller, but already ostracized group, namely Eastern European Roma. Their presence became a symbol of Germany's overextension, making their expulsion a top priority. This strategy is evident today, too: as I write these lines in 2015, Roma activists are occupying St. Michael's Church in Hamburg to protest looming mass deportations to newly "secure countries of origin," like Serbia, Bosnia, and Macedonia.[5] In the years following reunification, Roma were among the primary targets of an increasingly socially accepted racism, and they were the main victims of tightened asylum and migration policies, state regulations that legitimized and stoked popular racism. This was confirmed in 1993 after Germany finalized a deportation agreement with Romania,

---

3. Hielscher and Herder, *Gelem, Gelem*.
4. See Tagesschau, "Tagesschau vor 20 Jahren, 09.11.1989."
5. Romano Jekipe Ano Hamburg, "Romano Jekipe Ano Hamburg" and Baeck, "Verfolgung geht von der Polizei aus."

which—like a similar agreement with Yugoslavia—many Roma aptly describe as a "sale," as these states agreed to accept the deportees in exchange for financial support from Germany.

RCU activists in Hamburg staged another occupation at Neuengamme on May 16 to prevent these mass deportations to Romania, calling the action *Fluchtburg Konzentrationslager* (Concentration Camp Refuge). The date was of symbolic importance, exactly fifty-three years after the first Roma and Sinti were deported from Hamburg to concentration camps. Just half a year after the pogrom in Rostock, however, it turned out that the new German normality had even less capacity for reckoning with the past than the old one. At the behest of Christina Weiss, senator for cultural affairs, police were sent to block activists from the site; according to Weiss, arguing like a true Hamburg bureaucrat, this was all about protecting a "German cultural asset" from "improper overuse." The response effectively confirmed a statement published by the Roma National Congress (RNC) in the lead-up to the protest: "The situation for Roma in reunified Germany is defined by deportation agreements, expulsions, demagogic treatment in newspapers, non-recognition as a people, and political defamation in the form of blunt banish-the-Gypsies moves. . . . After Auschwitz and half a million murdered Roma, normality between Germans and Roma will never exist. Set against this backdrop, the actions of the German government amount to a reckoning with the past through continued injustice."[6] As though this analysis wanted further confirmation, in 2001—eleven years after a case had been brought against him for "coercion in traffic" during nationwide protests—Kawczynski was summoned to start serving time in Vierlande Prison, on the grounds of the former concentration camp Neuengamme.

"German Sinti and Roma Opinions Are Decisive"

In retrospect, what is striking about the debate is the idea that the occupation of Neuengamme would be seen as a breach of propriety, as

---

6. Roma National Congress, "Fluchtburg Konzentrationslager."

exploiting historical truths, or even as a mockery of Nazi victims (as Senator of the Interior Hackmann would suggest).[7] The real question is, Whose is the history that was subject to such supposed exploitation? RCU activists chose that location deliberately, of course, but not to downplay the genocide that had occurred there; on the contrary, referencing the Porajmos seemed the only way to establish a context in which anti-Roma racism would be seen as taboo. The RCU tried to leverage into state action the rhetoric of responsibility Germany had employed for the mass murder of Roma and Sinti. Instead, said democratic German nation accused them of trivializing this legacy. The majority population could deny its moral responsibility because Roma were not "good" victims (to quote Hackmann, "I can't imagine the Jews would ever pull a stunt like the one Herr Kawczynski is pulling. Besides, the Jews have a state.").[8] The practice of pitting victims against each other—descendants of the perpetrators deciding who "deserves" special treatment—was also evident in the disputes over the memorials in Berlin, which intensified around the same time as the RCU campaigns. These discussions were not about the "exploitation" of memorials to Nazi victims but about the creation of the first central Holocaust memorial in the united republic. The outcome, though, was the same—Roma and Sinti were lesser or even "bad" victims.

Discussions about a memorial of this kind had begun years earlier in West Germany but gained new significance after reunification and Berlin's designation as the new capital. A group called Perspektive Berlin, under the leadership of historian Eberhard Jäckel and journalist Lea Rosh, quickly took charge in arguing for a central memorial to the murdered Jews. It was important that the initiative arose from civil society, driven by citizens rather than the state, and that it was conceived as an expression of the perpetrators' responsibility (so at first the group did not recruit any Jewish members).[9] The public

---

7. The title of this section is a quote from Zentralrat Deutscher Sinti und Roma, "Stellungnahme des Zentralrats."

8. Kawczynski and Hackmann, "Sie haben mich reingelegt." True to form, Hackmann was saying more here than intended: if there were not a nation (one outside the continent, no less) that was willing to take in the Jews, their situation in Europe would undoubtedly have been far more precarious.

9. See Kirsch, *Nationaler Mythos oder historische Trauer?*

quickly embraced Perspektive Berlin's ideas, as did the federal government, which by 1992 had joined in the planning. The other part of the project, meanwhile, was riddled with conflict—as is so often the case with well-meaning attempts to act on other people's behalf. The Central Council of German Sinti and Roma was vehement in demanding to be included. Council chair Romani Rose presented the case in a statement published in *Die Zeit* in April 1989, outlining similarities between the forms of persecution both groups suffered: "Only when it came to Jews and Sinti and Roma was racial affiliation (as assumed by the Nazis), their mere biological existence, set as the sole reason for their extermination, whether they be old people or children. This intended annihilation typifies the singularity of the National Socialist crime of genocide."[10] Rose was met with dogged opposition, unlike Ignatz Bubis, chairman of the Central Council of Jews in Germany, who was often cast—willingly or not—as the authoritative voice for all (German) Jews by Perspektive Berlin and the federal government. Rose's criticism of the initiative certainly contributed to this response, but it was not the only reason. He was not recognized as an authority, nor did Perspektive Berlin plan to do anything "for" Roma and Sinti victims in the name of the descendants of the perpetrators. Rather, until the Central Council got involved, they had simply been forgotten.[11] Although Jäckel acknowledged that systematically "forgetting" the Porajmos was an "injustice," he ultimately drew on his authority as a historian and Holocaust expert in endorsing the original plan, without including Roma and Sinti.[12]

The familiar conflict between experts and impacted groups, categories that are often treated as mutually exclusive, is combined here with a contradictory perception of the Porajmos in postwar German history, yielding incompatible narratives: on the one hand is expert

---

10. Rose, "Ein Mahnmal für alle Opfer."
11. To this day, the website for the Memorial to the Murdered Jews of Europe does not mention Roma and Sinti victims in its timeline of the memorial's creation. [This was true at the time of the publication of the German original in 2016 but has now been corrected. See "Memorial to the Murdered Jews of Europe," Stiftung Denkmal für die ermordeten Juden Europas, accessed July 16, 2024, https://www.stiftung-denkmal.de/en/memorials/memorial-to-the-murdered-jews-of-europe.]
12. See Jäckel, "An alle und jeden erinnern?"

opinion, increasingly asserting that Roma and Sinti did experience systematic racist persecution under the Nazis, and on the other is the survival of structures that led to this persecution through the categorization of Roma and Sinti as antisocial, criminal, dangerous, and "foreign." In an effort to counteract the latter narrative, the Central Council of German Sinti and Roma had argued since its inception that the people it represented were (regular) Germans. The strategy had some success, securing the group's legal classification as a German minority and pushing the West German government to officially recognize the genocide in 1982. Its exclusive focus on national integration, however, meant it did not engage with non-German groups (or German Roma, for that matter, who are hardly represented in or by the Central Council). As we have seen, partially in response to the Central Council's strategy, the RCU and its pan-European offshoot RNC pursued radically different tactics, a strategy that in turn delegitimized them in the eyes of the state. With the Central Council acting as the official interlocutor with state and federal governments, representatives of non-German Roma and Sinti were roundly excluded, even when the council obtained a concession in 1992 for a separate monument in Berlin, and even though the majority of those murdered by the Nazis had come from eastern and southeastern Europe, as was true for Jewish victims.

The Central Council's failure to push through what it favored, namely a joint memorial to Jews and Roma and Sinti, indicated that its authority would always be limited when it came to direct conflicts with dominant society. This only grew more obvious as planning for the memorial progressed. The Central Council was the sole "authorized" point of contact for the government, that is, the one group that could request dialogue without risking vilification, unlike the RCU. That said, when it came to conflict, the state was quick to demonstrate that it held all power to determine legitimacy. The text the Central Council wanted for the memorial was a quote from former German president Roman Herzog, who equated the Porajmos with the Shoah,[13] an equation that underpinned the council's

---

13. "The genocide of the Sinti and Roma was motivated by the same obsession with race, carried out with the same resolve and the same intent to achieve

strategy for the recognition of the Nazi genocide of Roma and Sinti: linking it to extant discourse on historical responsibility. Given the postwar "reckoning with the past through continued injustice" against Roma and Sinti in West and East Germany alike,[14] this was a reasonable and often successful tactic, but it brought the Central Council into conflict with the assumption that the Shoah cannot be compared to any other genocide. One of the loudest voices for this stance was Jäckel, who pushed for the Memorial to the Murdered Jews of Europe and was one of the staunchest opponents of it being a shared monument. He was not even appeased when the federal government decided to create separate sites. An inscription that restored a connection between the Porajmos and the Shoah was unacceptable to him. I am not going to expand on this conflict here, as we will address it in Part 3. Instead, I would like to return to the expert-victim dichotomy and another question that has come up several times (and will keep doing so), regarding the right to (self-)designation.

An alternative inscription for the memorial was brought forward by the Sinti Alliance, a tiny group founded in Cologne in 2000, and read, "In memory of all the children, women, and men persecuted as Gypsies by the Nazis in Germany and occupied territories of Europe, and the countless victims of merciless killing among them." It not only insisted on using the term "Gypsy," which the Central Council had categorically rejected, but also denied the reality of modern-day discrimination and upheld the uniqueness of the Shoah as compared to the genocide of "Gypsies." The prominence the Sinti Alliance gained in the debate can be traced back to the mainstream German expert Eberhard Jäckel, who supported—some might say exploited[15]—the splinter group and aggressively laid claim to the right to decide on

---

their methodical and final extermination as the genocide against the Jews." "Recognition of the Nazi Genocide."

14. Roma National Congress, "Fluchtburg Konzentrationslager."

15. The statements Jäckel made about the organizations' roles are pretty dubious, including the claim that it was impossible to comment on the size of either group, as they did not keep membership rolls, given an "age-old sense of skittishness"—not a terribly tactful thing to say, in light of the continued use of "vagrant files," which facilitated active state discrimination against Sinti and Roma into the 1980s. See Jäckel, "Sinti, Roma oder Zigeuner?"

proper terminology: "Arguing that the word 'Gypsy' is derogatory does not hold water. Naturally adversaries intended it to be derogatory (just as antisemites used the word 'Jew'). But that is no reason not to use it anymore."[16] He embraced its use and deemed the classification "Sinti and Roma," names used among these populations, as "nonsense." He was similarly unequivocal about who was to blame for the faltering implementation of the memorial:

> Whereas the memorial for the murdered Jews of Europe is approaching completion in Berlin and slated to open in May, the memorial for the Gypsies—which has been in planning for as many years—still has a long way to go.
> The money is there (two million euros of federal funding), as is the plot on Simsonweg in Tiergarten (granted by the state of Berlin) and even the design (by Dani Karavan). The reason for the stalemate is a fight over the inscription. . . . Whoever wants to keep calling the Gypsies "Sinti and Roma" may do so. On the monument, however, the victims (and this really is indisputable), who were persecuted and murdered "as Gypsies," should be designated as such. It is a compromise that still falls short of historical accuracy, but that meets Romani Rose's obstinacy more than halfway. One thing is for sure: if he does not relent soon, it will be a long time before Berlin sees this memorial built.[17]

Federal and state governments have generously contributed the cash and location; the famous architect has drawn up his plans—everyone is primed and ready to go, but the "Gypsies" can't make up their minds (here, as with Hackmann, the comparatively "easy" process with Jews is implied). Difficulties in negotiation and implementation processes, which were certainly influenced by the vastly different positions held by German Jews and German Sinti and Roma in contemporary Germany, were thus written off as community in-fighting. This in turn was regarded as characteristic of "Gypsy" mentality, which gave the argument greater punch.[18] Again, the German public

---

16. Jäckel, "Sinti, Roma oder Zigeuner?"
17. Jäckel, "Sinti, Roma oder Zigeuner?"
18. Former Hamburg senator Christina Weiss, who in 1993 had ordered police to guard the grounds of Neuengamme concentration camp against "improper overuse" by Roma activists, was now heading up the memorial project in her new role as the federal government commissioner for culture and the media. She help-

was vexed by the group's refusal to accept the dominant (objective, universal) opinion and insistence on voicing their own (subjective, particularist) views.[19] The absurd, crude conviction that it should be the Roma and Sinti who "give in" was irrefutably justified by invoking "historical accuracy," to which all must yield, whether victim or perpetrator.

We have seen that in the debate regarding Roma and Sinti as targets of Nazi genocide—a faltering discussion that only got on its feet after repeated interventions by activists—the image of the bad victim prevailed, while at the same time, members of this community were increasingly styled as perpetrators in contemporary German society. In a statement, Frankfurt Roma Union chairman Hans-Georg Böttcher challenged the discourse on "quarrelsome" Roma and Sinti as well as the separation between migrant and German communities:

> Without having to fear a lobby or diplomatic or political objection, those parts of the populace inclined toward nationalism and neo-Nazism can unleash their fury most easily on Roma and Sinti. All this in a country historically responsible for the unparalleled industrial annihilation of our families, culture, and character. We German Roma and Sinti have lived here for centuries. We understand all too well that the new hatred toward refugees from Eastern Europe is ultimately aimed at us too, and that the fundamental reasons for this hatred rest in the fact that an open, honest, critical reckoning with the recent Nazi past has never happened.[20]

"Fortress Europe Is Built Deep Within Our Hearts"[21]

The climate in Germany after reunification became increasingly openly racist. Pogroms in the East and murderous arson attacks in

---

lessly proposed to circumvent the problem by using the English term "Gypsy." See Bakirdögen, "Streit um Text auf Mahnmal."

19. See Blumer, "From Victim Hierarchies to Memorial Networks."
20. Roma Union Ffm., Leidgeb, and Horn, *Opre Roma! Erhebt Euch!*, 8.
21. The title of this section is taken from Roma Union Ffm., Leidgeb, and Horn, *Opre Roma! Erhebt Euch!*, 7. Words spoken by Hans-Georg Böttcher, chairman of the Frankfurt am Main Roma Union. The extent of the open racism has never been assessed adequately, nor have the consequences. According to a study by

the West shocked some parts of the public, at least, but ultimately prompted a general shift to the right, which made nationalistic and racist views more acceptable in polite society. Yet, at the time, people of color and Antifa were practically the only ones using terms like *racism*. The insistence on the term *xenophobia*, even on the part of those who opposed it, expressed a clear sense of possessiveness: only those who were not "foreigners" (i.e., white Germans) were entitled to have a say, feel a sense of belonging, or enjoy the rights to residence or interpretive sovereignty. While political debates concentrated on asylum law, the social climate also became more hostile toward racialized Germans and migrants who had lived in the country for a long time. This routine racism went unnamed for years before Germany finally declared itself an *Einwanderungsgesellschaft*, or "society of immigration" (only to pronounce multiculturalism a failure a few years later), which had long-term consequences for the cohesion of German society. Among other things, it perpetuated a selective racist amnesia that allows Germany to repeat the process today and to keep blaming "foreigners" for metastatic racism. Within the asylum law debate back then, "bogus" asylum seekers—people supposedly gaming the system, out to score a life of luxury in the German welfare state—were scapegoated for the incipient and very real neoliberal dismantling of social rights. Roma and Sinti epitomized the image of the bogus asylum seeker, not least because the biases associated with that image were the same as those projected onto Roma and Sinti for centuries: that, collectively, they were unwilling to work, lazy, dishonest, and irrevocably foreign.[22]

---

the national weekly newspaper *Die Zeit*, the government has underreported the number of murders by right-wing perpetrators since reunification (according to the state, there have been 76 cases, whereas *Die Zeit* in 2015 verified 156 deaths). See Jansen et al., "Todesopfer rechter Gewalt."

22. The case of four-year-old Mohamed Januzi from Bosnia and Herzegovina, who disappeared in October 2015 at the Berlin State Office for Health and Social Affairs (LAGeSo), the notoriously chaotic drop-in center for refugees, highlights the effects of this persistent prejudice, which caricatures racialized people as dishonest, unscrupulous, and money-grubbing. It later turned out that he had been kidnapped, sexually abused, and murdered by a white German man, while the police had assumed that the child's mother was faking his disappearance to avoid deportation,

"We Are the Volk" 113

Six-day pogroms in Hoyerswerda in September 1991 and the almost daily racist attacks that ensued across Germany failed to generate any meaningful political response; barely a year later, the violence escalated in Rostock-Lichtenhagen.[23] The Zentrale Aufnahmestelle für Asylbewerber (Central Reception Center for Asylum Seekers;ZASt) located there was hopelessly overcrowded. The refugees, mostly Roma from Romania, were deliberately housed in squalid conditions and sometimes forced to sleep outside for days, as Rostock authorities did not want the situation to become "normalized," which they feared would attract more refugees.[24] While those authorities delivered the familiar refrain about being overwhelmed, it was a condition they had manufactured, to the detriment of human beings who were legally entitled to protection. The result seemed to prove them right, because in response to the racist riots, the vast majority of refugees and foreign contract workers (who had lived in Germany for a long time) were deported posthaste. Twenty years later, anniversary commemorations highlighted attacks on the apartment building that had housed primarily Vietnamese laborers, whereas Roma were scarcely acknowledged. (In the film *Wir sind jung. Wir sind stark.* [*We Are Young. We Are Strong.*], which excavates the souls of East German youths, Roma are no more than mute extras.)

Easily stoked anti-Roma prejudice undoubtedly fed the violence as well as its broad justification. The deplorable conditions at the reception center did not inspire sympathy or solidarity among the white German residents of Rostock-Lichtenhagen; instead, they were seen as having been created, and even preferred, by the refugees, an alleged propensity linked directly to ethnicity. Politicians

---

just as authorities had for years suspected that "foreign organized criminals" were behind the National Socialist Underground serial killings of 2000–2007. See "Der Fall Mohamed."

23. The pogroms were a grim illustration of the importance of the silent majority, those people who helped to normalize racist violence by ignoring it, even when it was happening before their eyes. The perpetrators were right to feel encouraged; it was safe to assume that if they were not met with widespread sympathy, they could at least count on apathy. For potential victims, on the other hand, the hostility was amplified by the likelihood that no one would help, even if the attack took place in a busy area.

24. The catastrophic conditions at LAGeSo in 2015 suggest similar motivations.

also fanned the flames of old prejudice. In May 1992, Berndt Seite, minister president of Mecklenburg-Vorpommern, the northern German state in which Rostock is located, declared, "Anyone in our state who hasn't lost touch with the population can tell you: our people are deeply troubled by the unabated arrival of asylum seekers whose request for asylum is primarily economically driven."[25] He refrained from providing any evidence for the claim, not that there was any need: by then the conflation of Roma and bogus asylum seekers was a given. Senator of the Interior Peter Magdanz spoke even more bluntly: "It's no secret that shoplifters in Rostock are often Romanian Gypsies."[26] News coverage reveals why politicians saw no issue with making such statements. The Rostock daily *Norddeutsche Neueste Nachrichten*, for instance, published this in July 1992: "Anything shiny is basically dismantled. Toilet use is rare.... Spiering just barely managed to avert the worst, when he recently surprised a Roma family grilling in their one-room apartment: seagulls caught on the balcony were roasting over an open fire stoked with ZASt furniture."[27] Public discourse construed the "Gypsies" as a fundamentally foreign threat by harnessing centuries-old stereotypes. Unsurprisingly, the result also had a centuries-old precedent: the racist pogrom.

Although the arson attacks in Solingen (1993), Mölln (1992), and other former West German cities indicate otherwise, racist violence in East Germany was and often still is attributed to democratic deficits, the assumption being that East Germans must catch up to West German standards and develop the capacity to live in peace and multicultural harmony. It is without a doubt true that GDR scripts about the international friendship of peoples provided little concrete guidance on how to achieve equitable coexistence. What this argument ignores, however, is that aggressively distancing themselves from anything "un/German" allowed East Germans to unleash their frustration with the new hierarchy (in which they were

---

25. Prenzel, *20 Jahre Rostock-Lichtenhagen*, 14.
26. Prenzel, *20 Jahre Rostock-Lichtenhagen*, 18.
27. Bentzien, "Möwengrillen" quoted in Prenzel, *20 Jahre Rostock-Lichtenhagen*, 18.

treated as wholly inferior to West Germans) on people who occupied a rung even lower than theirs. At the same time, they had a vested interest in maintaining this relatively higher ranking, certainly more so than those at the top of the heap, mainstream West Germans, whose hegemony is not threatened by racist violence in East Germany. On the contrary: the belligerence seems to involve groups that lack white West Germans' innate ability to resolve conflict rationally. East Germans and communities of color still not acknowledged as being part of Germany (like Roma or Muslims) are thus confirmed as backward in the internalist-evolutionary model. Both groups must therefore endeavor to achieve West German levels of development, for instance by participating in state intervention programs like antiradicalization training. White West Germany thus remains the idealized norm, while ethnonationalism as a fundamental structure in its national understanding remains unacknowledged. In contrast, shortly after the Soviet Union collapsed, Stuart Hall had already observed this in relation to escalating nationalist conflicts in Eastern Europe: "These emergent nationalisms are not simply revivals of the past but reworkings of it in the circumstances of the present—entry tickets to the new Europe. Though they look like a return to a pre-1914 historical agenda, they are functioning as a way of evading the past and making a bid for modernity (i.e., entry to the Euro-club)."[28]

"A Poisonous Brew Is Bubbling Up Here"[29]

That an ethnonationalist understanding of German identity was prevalent in the West too is reflected in the preunification presence of racist groups and debates there. After all, the deadliest terrorist attack in postwar Germany, the 1980 Oktoberfest bombing in Munich, was committed by a neo-Nazi—there is only uncertainty as to whether Gundolf Köhler acted alone. Relying on the lone wolf hypothesis to explain right-wing violence, meanwhile, is not only

---

28. Hall, "Europe's Other Self," 18.
29. Barth, "Hier steigt eine Giftsuppe auf."

symptomatic of the response to attacks like those in Solingen and Mölln, which are rather firmly rooted in national memory, but also explains the ease with which similar events are forgotten. There was the neo-Nazi attack on a building that housed mostly Turkish families in the Upper Palatine town of Schwandorf in 1988, for instance, in which four people died and many more were injured. To this day, the arson is viewed as an isolated incident, despite the perpetrator's involvement in neo-Nazi circles and his continued adherence to extreme right-wing and racist views.[30] Countless other examples could be cited here: the prevalent model for explaining right-wing terrorism clings to the notion of lone wolves whose actions are ultimately based in psychopathic tendencies. This model, which is used for perpetrators from dominant population groups—for example, white, Christian, German—differs from the one used to make sense of terrorist acts by people from marked groups, like Muslims: in this case, the pathology is treated as cultural, a collective responsibility, and ultimately a group trait. To a certain extent, this applies to standard explanations of xenophobic violence committed by East Germans, though in this case the deficit is considered social rather than cultural.

In fact, East Germans did receive immediate aid when it came to adapting to Western levels of racism: by June 1992, months before the pogrom, an extremist fringe party from Hamburg called Hamburger Liste für Ausländerstopp (Hamburg List for Halting Foreigners; HLA) was active in Rostock with such slogans as *Widerstand gegen die Asylantenflut* (Resistance against the flood of asylum seekers) and *Rostock bleibt deutsch* (Rostock stays German).[31] The HLA first campaigned in Hamburg state elections in 1982, the same year in which 66 percent of German citizens said they wanted "guest workers" sent back home, something Chancellor Kohl tried to do the moment he took office. There was no "refugee crisis" to speak of in 1982, nor was reunification in sight, but there was the standard interplay of everyday racism, right-wing extremism, and political handwringing over "concerned citizens." As we have seen, racism against Roma and Sinti was as active in the West as in the East and

---

30. "Der totgeschwiegene Anschlag."
31. Prenzel, *20 Jahre Rostock-Lichtenhagen*, 19.

extended deep into mainstream society. In 1991, for instance, the respected news magazine *Der Spiegel* (based in Hamburg) published a ten-page piece describing nightmarish conditions in the Karolinenviertel, a city neighborhood allegedly overrun by criminal hordes of Roma. Reporter Ariane Barth goes into great detail about the terror German residents have endured in the neighborhood—located adjacent to the famous Hamburger Dom fairgrounds—and how the Roma have made their lives a living hell, all while police stand helplessly by.[32]

The article is manipulative and seethes with racism. What makes it noteworthy isn't its dubious claim to truth—later that year, the journalist Oliver Tolmein published a meticulous counterargument that proved Barth played fast and loose with the facts[33]—but the insight it grants into liberal, middle-class mindsets. For that reason, I have excerpted a lengthy passage from the *Spiegel* article, along with the notes I jotted down two decades ago, when I was still living in Hamburg's Schanzenviertel, right next to Karolinenviertel. My comments address the perception of a racialized Other that crops up again and again—for example, fifteen years later with regard to Muslim youth in Berlin's Neukölln neighborhood. This is a perception that can target new groups at will, since it is not based on these groups' actual characteristics but on German thought patterns that may be projected outward whenever necessary. Another example is the reports about the "unprecedented" sexual violence of "North African gangs" on New Year's Eve 2015 in Cologne.[34] I was moved

---

32. Barth, "Hier steigt eine Giftsuppe auf."
33. See Tolmein, "Die rassende Reporterin."
34. By no means do I wish to minimize what happened or dispute that the violence warranted a collective response. What concerns me is how violence is debated, rationalized, spun as scandal, or concealed, depending on how it fits into preexisting perceptions. Many years ago, though I can't remember exactly when, I attended a seminar hosted by the TV broadcaster Norddeutscher Rundfunk (NDR). What I do remember is heated debate about the construction of housing for asylum seekers and assertations that it didn't make you a racist to worry about your property value tanking if one of these homes was built nearby (such were the concerns of NDR editors back then)—so it must have been sometime in the early to mid-1990s. One of the seminar leaders, a journalist, told us about a report he had done on border skirmishes between the German *Freikorps* and the Polish army in the 1920s. He had interviewed a man who recalled that his comrades had slit the belly of a Pole they

to mark up the *Spiegel* piece less because of its stunning racism than because of its reflection of a German reality that, though the dominant majority seemed blind to it, racialized people like me could not help but notice—from the "N——out!" graffiti I passed daily on the way to my girlfriend's place in the trim neighborhood of Eimsbüttel to university classes in which mainstream German students proclaimed, unopposed, that "white people invented literature," meaning the exclusion of non-white writers from the canon could not possibly come down to racism. Here is my visualization attempt from all those years ago, which seems no less relevant today:

> When the weather is nice, Roma gather here, enormous clans with throngs of children. Twenty-one units of government housing have been rented out to four extended families:[35] all Roma, no Sinti tenants.[36] They once arrived here[37] from Yugoslavia and, in a process of adjustment that often lasted for decades, blended inconspicuously[38] into the vibrant neighborhood.[39]
>
> When the ethnic conflict in their former homeland came to a head, family members arrived from all corners, friends and friends-of-friends, upwards of 500 people,[40] some of whom pitched tents in the square outside City Hall until the Mitte district office eventually put them up in hotels around Karo[linenviertel].[41] Shaped by the struggles of life in the

---

had captured, pulled out his intestines, nailed them to a tree, and then made him run around the tree until he had disemboweled himself and collapsed. The journalist agonized over including the scene in his piece and ultimately decided against it. I can understand why, yet it is something I have often come back to, especially when I hear or read about "Others" committing unthinkable or—*here in Germany*, at least—unprecedented atrocities. Such notions of a civilizational watershed rely on the fact that this manner of journalistic restraint is only ever exercised unilaterally.

35. Flood/undifferentiated mass/overpopulation: throngs of children, twenty-one apartments for four extended families: organized abuse of social services; German nuclear family versus "enormous clans."

36. Author not racist: can distinguish between Roma and Sinti! Assimilated, good Sinti—bad, foreign Roma.

37. Fairy-tale language: battle of mythic proportions, Lord of the Rings.

38. The enemy within, infiltration, everywhere.

39. Intolerant foreigner a threat to the vibrant multicultural mainstream German neighborhood; socially dominant mainstream Germans are the true hip hybrids, they can handle multiculti. The foreigners are the racists.

40. Five hundred relatives from four families! These people are different (like bunnies); first one comes, the rest will follow.

41. Asylum seekers in hotels instead of tourists! Very presence of Roma preventing economic upswing in Karo-Viertel.

ghetto,[42] the asylum seekers' children brought a roughness that seemed to infect[43] the children of integrated Roma. They slipped out of their parents' grasp, into a society of street urchins.[44] According to police counts, 50 to 60 of them can be found loitering around the neighborhood, unless they are at the center of the action, at the corner of Marktstrasse and Glashüttenstrasse. Shrieking activity fills the square, little imps scurry about.[45] . . . Roma children, instructed by their elders,[46] deal hash[47] while guards posted at the ends of the street secure the area with an elaborate communication system of whistles and hand gestures. . . .

Horst Krigel (33), at 6-foot-4 a kind of Superman,[48] whose "physical charisma" naturally helps him avoid trouble with the Roma, is nevertheless outraged by "the kind of mayhem these people are causing every day. . . ." Krigel has played out what might happen if he called in some of his "buddies" from the Antifa[49] movement: "It would land those clans[50] in the hospital. Within a few hours, though, the Gypsies[51] would come from the outskirts, where 10 out of 100 policemen were roughed up so bad recently, they couldn't report to work.[52] In a pinch, the Gypsies can put out a nationwide call,[53] and within two days, all hell would break loose.[54] Forget about it."

Barth's report fails to address or analyze long-standing conflicts around aggressive gentrification efforts in Karolinenviertel (especially by slumlord Niklas Rabels, a big name in the city) that aimed to drive out financially uninteresting residents by deliberately leaving

---

42. Social Darwinism.
43. So it really *is* in their blood.
44. Street gangs the natural form of organization for Roma: kids instinctively return to this state, slip away from assimilated parents.
45. Noise pollution and drug deals both essential expressions of foreign Roma culture.
46. Organized crime, always send the kids out.
47. To deal drugs, of course.
48. Superman in every sense, not just physical: educated, politically correct, German Antifa-multiculti man: powerless against gangs of children.
49. Full spectrum of German society, from Antifa to police, are against the Roma, yet all are powerless.
50. (*Sippe*—Trans.) Nazi term—used by Antifa?
51. See above.
52. Not even one hundred policemen can protect us from Roma gangs! In times of emergency, everyone comes together, cops and Antifa.
53. The enemy walks among us, all around, strategically placed, ready for military action.
54. The apocalypse approaches.

properties abandoned and effecting structural neglect. This is by no means unique to Hamburg: it has become part and parcel of postreunification political discourse to turn crises caused by neoliberal urban policy into talk about scary racialized groups taking over economically underdeveloped neighborhoods—areas that are attractive to speculators but rendered uninhabitable by those threatening groups.[55]

The feeling of being besieged by adversarial hordes of antisocial foreigners, who must be met with violence because that is the only language they speak, was intentionally constructed here and again in Rostock, where a year later upstanding citizens complained that women and children could no longer walk down the street unmolested by "Gypsies": "Our kids are only allowed to play in the courtyard now. It's been ages since we allowed them to go to the store or ice cream parlor. Their pocket money was stolen on the way by child asylum seekers far too many times. Even as an adult, I never walk that way by myself."[56] Just days after the pogrom in Rostock, Lothar Kupfer, minister of the interior of Mecklenburg-Vorpommern, sent a letter to Romani Rose, chair of the Central Council of German Sinti and Roma, in which he put all the blame for the attack on the victims: "Our people quite rightly expect ... foreigners living here to respect our norms of coexistence and to behave accordingly.... There have been many instances of shoplifting by members of this ethnic group. Considering our generous asylum law, ... the population can no longer be expected to tolerate such social behavior. I would therefore appreciate if you could relay this message to your fellow countrymen. In my opinion, if foreigners conformed to standard behaviors, it would help ease existing reservations."[57] Again, this letter was sent *after* the attacks on the Central Reception Center for Asylum Seekers,

---

55. The scenarios are similar, even if the targeted racialized groups change. See, for example, discussions about African drug dealers in Hamburg's Schanzenviertel in the mid-nineties and in Berlin's Görlitzer Park in the mid-aughts, or about Muslim youth in Berlin's Kreuzberg or Neukölln neighborhoods during the same period. In the early twenty-first century, the scenarios came to center on homophobic hate crimes committed by Muslim men (see Haritaworn, "Queer Injuries").

56. Prenzel, *20 Jahre Rostock-Lichtenhagen*, 61.

57. Prenzel, *20 Jahre Rostock-Lichtenhagen*, 64.

thus implying that the riots were a reasonable response to "nonstandard" behavior among Roma. Veracity of the allegations aside, shoplifting is not a crime punishable by lynch mob—and it is troubling in the extreme that this logic of disciplining has become the norm in addressing conflict between the majority and racialized groups. The generous asylum law referenced in the letter was curtailed soon after, confirming Kupfer's stance that it was less a policy defending human rights—in this case, the right to protection from persecution—than it was a generous gesture made by the gatekeepers, who could deny access to those protected if they did not conform to standard behaviors or if simply too many of them showed up. The political center still tends to respond to racially motivated violence in this way. Not long before asylum law was tightened again in 2015, Minister of the Interior Thomas de Maizière revived the image of brazen "bogus" asylum seekers: "We are seeing a lot of refugees now, who think they can move about freely.[58] They leave facilities; they'll call a cab and amazingly have the money to travel hundreds of kilometers around Germany. They strike if they don't like their accommodations, make a fuss if they don't like the food, and brawl in the facilities for asylum seekers."[59] The moral panic the *Spiegel* article successfully unleashed about the "Roma invasion" in the early 1990s contributed to the charged atmosphere that found release in Rostock (and elsewhere), and it also helps explain the forceful response to the attempt to occupy Neuengamme in 1993. By then the Roma were classified discursively as besiegers of the Germans, their every action read as manipulative and threatening, including references to their persecution and mass murder by the Germans.

The Germanophobes

The narrative of certain populations—who, compared to civilized Europeans, are less self-conscious, less sophisticated, less plagued by

---

58. Asylum seekers in Germany are assigned to facilities and are not allowed to leave the surrounding area without prior permission.
59. "De Maizière will Dank."

unwarranted self-doubt—threatening and laying siege to Europe can be seen as a continent-wide response to disputes over social inequality and historical guilt.[60] In Germany's case, however, these discussions veer toward the assertion that shameless groups are sponging off Germans' excessive sense of responsibility for Nazi crimes.[61] Barth's article represented a low point in the racist journalism during the years between reunification and the tightening of asylum laws, but by no means was it anomalous. In January 1992, for instance, *Der Spiegel* published a piece poetically titled, "Jeder streichelt seinen Bimbo" (And they all coddle their Negro), in which the author laments Germans' habit of beating themselves up over such peccadilloes as the Hoyerswerda pogroms.[62] The rest of the world, the unnamed journalist argued, was watching in disbelief as the German people indulged in boundless tolerance for multiculturalism, letting fake asylum seekers get away with whatever they liked, all because of the "psychosis of guilt" elicited by the country's Nazi past. True to its role as the paragon of German opinion journalism, *Der Spiegel* catalogs the dominant defense strategies mainstream society still employs against accusations of racism today: in a year that saw more than two thousand far-right crimes, the article focuses primarily on violence targeting right-wing extremists (or on left-wing "violent fantasies") who are thus made out to be victims—marginalized young men whom society has inculcated with the belief that, because they are German, they are *Scheisse*, who have trouble with the opposite sex and who don't receive any help from social workers because the social workers are spending all their time helping foreign kids;

---

60. See European Network Against Racism, "Black People in Europe."

61. A high, or perhaps low, point in this debate was Martin Walser's acceptance speech upon receiving the Peace Prize of the German Book Trade in 1998, in which he described Auschwitz as a "moral bludgeon" used against the German people (he was especially galled by the planned Holocaust memorial in central Berlin). Although he was taking aim primarily at collective memory ("Every person is alone with his conscience. Public displays of conscience are therefore at risk of becoming symbolic, and nothing is more foreign to the conscience than symbolism, however well intended"), Walser quickly (and willingly) became a poster child for the "We've felt guilty long enough" attitude within the new German normalcy. See Hagestedt, "Der Streitverlauf."

62. "'Jeder streichelt seinen Bimbo.'"

those kids, meanwhile, can freely express pride in being Turkish or Italian and spend their time scrapping with skinheads. On the other hand, societal racism is reduced to a small, pathologized group: the real problem is that, because of the Nazi past, a self-flagellating but ultimately blameless majority is unnecessarily concerned with coddling its Negros.[63] In essence, the response to racist violence has gotten out of hand and threatens to turn in the other direction, unless someone rights the ship: if racism among "Turks", "Italians", and "Negros" goes unchecked, it's Germans who will emerge as the true victims (a danger identified fifteen years later as "Germanophobia" [*Deutschenfeindschaft*] by Frank Schirrmacher, the former publisher of the *Frankfurter Allgemeine Zeitung*).

Collective panic in dealing with marginalized groups—whose foreignness is construed as insurmountable, then cited as the reason for their exclusion—is especially prevalent in recent German history and probably peaked in 2002, in the hysteria surrounding Rütli, a high school in Berlin's Neukölln neighborhood. The school became emblematic of the (renewed) destruction of German culture by inimical foreigners. Whereas Barth highlighted old people being terrorized by Roma youth, now the future of German children was at stake—*German* children, that is, and not kids *nichtdeutscher Herkunftssprache* (those whose mother tongue is not German, abbreviated as NdH) or "German-African" youngsters. The horrors they face look the same, though, only now the perpetrators are teenage Muslim thugs instead of Roma juvenile delinquents. The siege imagery and descriptions of hapless, civilized do-gooders who just want to understand and help, instead of lashing out like intolerant foreigners, also remain the same, as does the message: Germany is being overrun by violent, primitive, aggressive migrants, for whom

---

63. Although the article's extremely racist title is set in quotation marks as a precaution, its aggressive symbolic function is crystal clear. At the same time, the author is taking a brave stand against another existential threat to German identity: political correctness, which is out to rob the land of poets and thinkers of its language (and impose upon it such nonsense as the *Binnen-I*, with the medial capital *I* intended to signal gender inclusivity in plural nouns). Intellectuals from Harald Schmidt to Deniz Yücel have set out to show how important racist language is in defending free speech—the use of the N-word and its variants in particular.

tolerance, gender equality, and education are not only foreign terms but are practically anathema. The attempt to make them more like us (i.e., "normal") is therefore certain to fail, and the only reasonable alternative is to acknowledge their inherent alterity.

An article published in the Berlin weekly magazine *Zitty* toward the end of the school debate is symptomatic of its overall tenor. "Schulwahl: Flucht vor Multikulti" (School choice: Fleeing multiculturalism) tells the story of Sarah, who was bullied at school after announcing she didn't believe in God.[64] The following lines reveal how that could be: "Sarah is in the fourth grade at a school in Kreuzberg. She has two friends: Marlene, who is German, and Kia, who is a German-African. The rest of the class comes from Turkish or Arab families." Sarah, it goes without saying, is also "German" and does not belong to either of those divergent categories. Therein, we quickly learn, lies the problem: "Many parents are familiar with Sarah's story, or something similar, because their own child has experienced it. Tanja and Kai, in Moabit [another rapidly gentrifying multiethnic neighborhood], for instance, send their daughter to a Catholic school, although they are atheists." Catholic schools as a last resort for atheists whose kids are being harassed by NdHs because they don't believe in God—this is what it's come to in postmigrant Germany. However absurd this assertion, I am not interested in poking fun at the article's dubious line of argument. Unfortunately, of far greater relevance is the fact that said argumentation is accepted as logical, though it flagrantly distorts reality. It starts with the division into Germans, German Africans, and Arabs and Turks: naturally it's the unmarked Germans who hold the keys to the castle. Unmarked necessarily means white and Christian, or at least culturally Christian. If the "Germans" did not meet those criteria, they would of course be Something-Germans or come from Arab or Turkish families. The unmarked status for (culturally) Christian white people is thus only possible if the others remain qualified and are never allowed to become just normal "Germans"— if that happened, people wouldn't know where they stood with Germans and might unwittingly end up with an NdH on their hands.

---

64. Brakebusch, "Schulwahl."

The "German-*x*" designations are preposterous as it is, in that they name nationalities—German-Turks, German-Ghanaians, German-Moroccans, and so on—when what they really mean is ethnicity or heritage. The construction, though superficially analogous to what is used in the United States, has the opposite effect: whereas German American, Irish American, or similar identifiers divide Americans into ethnic categories and ostensibly celebrate the melting pot ideology of a nation of immigrants (vertices provided by such occasions as Oktoberfest, St. Patrick's Day, or Cinco de Mayo), the labels used in German cement racialized people's roles as eternal foreigners—the emphasis is on the second part of the term, not the first: Turks are Turks, even if nominally "German-Turks," never mind if an individual doesn't speak Turkish or has never set foot in Turkey, or that they hold a German passport and maybe even identify as German. The "German-African" formulation the *Zitty* author uses is even more ludicrous, as it encompasses an entire continent that one is unwilling or unable to break down into its constituent nations. (This, too, differs in usage from "African American"). It is obvious what the squishy term "African" connotes—Black—so why not simply say Black Germans, which has the tremendous advantage of being this group's preferred self-designation?[65] The answer is that these formulations are not intended to augment the term "German," to highlight different versions of Germanness, but are meant to underscore the contrast between "Germans" and those whose national (or continental) identity is primarily different. In other words, German and not (really) German. (In contrast, in the United States, white groups are ethnicized too, all the way up to socially dominant WASPs—White Anglo-Saxon Protestants—who consider themselves the default.) In Sarah's tale, her "German-African" friend Kia occupies a liminal space: although not as German as her pal Sarah, Kia is compatible (so what

---

65. To be very clear: Most "African Americans" do not know where exactly on the continent their ancestors came from, as the systematic destruction of the abducted Africans' cultural identity was a cornerstone of the transatlantic slave trade. Germans of African descent are in a fundamentally different situation—and it is safe to assume that the author here is referring to a Black child socialized as German, not one who migrated from somewhere in Africa, since otherwise "African" Kia would have been grouped with the insufficiently assimilated "Arabs" and "Turks."

we're dealing with here is not racism, at least not coming from the Germans), which explains why she, too, transfers out of the school dominated by Arabs and Turks. The school itself becomes an extraterritorial area, the foreignness of its occupants reflected in the fact that they are even denied the "German"- prefix.

As it happens, I faced problems similar to Sarah's in grade school: I brashly declared that I did not believe in God (and what's worse, I maintained that God did not exist), much to my classmates' horror. In the small conservative town in Lower Saxony where I grew up (where religion was a required course in public schools and consisted solely of Christian teachings), this stance—which my secular Muslim father happened to share—made me part of a tiny minority (certainly among resident nine-year-olds). I was not bullied too terribly in this instance, though the bullying related to the unforgivable fact of my Blackness is another story altogether. I do not wish to minimize the gravity of what the many Sarahs out there are facing, nor downplay school bullying or present migratized people as irreproachable victims of racism. All I want is to point out that what was treated as an unpleasant but normal and unavoidable aspect of school life as long as it came from mainstream German kids (bullying those deemed different, whether based on looks, beliefs, or very being) is now presented as a wholly new, wholly unacceptable phenomenon— because it is coming from a group itself perceived as unacceptable, whose presence seems to represent an intractable conflict. This is what the *Zitty* article and countless others do: they identify a set of issues that seem both unacceptable and intractable. Unlike the first scenario (mainstream German children bullying each other or, more likely, their minoritized peers), the problem does not arise from structures but from a group identity—more precisely still, it arises from a group whose presence is the root cause of this "foreign" problem, making their removal seem the only logical solution. This is for the protection of the "German" public at large but also in particular for that of German youth, who are not only being terrorized but contaminated: "Then she describes Sarah's miserable spelling and grammar skills. 'I'm a German teacher, and my daughter can't form the dative case.' Furthermore, her mother continues, Sarah has adopted the sociolect of her classmates, dropping prepositions at will."

Yet again, Sarah's story reminds me of my own family. In this instance, I can't help but think of my "German-African" sister, who still lives in our hometown, and the dismay she felt whenever her children used the regional white dialect, which has its own deviations from grammatical accuracy (unlike Sarah's mother, my sister somehow managed to teach her kids High German without them transferring schools). None of this is meant to suggest that Rütli and other schools don't face real problems, or that it isn't a cause for concern when 90 percent of the student population does not speak German as a first language. The concern, however, is not uncontrollably violent and fanatically religious ten-year-old "Arabs and Turks" bullying defenseless "Germans" out of their school. There is an actual concern, and it is readily named: the racialization of poverty. The problems at Rütli were not remotely exotic or inexplicable: poverty and a lack of prospects, paired with underserved *Hauptschulen*—schools for children assigned to the least academic track, usually ending after the ninth grade—led to conditions also found elsewhere.[66] What should surprise us here is the insistence on a culturalist explanation that exempts broader society from any responsibility and justifies a neoliberal social Darwinism that not only allows weaker groups to fall to the wayside but pathologizes and criminalizes them for their own "failure." The disgust, fear, and guilt triggered by poverty and its attendant ills in liberal, middle-class residents of formerly hip areas like Kreuzberg or Neukölln (or Hamburg's Karolinenviertel or Schanzenviertel) are channeled into racism, as generally accepted now as it ever has been.

But come on, it's not racism when the real aggressors are racialized people, whether we're talking aggressive, criminally inclined, misogynistic Roma or aggressive, fundamentalist, misogynistic Muslims—they hate us, *they're* the intolerant ones driving us from our schools and neighborhoods, while we don't dare fight back, because we don't want to be racist. This can't end well, which brings us back to the concerns of regular citizens, Alternative für Deutschland (Alternative for Germany), and Pegida (Patriotische Europäer gegen die Islamisierung des Abendlandes or Patriotic Europeans

---

66. See Randow, "Unter Polizeischutz."

Against the Islamization of the Occident), as well as the racism found at every turn, even in the left-most fringes of mainstream German society. Everyday racism explains why the backlash to a kid saying "I don't believe in God" embodies everything that makes (underserved, understaffed, and otherwise troubled) "Arab- and Turkish-dominated" public schools unacceptable, whereas the same backlash *is* acceptable in a private Catholic school that, more importantly, has the resources it needs and few, if any, students from disadvantaged or Muslim households. After all, being a liberal who has failed because of their own idealism and the insuperable Otherness of non-whites is more romantic than the banal reality of economically motivated, racist white flight.

The postulated fundamental Otherness of racialized people implies that these groups must be treated differently, too, that *our* ways of conducting ourselves and solving problems do not work for *them*, and that other, tougher measures are required. Deportation was the go-to method for dealing with Roma in Hamburg and Rostock and remains a crowd favorite when it comes to unwelcome "foreigners." Things get tricky when these so-called foreigners are Germans, unless—so the argument goes—they flat-out don't want to be. The whole discussion surrounding the failure of multiculturalism was built on this premise: Germans (white and Christian, as ever) have made an honest effort, but the others simply refuse to cooperate; they cling to their old, intolerant ways, central among them sexism, homophobia, antisemitism, and yes, Germanophobia.

The debate escalated in 2008 following an article by *Frankfurter Allgemeine Zeitung* thought leader Frank Schirrmacher about two young men brutally attacking a senior citizen. Though a woefully familiar occurrence, in Schirrmacher's telling it represents an unprecedented phenomenon in the history of humankind: "It was historically unknown to us that a majority could attract the racist hatred of a minority."[67] (The author seems to have missed the memo on apartheid South Africa.) As it happens, all three parties—the retiree and teens—were German, but not *really*: the perpetrators, of

---

67. Schirrmacher, "Junge Männer auf Feindfahrt."

Turkish and Greek descent, had called the victim a *Scheissdeutschen* ("fucking German," or "piece of shit German"), thus revealing their true un/German identity. What was new and scary about this scenario wasn't the violence or "group-specific misanthropy" (by 2008, more than one hundred people had been murdered in racist attacks in reunified Germany), it was the target: normal Germans.

True terror is when bad things no longer just happen to other people but come home to roost. This naturally invites comparisons to Nazism and the familiar refrain that Germans are so concerned (i.e., overly concerned) with their Nazi past that they fail to notice they are the victims of new Nazis: "If the aim behind embracing such positions is to preserve an old image of the German majority as morally dubious—because Nazism can be suspected at will—then what we are now witnessing is a fortunate end to this madness."[68] Schirrmacher's pseudoanalysis of mainstream Germans as the new victims and racialized groups as the new Nazis was not exactly novel: *Spiegel* author Barth had already concluded sixteen years earlier that elderly assault victims symbolized the horror of un/German minorities rising up against the German majority. The constant is the differentiation between Germans (as in white, Christian, or culturally Christian people) and the Others, whether they are classified as Roma, foreigners, Turks, or Muslims. Most important is that they are not German. The evidence: they hate Germans and act on their racist Germanophobia. In other words, Germans have repented plenty; they can cast off their sense of guilt for the Nazi past and not feel bad about it, and indeed, this is what they need to do, as hanging onto that guilt has become counterproductive and emboldens the new (non-German) Nazis.

What was new about Schirrmacher's article and the heated debate it triggered was the introduction of the term *racism* into the general vocabulary. The very people who had insisted on calling racist conditions "hostility toward foreigners" or—among the more intellectual set—"xenophobia" now thought the term appropriate when talking about discrimination against (real) Germans. Although

---

68. Schirrmacher, "Junge Männer auf Feindfahrt."

this is an obvious misnomer when applied to mainstream Germans, it actually works, because it maintains the strict delineation between Germans and "foreigners" (that is, non-white, non-Christian Germans): it's the others who see themselves as fundamentally and forever different from Germans, not Germans who have a problem with the others. The term is also effective, if at the level of playground politics, because it turns excluded groups into the real racists: Germans represent a "tradition that does not allow radical ideologies and racist attacks in their midst to go unpunished. The Turkish community in Germany is clearly not doing enough of the same."[69] (As Schirrmacher penned these lines, the National Socialist Underground was carrying out its murders unchecked and, for the next ten years, unpunished.)

German normalization meant finding closure with the Nazi past, not encouraging debate by challenging East Germany's self-definition as an antifascist state, for instance, or pushing West Germany to grant victimized groups a real say in issues that concerned them. One need look no further than the failed attempt of Roma, Nazi victims who still suffer from racism today, to appeal to a German sense of responsibility. Instead, reunification helped establish a growing consensus that enough was enough—it was time to leave the "guilt complex" behind and finally turn toward the future. Mounting racism accompanied this shift and culminated in racialized groups being cast as the new Nazis. It comes full circle in discussions about Muslims, the Nazis' modern-day heirs, victimizing mainstream Germans, with racism framed as antifascist self-defense. As I have demonstrated, this process was not linear but circular, with certain tropes repeated enough times that they ultimately took center stage. Though their focus jumped between groups, these tropes essentially had the same objective: keeping the Other othered. This was accomplished by means of creating enemy images that tied old stereotypes about "Gypsies," "Mediterranean types," or "Orientals" to Nazism, hitherto defined as typically German. Schirrmacher describes the duties of German intellectuals in just this vein: "[It behooves us] to state that the mixture of juvenile

---

69. Schirrmacher, "Junge Männer auf Feindfahrt."

delinquency and Muslim fundamentalism is potentially the closest thing we have today to the deadly ideologies of the twentieth century."[70] Although this scenario is specifically German in some regards, pegging Muslims as the new Nazis reveals connections to debates taking place more widely in Europe and around the world.

---

70. Schirrmacher, "Junge Männer auf Feindfahrt."

Part 3

Post/Fascist Multiculturalism

5

Germany Is(n't) a Land of Immigrants

Europe's Others

Western Europe, which after World War II was primed for a leading role on the global stage, nominally stood for everything Nazi Germany had wanted to destroy: freedom, peace, human rights, and democracy. It presented itself as the successor to Hitler's democratic opponents, now defending the continent against the equally antidemocratic communist Eastern bloc. This allowed Western Europe to delegitimize the antifascist narrative of the socialist East and distance itself from the legacy of fascism (despite the system's persistence in Spain until the late 1970s and resurgence in Greece in the 1960s, neither of which prompted the Council of Europe to intervene). During the Cold War, it was politically opportune for the West to keep the memory of democratic Europe's fight against the threat of National Socialism alive. The Federal Republic of Germany, the driving force behind a continental union, had to switch sides in this equation, from the (Nazi) German to the European side. Tensions around the already fraught process worsened after the USSR collapsed and the two Germanies were unified, as the country's newfound power revived dormant fears. These fears were also informed by the open question regarding the identity of the European continent, itself newly reunited.

It soon became clear that Germany would play a central role in the new Europe, but no one could really say what that new Europe would look like: What about the socialist legacy and post/socialist nations? Should the European Union (EU) be expanded, and if so, how far? How should the relationship with Russia and the unresolved question of Turkey be approached? What about migrants? An increasingly anxious debate arose about threats to European identity, which was vaguely defined at best—sometimes it was presumed to be Christian, or maybe secular, or maybe Judeo-Christian, while whiteness was generally implied. Accordingly, the threat to Europe seemed to emanate from those who defied these definitions, namely communities of color—Black, Roma, and Muslim, especially in recent years—as though excluding these groups, deemed unEuropean in every regard, would put an end to uncertainty about European identity and the continent's economic and political future.

This strategy is nothing new, of course. Scapegoating racialized groups for problems within Europe is key to the internalist narrative, which strives to prevent any blurring of European identity, whether by defining it against the East and Global South or internally, by creating a hierarchy of Europeanness. (The countries in the Northwest occupy the top, as far as possible from those suspect border regions of the Balkans and Mediterranean.) This process goes back to the age of the nation-state. While the exclusion of certain groups had existed well before then, the goal now was to create collective territorial identities. From the first, constructing a European nation-state as the "natural" homeland of the people who lived there required the creation of a normative national identity. This identity had to be distinguishable from the collective identity of other constituent people, which automatically produced national minorities. No population is as homogeneous as it is imagined to be, and borders—no longer pragmatically separating spheres of influence but instead defining quasi-natural nations—tore apart cultural and linguistic communities.

This separation process went smoothly at times, as in the case of the Danish minority in Schleswig-Holstein, which has been governed by a bilateral agreement with Denmark since 1955.[1] More often than not, however, national homogeneity was forced into being. In 1885–86, for instance, around thirty thousand Poles were deported from Prussia, while East Prussia, which had been Polish, underwent a process of "Germanization."[2] People perceived as not belonging to the ethnonational community were assigned a different, distinct identity, considered either compatible with the dominant collective (as with the Danes) or not (as with the deported Poles). Those excluded in this fashion were disallowed from identifying with their homeland—that is, the land they lived in—and were forced to adopt a different national identity, at times with far-reaching consequences. In any case, what mattered most was the ascription of one—and only one—national identity. This majorly impacted groups that were defined in the dominant discourse of their homelands as not belonging and could not be assigned to any other nation-state. This applied to Jews and Roma across nations; classified first as un-German, un-Polish, and so on, they were ultimately regarded as un-European.[3] The postwar Europeanization process did not fundamentally change this: whereas Jews were allotted Israel as their home state, the fact that Roma are present throughout Europe without striving for their own nation-state is by no means seen as an affirmation of European identity; instead, it furthers their exclusion from the diverse national collectives that comprise post/national Europe. The racialization of European people of color likewise lives on in the assumption that their true home is somewhere outside the continent. After the mass expulsions

---

1. Bundesministerium des Innern, "Gesellschaft und Verfassung."
2. See Ther, *Die dunkle Seite*.
3. See also Matti Bunzl's theory on modern antisemitism as a product of the rise of the nation-state, whose objective was to secure the "purity" of the nation. Bunzl argues that modern Islamophobia, on the other hand, is a product of the postnational world order. In this case, the goal is to safeguard the purity of Europe's identity. Bunzl, "Between Anti-Semitism and Islamophobia."

of World War II, Western Europe distanced itself from the kind of explicit ethnonationalism that would have allowed for the forced displacement of minoritized groups. Nevertheless, ethnonationalist thinking continued in postwar Europe, with concrete political consequences from Northern Ireland to Spain, and in the Federal Republic of Germany as well.

Upon taking office in 1982, Federal Chancellor Helmut Kohl started crafting plans to halve the country's "Turkish" population, a fact that first came to light decades later. The plan was built on the assumption that, given their cultural alterity, millions of "guest workers" and their descendants had not put down roots and, if provided a modest financial incentive, would jump at the opportunity to abandon the lives they had built over many years in Germany and go "home"—the other assumption, of course, being that it was necessary or advantageous for the nation to decimate this demographic. Kohl's idea, which was only partially implemented, reflects a perception that has persisted in Germany for far too long:[4] non-European "guest workers" as eternal aliens who arrive with an incompatible and static "foreign" identity that they preserve until they head back to the foreign country whence they came (two-thirds of West German citizens supported this kind of "repatriation" in 1982).[5] Although this perception was certainly not limited to West Germany, it manifested there with profound clarity and consequences in terms of the right to citizenship by descent: a growing group of migratized people emerged, born and raised in Germany but denied German status. Legally, this was because they lacked "German blood" (which, until 1976, only secured citizenship rights if it came from the paternal side), but the fact that legitimate "Germanness" was inseparable from the idea of descent from "ethnic Germans" naturally had thornier implications: those who fit the image could pass in society as

---

4. In 1983, the federal government resolved to offer "repatriation grants" of 10,500 deutsche marks (plus 1,500 deutsche marks per child) to migrants from non-EU nations with which West Germany had signed recruitment agreements between 1955 and 1968. Despite high unemployment at the time, relatively few people took the state up on the offer, which expired after one year. See Schmidt, "Türken waren Kanzler Kohl fremd."

5. See "Ausländer: 'Das Volk hat es satt.'"

German, even if their legal status indicated otherwise, whereas those who did not look the part were perceived as un/German, despite their German passports. While Eastern European migrants faced systematic discrimination, even if they were white and Christian, these two characteristics were often all it took for their children to become "Germanized," as their language skills allowed the younger generations to be perceived as native. For others, like Black Germans, language—which was otherwise seen as the deciding factor—was secondary to the belief that German means white; in this instance, neither having the right passport nor proof of Teutonic lineage was enough to secure popular perception that they belonged.[6] The link between belonging or citizenship and "German blood" thus produced reliable and inevitable racialized categories of exclusion that were reflected in German citizenship laws until the turn of this century.

Inborn Foreignness: The Origins of German Citizenship Law

With the creation of nation-states in eighteenth- and nineteenth-century Europe, where people had long formed local or regional communities, national identities first had to be constructed, then defined in concrete, constitutional terms. Citizenship regulations echoed prevailing concepts of what it meant to represent a given nationality. Places that favored a cultural notion of belonging, like France, abided by the jus soli (right of soil) principle, which holds that one's birthplace and permanent residence in a country constitute one's citizenship. In contrast, the jus sanguinis (right of blood) principle determines citizenship based solely on parentage. While most European constitutions mixed the two approaches, central Europe tended toward jus sanguinis. The first modern German citizenship law, which replaced feudal birthright citizenship, was enacted in Prussia in 1842 and explicitly stated that a right to naturalization did not exist. The issue inherent to jus sanguinis regulations, however, is that they project concepts of state and people onto a period of time

---

6. See Foroutan, Canan, and Arnold, "Deutschland Postmigrantisch I."

before these definitions existed: citizenship is passed by descent from a citizen, that citizen having been passed citizenship by descent from another citizen, and so on. Prussian officials solved this problem by conferring citizenship to anyone born in Prussia *before* 1842, regardless of lineage, while those born after 1842 were deemed citizens only if their fathers were Prussians by birth. (In other words, a radical jus soli interpretation of belonging was practiced selectively to pave the way for a radical application of jus sanguinis.)

The German Empire, founded not quite thirty years later, adopted this principle. Imperial citizenship was acquired indirectly at first, through belonging to one or more German states. It was not until 1888 that it could be granted directly, without simultaneous federal citizenship. The ethnocultural definition of Germanness assumed an ideal of German national character, which had found heroic expression since time immemorial (quintessentially expressed in Johann Gottlieb Fichte's 1808 *Reden an die deutsche Nation* [*Addresses to the German Nation*]). This placed impossible demands on the actual founding of the state, however. The German Empire reflected the true composition of the German people, its ethnic and religious heterogeneity, but this was considered a problem. Whereas certain imperial citizens were not accepted as members of the German *Volk* (namely people of Jewish or Polish descent), citizens of other nations, like Austria, were viewed as belonging to the *deutsche Blutsgemeinschaft*, or "German blood community." Establishing a unified German people and expelling foreign bodies was increasingly seen as the real aim of nation-building. For all its severity in implementing jus sanguinis, the existing German state was never perceived as a satisfactory expression of the "German nation," as its constitutional framework contradicted the ethnic concept of the people. This prompted early attempts at making ethnonational changes to citizenship laws, with two main goals: (1) binding German expatriates to the state (after all, no European nation produced more emigrants than Germany) and (2) making naturalization harder for foreigners, including those born in Germany.[7]

---

7. See Brubaker, *Citizenship and Nationhood*.

As early as 1894, the influential Alldeutscher Verband (Pan-German League; AV) campaigned to abolish a clause that stripped Germans of citizenship after living abroad for ten or more years; in its place, the nationalist organization called for jus sanguinis to apply to Germans born abroad and their descendants, thus encompassing the great many emigrants living on other continents as well as "ethnic Germans" in Europe, especially Poland.[8] The Reichstag signaled unanimous support, and in 1901 the government accepted the proposal. The AV also demanded an immigration ban on *Sprachen- und Rassefremde*, or "linguistic and racial aliens," a request that AV president and National Liberal Party legislator Ernst Hasse brought before parliament. Similar bans already existed, if unofficially; from 1899 in Prussia, Poles and Jews seeking naturalization were required to appeal to the minister of the interior for special consideration,[9] while the Imperial Colonial Office quite simply did not accept such applications from Africans.[10] Conflict was inevitable when, in 1912, discussions started on reformulating

---

8. As its name suggests, the Pan-German League (Alldeutscher Verband; AV), founded in 1891, viewed itself as the representative of all "Germans." The group did not see this category as equivalent to that of citizens of the German Empire but rather as in opposition to it: the goal was to unite the "German race" in one nation, from which all citizens "foreign" to that race would be expelled. On the one hand, the AV was expansionist: the primary objectives of the association, which was cofounded by Carl Peters, included pushing German overseas colonialism as well as creating a Greater German Reich that included large parts of Poland, Czechia, and ideally Austria. On the other hand, the league was concerned with fighting internal enemies, meaning anyone who did not belong to the German "race" and those who threatened it politically, especially the Social Democrats. The AV's understanding of "German blood" as a racial category largely corresponds to what is implied by today's definitions of *white* and *Christian*: German blood was not enough; it had to be "pure." For the AV, "miscegenation" was one of the greatest threats to the German race. (Within Germany, Jews and Slavs were responsible for such "contamination," while in the colonies it was the "colored peoples.") See Hering, *Konstruierte Nation*.
9. Brubaker, *Citizenship and Nationhood*, 135.
10. Africans living in Germany could, however, gain imperial citizenship by becoming naturalized in their respective federal state. This happened quite frequently, as one can infer from the number of cases in which this citizenship was revoked after 1933. See El-Tayeb, *Schwarze Deutsche*, 139.

the German Imperial and State Citizenship Law. On one side were those who wished to make these commonplace exclusionary practices official and who, like the National Liberal Party deputy Anton Beck, affirmed that "the purpose of this law . . . is to prevent unwelcome foreigners from becoming Germans; it is intended to prevent non-German blood from being admitted to the German fatherland."[11] On the other side were the Social Democrats, who wanted elements of jus soli introduced to allow for the conditional right to naturalization for certain groups. The Reichstag commission tasked with producing a preliminary draft of the law accordingly failed to reach consensus about the connection between the terms *race*, *people*, and *state*. The attempt to define Germanness, instead of strictly legal imperial citizenship, ushered in immediate conflict, as evidenced in the commission minutes:

> Germans are
> 1) those who hold citizenship in a German federal state. . . .
> 2) those who directly obtained imperial citizenship.
>
> Members of the commission further opposed the proposal on the grounds that it blurred the concept of nation and race and disregarded the national moment. Were one to replace "imperial citizen" with the word "German," the consequence would be that a German who does not hold imperial citizenship—such as a German-Austrian or a Balt—could no longer feel and consider himself German, whereas a Slav who has acquired imperial citizenship would be German.[12]

The manufactured dichotomy between imperial citizens and Germans was not subsequently resolved; instead, it became clear that for most commissioners, the latter category was the one that really mattered. The final draft provided for "ethnic Germans" abroad to retain German citizenship (or to obtain it upon application) and to pass it on to their descendants, even if they did not live in Germany; dual citizenship did not pose any problems in this regard. By contrast, the Social Democrats' attempts to secure the right of naturalization for children of foreigners born and raised in Germany failed. In light of the situation of stateless Danes in northern Germany,

---

11. Hansen, "Deutschsein als Schicksal," 7.
12. See El-Tayeb, *Schwarze Deutsche*, 140.

liberal Reichstag delegate Max Andreas Blunck proposed that citizenship be granted to children born of marriages between German women and their non-German husbands. With explicit reference to children from "racially mixed marriages," this proposal was also rejected, as the majority of the commission objected to the implication that "German" and "white" blood were not one and the same.[13] Only when it came to foundlings did the commission agree on jus soli regulations: subject to withdrawal, children whose parentage was unknown should initially be considered citizens of the federal state in which they were discovered—naturally this did not include German "protectorates," as the colonies were officially known. The government swiftly killed the resolution, though, reasoning that it could have extended to babies who "could not possibly be German, such as Mongol or Negro children."[14] The Reichstag also rejected the Social Democrats' proposal to ease the naturalization process for foreigners who had resided in the country for a long time.

The claim that the term "German blood"—which remained the only venue to automatic citizenship rights—has no racial connotations, since it does not necessarily exclude non-white persons with German ancestry, is suspect considering its explicitly racialized genealogy. "German blood" is not a real thing, of course, but rather a construct aimed at limiting the category of Germans to a set group of people, which it managed to do for nearly a century. Despite its ambiguous terminology and ethnonationalist, racist undertones, the German Imperial and State Citizenship Law of 1913 was not overhauled until 2000.[15]

---

13. El-Tayeb, *Schwarze Deutsche*, 140.
14. El-Tayeb, *Schwarze Deutsche*, 141.
15. Among other things, this meant that West Germany adhered to a uniform German citizenship that included East Germany (where, in 1967, a new citizenship law specific to German Democratic Republic territory replaced the 1913 statute). Also included were "ethnic Germans" living outside the Federal Republic's borders, while naturalizations of "foreigners" born in Germany remained exceptions to the rule. The debate on reforming the citizenship law after reunification focused on the issue of naturalization and dual citizenship. The Christian Democratic Union (CDU) and Christian Social Union (CSU) opposition used this to launch a racist petition campaign, which led to Roland Koch's electoral victory in Hessen. This altered the majority in the Bundesrat, the representative organ of the German states, whose

Citizens "with a Migrant Background" and the Failure of *Multikulti*

A striking contradiction lay at the heart of the German understanding of citizenship for all of the twentieth century: aggressive calls for "foreigners" (i.e., people without "German blood") to assimilate paired with the belief that assimilation was essentially impossible for racialized groups, since the concept of Germanness itself was deeply racialized. It was difficult, if not impossible, for "racial aliens" to gain citizenship—the model equated dual citizenship with divided loyalties and thus denied it. Even today, it is granted only in special cases when the second nation is outside the EU, which puts the large Turkish German population in a tight spot.[16] Ethnic Germans living abroad were always the exception: the government did everything it could to prevent individuals of German descent in other countries from assimilating and to encourage them to identify as "German," efforts that included offering the possibility of dual citizenship. This kept alive the tension between an "ethnic," racialized notion of Germanness and modern definitions of citizenship.[17]

It also explains why foreignness was transferred to the children and children's children of "racially alien" migrant laborers in the Federal Republic. Until the beginning of the twenty-first century, they were legally, culturally, and socially considered foreigners despite being born and socialized in Germany. The inevitable result was the rise of a two-tier society, in which nonbelonging was actively produced by projecting foreignness onto minoritized groups (who could never be anything but "foreign," given the prevailing dogma), only to fault them for that alleged foreignness, which largely

---

agreement was required to change the law. As a result, dual citizenship was jettisoned from the reform package and replaced by the contentious "option model." See Klärner, *Aufstand der Ressentiments*.

16. See Yücel, "Mal eben ausgebürgert"; "48.000 Türkischstämmige"; and "Entzug der deutschen Staatsbürgerschaft."

17. See El-Tayeb, *Schwarze Deutsche* for an examination of how Black Germans fit into the racialization of a German concept of nation.

barred them from fair participation in society.[18] Then as now, mainstream Germans have responded to these inevitable consequences with naive or feigned astonishment, then rushed to blame faltering integration on cultural deficits in people they were never prepared to recognize as equal, let alone as German. The new citizenship law of 2000 acknowledged the untenability of this essentialist view, at least in part, though not without faulting the potential new Germans for the alleged failure of this halfhearted strategy, in which terms like "citizens with a migrant background" ensured the survival of old hierarchies. (What exactly *is* a "migrant background"? Why is it relevant? When does one's background come to the fore? And how does the term help reduce casual racism—or, for that matter, produce it?)

This is still most evident in the treatment of Germans of Turkish origin, a population usually referred to today as Deutschtürken ("German Turks"), which anchors them linguistically and symbolically in Turkey, not Germany. In 1982, Kohl's justification for the need to remove Turkish families from Germany had been their "very different culture," which distinguished them from migrant groups that the chancellor deemed European and therefore capable of integration.[19] Cultural compatibility remained a central concern for decades to follow, though the benchmark now is European, not national, culture (outside of right-wing nationalist circles, at least, and increasingly within them too, as one can infer from such names as Patriotic Europeans Against the Islamization of the Occident [Patriotische Europäer gegen die Islamisierung des Abendlandes], or Pegida). Rather than trotting out discredited ethnonationalist ideas, a threatened liberal European identity can be used to justify exclusionary measures: instead of preserving the purity of a given *Volk*, now it is all about freedom, tolerance, equality, and other buzzwords of neoliberal multiculturalism.[20]

---

18. "Foreigners" born in Germany have fewer rights than Germans in many areas or are excluded from them altogether, ranging from youth athletics to the labor market.
19. Schmidt, "Türken waren Kanzler Kohl fremd."
20. As extreme right-wing nationalist organizations become more European, their rhetoric has also shifted toward the alleged threat (posed by Muslim Europeans)

Almost thirty years after Kohl's initiative, in October 2010 Chancellor Angela Merkel proclaimed multiculturalism a failure—a radical move, in light of German society's chary commitment to the model, but for all its radicalism, Merkel's statement was broadly received as an overdue acknowledgment of a glaring reality.[21] The end of multiculturalism translated rapidly into an end of tolerance toward those who were never recognized as Europeans, anyway—post/colonial and labor migrants from the Middle East, Asia, and Africa, along with their descendants. Without them, Europe could reclaim its imperiled common identity, or so the argument went. It was an identity defined by the following values, as outlined in the 2004 European Constitution, which never took effect: "respect for human dignity, freedom, democracy, equality, the rule of law and respect for human rights, including the rights of persons belonging to minorities."[22] Most defenders of Europe either missed the irony in using these values to exclude racialized communities or argued that the new Europe was only excluding those who rejected its basic values (by which they certainly did not mean the racist, right-wing, anti-European parties and nonparliamentary groups that were gaining momentum).

Ultimately, the positive response that Merkel's verdict garnered among European heads of state confirmed Germany's status as normatively European—across the continent, the end of the multicultural experiment was interpreted not as unique to Germany but as the German variant of a European situation: British prime minister David Cameron and French president Nicolas Sarkozy soon issued similar statements.[23] These reactions seemed to confirm the perception of Germany as representative of a united Europe confronting

---

to fundamental European values—values these far-right groups themselves actively violate. See El-Tayeb, "Gays Who Cannot Properly Be Gay."

21. According to the German Press Agency, most European media outlets responded positively to Merkel's declaration, whereas reactions overseas were mixed. See "Lob und Empörung."

22. Marzocchi, *Protection of Article 2 TEU Values*. Following negative referenda in France and the Netherlands, the EU backed away from introducing a European constitution.

23. See Wright and Taylor, "Cameron," and "Auch Sarkozy erklärt Multikulturalismus."

problems caused by non-Europeans that demanded transnational maneuvering. In addition to shared migration policies, the strategy focused mainly on Turkey's potential EU membership; throughout Europe, but especially in Germany, the majority of non-EU migrants hail from Turkey. (Russia comes in a close second, but Turkey—also positioned on the periphery of Europe—is interested in joining the European collective, unlike Russia. Also unlike Russia, Turkey is a Muslim-majority country.)

It took a long time for society to accept the fact that Germany is a land of immigrants, and everything that has happened since Merkel's declaration—from the emergence of Pegida to the rise of the Alternative für Deutschland (Alternative for Germany) party—demonstrates that the concept of an immigrant society remains controversial. There is little common knowledge of the tradition of migration in Germany, which began centuries before the first "guest worker" recruitment agreement in the 1950s, and people also seem to have forgotten that Germany was unrivaled in the eighteenth and nineteenth centuries in the number of emigrants it produced.[24] Over the course of reunification, the dogma that Germany was *not* a land of immigrants was so central to discussions about citizenship, migration, and right-wing violence that its significance to a national sense of self seems safe to assume. There was far more at stake here than legal constructs. Still, however hesitantly, Germany did say goodbye to its monoethnic, immigration-unfriendly identity. The separation of nationality from ethnicity within German concepts of identity is possible, as shown by the overdue introduction of jus soli elements into citizenship law and the attempt to legally regulate migration (thereby conceding that this is a long-term reality).

---

24. Since the early 2000s, at least within scholarly circles, the topic of migration has gradually shed its long-standing outsider status. Notwithstanding groundbreaking work, for instance that of Klaus J. Bade and the Osnabrück University Institute for Migration Research and Intercultural Studies (see Bade, *Deutsche im Ausland* and Motte, Ohliger, and Oswald, *50 Jahre Bundesrepublik*), and the founding of the Council for Migration (Rat für Migration) in 1998, the field of migration studies in Germany still has a long way to go. Too often in its research, as in society as a whole, migrants and migratized people are treated as passive objects for study (seminal early exceptions to this include Ha, *Ethnizität und Migration* and Gelbin, Konuk, and Piesche, *AufBrüche*).

The rancor regarding these circumscribed concessions to a cultural, rather than biologistic, definition of national identity also indicated that this process will not continue automatically or irreversibly. Time and again, migration and the question of who is German (or who can become German) prove to mobilize mainstream society and polarize debate more than any other topic.

In 1999, minister president of Bavaria Edmund Stoiber (who later ran as the Christian Democratic Union/Christian Social Union candidate for the chancellorship) declared that dual citizenship posed a greater threat to Germany's domestic security than the Red Army Faction terrorist attacks of the 1970s had.[25] Although Stoiber's thinly veiled equation of migration and terrorism was unusual at the time, it took on the platitudinous quality of the state response to the September 11 attacks. Around the world, 9/11 was used as an occasion to restrict civil rights in the name of "domestic security" and to present repressive legislation aimed at foreigners as an appropriate tool in the fight against global terrorism. Paradoxically, the botched "war on terror," which created failed states across the Middle East, was used as proof of this polarizing strategy's success. (George W. Bush summed it up in 2001: "Either you are with us, or you are with the terrorists."[26]) Muslim migrants and migratized Muslims fall under general suspicion and need to keep proving that they belong to "us" and not "the terrorists." These developments illustrate just how precarious a nonbiologistic understanding of Germanness still is. Those who visibly embody Germany's refuted history of migration are left to navigate the tension between the dominant line about the nation never having been a land of immigrants and the counterevidence (often buried) of its actual diversity—especially in moments of crisis, as regular as clockwork, in which the presence of the cultural/religious/ethnic Other is styled as an unprecedented challenge for what was once a homogeneous national (and continental) collective.

---

25. "Unterschriftenaktion zur Ausländerpolitik."
26. Bush, "Address to a Joint Session of Congress and the American People."

Germany and Turkey

The last few decades have seen certain tropes flourish, from Islam's incompatibility with European values to the impossibility of Muslims being (authentically) German or European—twenty years ago, despite existing hostility to Islam, it would have been hard to imagine a mass movement called Patriotic Europeans Against the Islamization of the Occident.[27] Recent surveys show that significantly fewer German citizens—all of 34 percent—agree that Islam belongs in Germany compared to a few years back.[28] This development is more than a little unsettling, considering the existence of millions of German Muslims: if there is no place for Islam in Germany, as two-thirds of the population seem to believe, then that same majority would argue that German Muslims don't belong here either. The September 11 attacks and subsequent war on terror helped shape this stance, but the roots go back much further, as President Bush's word choice suggested when he spoke of a "crusade" against terrorism.[29] In fact, these roots go all the way back to the beginnings of Islam. From their earliest days, Islam and Christianity, Islamic and Christian realms have been in competition with each other, whether theologically, economically, or militarily. At the same time, commonalities and intersections have always existed, though *Clash of Civilizations*–type scenarios

---

27. Interestingly, Islam as the bogeyman has galvanized traditionally anti-EU right-wing extremist groups into embracing Europeanization. Consider Städte gegen Islamierung (Cities against Islamization), founded in 2008, a Europe-wide alliance of such organizations as the Freiheitliche Partei Österreichs (Freedom Party of Austria), the Initiative Pro Köln (Pro Cologne Citizens' Movement), and Vlaams Belang (Flamish Interest)in Belgium, which succeeded the banned Vlaams Blok (Flamish Block)party. Further information can be found on the right-wing extremist blog *Gates of Vienna*, whose header reads, "At the siege of Vienna in 1683 Islam seemed poised to overrun Christian Europe. We are in a new phase of a very old war." See Krake, "European Initiative 'Cities against Islamization.'"
28. "Für jeden dritten Bürger."
29. Waldman and Pope, "'Crusade' Reference Reinforces Fears." This *Wall Street Journal* article quotes Bush as saying, "This crusade, this war on terrorism, is going to take a while." The statement, panned in Europe as insensitive and ahistorical, seems comparatively restrained today.

may deny it: "As a concept designed to help us understand the rapidly shifting relations between the different 'worlds,' fundamentalism is virtually useless. Islam, the principal culprit in this fundamentalist discourse, is an immensely diverse set of peoples, beliefs, traditions and practices. What it shares with Christianity is more extensive than that between any other world religion. It may be the fact that they are so close which makes them such implacable enemies."[30] I can't delve into this tortuous history here, as fascinating as that would be. However, fraught ties between Turkey and Europe exemplify the debate about European Islam: negotiations over Turkey's potential membership in the European Community have lasted more than fifty years, the latest chapter in a centuries-old relationship, as close as it is complicated.

This example reveals one of the continent's central problems: although superficially defined by geography, Europe's physical boundaries never have been and never will be clear-cut. Continental borders must be determined in a different but no less definitive way if the idea of Europe and the tremendous political, economic, and political privileges tied to being European are to be preserved. In a case like Turkey's, where a nation lays claim to this Europeanness and the perquisites that go along with it, Europe's identity is revealed to rely on a set of properties that sometimes clash but whose inconsistencies nevertheless determine continental politics. For example, Europe's Christian Democratic politicians will cite Turkey's Muslim identity as a reason to deny it European membership, without themselves appearing as a threat to Europe's secular principles. Turkey first applied to join what was then the European Economic Community in 1959, an application that was denied in 1989 by the European Community (EC). The successor to the EC, the EU, declared Turkey an official candidate country in 1999 and in 2005 began the negotiations, which are nominally still ongoing. Little has actually happened, though, since the Spanish sociologist of religion José Casanova wrote, "Can 'secular' Europe admit 'Muslim' democratic Turkey? Officially, Europe's refusal to accept Turkey so far is mainly based on Turkey's deficient human rights record.

---

30. Hall, "Europe's Other Self," 19.

But there are not-too-subtle indications that an outwardly secular Europe is still too Christian when it comes to the possibility of imagining a Muslim country as part of the European community. One wonders whether Turkey represents a threat to Western civilization or rather an unwelcome reminder of the barely submerged yet inexpressible and anxiety-ridden 'white' European Christian identity."[31] After all, Europe did not necessarily define itself on its own terms, as is often imagined, but leaned heavily on what distinguished it from the Muslim empires with which it had sparred over territory since the seventh century. Fourteen centuries generate a great deal of shared history and cultural overlapping as well as symbolic differentiation.

All manner of Muslim images have left their mark on the European imagination, from the "Moors" to the Saracens. Central and eastern Europe most often conjure up the Ottoman Empire: from Vor Wien, a popular bar in Berlin whose name alludes to the Siege of Vienna, to the musical round still being taught when I was in school ("C-a-f-f-e-e, do not drink so much coffee! Not for kids, that Turkish swill, makes you jumpy, pale, and ill. Be not like the Mussulman, who drinks a cup whene'er he can!"), to the habit of casting a seven-hundred-year-old battle in Kosovo as decisive in ensuring the survival of the Christian Occident in the face of invading Mussulman masses (a battle that carries on today, from Pegida's rhetoric to Serbian extermination policies).

Given how far back these things go, historians' input is as important as politicians' in the debate over Turkey's suitability to join Europe; what needs preserving is the continent's "historical identity," after all. Germany plays a key role here too, for one because it was a driving force behind European unification (despite the EU's democratic structure, Germany's yea or nay carries more weight than, say, Belgium's). Furthermore, the majority of Turkish migrants within the bloc live in Germany, a fact that has raised the pitch of debate here about Turkey's compatibility with the EU. It was Hans-Ulrich Wehler (1931–2014), that leftist-liberal doyen of German social history, who spoke out against Turkey's accession to the EU

---

31. Casanova, "Der Ort der Religion."

and justified his opposition on the basis of (his version of) European history: "The country does not have a liberalized market economy, shows flagrant disregard for human rights, and persecutes its Kurdish minority, but as a Muslim state, what divides it most from Europe is a deep cultural border. Based on geographic location, historical past, religion, culture, and mentality, the consensus is that Turkey is not part of Europe."[32] It would seem that Wehler is less concerned with Turkey's lack of secularization than with its identity as a Muslim-secular nation. Religion is coupled with culture in an Enlightenment tradition in which the relationship between religion and secularism was not necessarily antagonistic. Instead, the hierarchy of religions was determined by their compatibility with modern, enlightened forms of rule. Within this secular/religious hierarchy, Protestantism (and with it, northwestern Europe) represented the ideal of civilized religion, whereas Islam—initially esteemed by many Enlightenment thinkers—was increasingly deemed inherently "premodern." (See, for instance, the common assertion that, unlike Christianity and Judaism, Islam never went through a period of enlightenment, meaning it has yet to enter the modern age.) Accordingly, Wehler views the question of Turkish accession as the "riskiest endeavor in the history of European unity," totally unlike granting membership to Catholic Poland or orthodox Christian nations in eastern Europe. These countries do not challenge the definition of the EU as a secular confederation of states, as Christian and secular identities are considered compatible; in the European view, Christianity is part and parcel of secularism: "EU expansion to the east will happen, and it must, to help this European zone finally achieve political stability and, in a sense, to bring it home to Europe after having been exposed to Sovietization and exploitation for more than four decades in the imperial satrapy of Russia as a result of the war waged by Hitler's Germans in the East."[33] "De-Sovietization" in eastern Europe occurred in tandem with a "re-Christianization" comparable to the strengthening of Muslim parties in formerly socialist Middle Eastern nations like

---

32. Wehler, "Das Türkenproblem."
33. Wehler, "Das Türkenproblem."

Yemen, Algeria, or Egypt. (The dictatorships in Iraq and Syria were mostly secular, too, unlike Saudi Arabia, which remains a close ally of the West.) Wehler does not see the connection. Instead, the author elaborates on the ways in which Islamists have successfully (and necessarily) undermined Turkey's secular Muslim structure since the mid-1980s, when the military dictatorship ended. Sure enough, Wehler renders the military as the (overly tentative) guardian of democracy, whereas the Justice and Development Party (AKP) and its voter base are its foes. The notion that in the Islamic world, secular democracy must be protected from religious fanatics at the ballot box, even if it takes military intervention, has increasingly influenced Western responses; a local military with Western support might take action when an Islamist party wins an election, as in Mohamed Morsi's Egypt, and if that local force fails, NATO may intervene directly. On this point, Casanova remarks, "One wonders whether democracy does not become an impossible 'game' when potential majorities are not allowed to win elections, and when secular civilian politicians ask the military to come to the rescue of democracy by banning these potential majorities, which threaten their secular identity and their power. . . . Unless people are allowed to play the game fairly, it may be difficult for them to appreciate the rules and to acquire a democratic habitus."[34] The question is not (only) how "democratic" Turkey is but rather how this term is defined, where the limits of what is acceptable are set, and how resilient democracy is thought to be. For instance, why are parliamentary victories for far-right parties within the EU viewed with concern—but not as the death knell of European democracy—while the Justice and Development Party's big win in Turkey signifies the population's limited capacity for democracy? As Wehler demonstrates in his polemic, printed in the national weekly *Die Zeit*, the answers to these questions are predetermined by the widespread assumption that Islam and democracy are incompatible—and that democratic systems in general remain alien to the Global South, thereby causally linking such systems to the West (while massive Western interventions in domestic affairs of non-Western states and

---

34. Casanova, "Der Ort der Religion."

the effect on their democratic structures are ignored). Anticipating Thilo Sarrazin's anti-Muslim treatise, Wehler casts Turkey as the "incarnation of antagonism" toward Europe, from "Jewish-Greek-Roman antiquity" and the Siege of Vienna to the "portent" represented by 9/11: "Across Europe, Muslim minorities are proving to be unassimilable, holing themselves up in their subculture. As is well known, the Federal Republic of Germany does not have a problem with foreigners—what it has is a *Türkenproblem*."[35] Paradoxically, West Germany's recruitment of Turkish guest workers reveals that the "Turkish problem"—an allegedly historical dichotomy of Islamic and European civilizations—is a rhetorical construct that obscures a much closer and more ambivalent relationship. As the German political scientist Karin Schönwälder explains, in the 1960s the German government deliberately prevented the recruitment of laborers from non-European nations, referred to internally as "Afro-Asians."[36] According to Schönwälder's examination, nonpublic discussions reveal the central role racism played in this decision-making process, a calculated state intervention aimed at keeping Germany "white" by preventing people of "Afro-Asian" descent from settling here permanently. Having this context is all the more important because it emphasizes that when in 1961 Germany signed a recruitment agreement with Turkey, the latter country was explicitly classified as European and there were no objections to the arrival of Turkish workers.

It is no coincidence that Wehler's historical outline omits this point and the fact that ethnoreligious homogeneity at Europe's southeastern border was violently established through League of Nation–sanctioned expulsions of Muslim and Christian minorities after World War I. Instead, he posits a static, antagonistic relationship between "Europe" and the Islamic world that has barely changed over the last thousand years. This unfortunately represents an exploitation of the past for contemporary political interests more than it does an accurate description of labyrinthine historical ties. The actual mutability of this relationship based on shifting geopolitical constellations

---

35. Wehler, "Das Türkenproblem."
36. Schönwälder, "Germany's Guestworkers," 249.

and Europe's fluid borders has most recently manifested in Turkey becoming whiter and more European as the "migrant crisis" escalates: as long as Turkey stems the flow of Middle Eastern Muslims (and other Afro-Asians), whose foreignness is even more egregious, the EU is willing to make concessions to Turkey on membership in the bloc and freedom of movement—and suddenly, the human rights violations that have long been cited as a primary impediment to accession are no longer so important. Despite the Justice and Development Party's landslide victories and increasingly open warfare against the Kurdish population there, Turkey is now a reliable third country and thus destination for deportations; more importantly, it hinders refugees in their progress toward Europe, using any and all (even undemocratic) means, just as Hungary is wont to do. In return, Turkey officially becomes more European. The fact that undemocratic behavior and human rights abuses can serve as justification for both European inclusion and exclusion plays out in border areas other than Turkey as well (see, for instance, Germany's "readmission agreements" with Yugoslavia and Romania in the 1990s, made with full knowledge that these countries' treatment of Roma was anything but democratic).

The notion that Islam and Europe are forever incompatible is not only historically refutable but also politically dangerous. This line of argument is still trapped in the ethnonational thinking that prefers to declare impossible such real conditions as the changing makeup of the continent's population when these realities contradict the European self-image. Recent history has made abundantly clear that the attempt to reverse reality through repressive measures yields nothing but devastation. The challenges of changing conditions require a constructive approach. The first step is acknowledging that this process of change is nothing new and that it makes sense to abandon old demarcation strategies and to examine a shared future as well as a suppressed shared past. This would entail both a rediscovery of historical European multiculturalism and an honest reckoning with the legacy of continental racism. Of equal importance, however, is a critical analysis of Germany's treatment of "non-European" societies.

"German Historicism's Fixation on the Occident Persists Unimpeded"[37]

Among those who responded publicly to Wehler's rendering of Germany's supposed *Türkenproblem* was another historian, Andreas Eckert, professor of African history at the University of Hamburg. His criticism took aim less at Wehler individually than at the German historical profession in general, which he accused of provincialism in its treatment of non-European histories. According to Eckert, this is what underlies Wehler's static image of a monolithic Islam as well as the facile view of the non-Western world as a whole.[38] This fixation on the Occident—which a decade earlier Stuart Hall had identified as internalist historiography—necessarily leads to the "outside" world functioning as a mirror for the West, much like the mirror that assured Snow White's stepmother she was the fairest of them all. And Germany is not much calmer than the fairy-tale queen in its response to those who threaten this comfortable setup by holding up a less flattering mirror to the nation, namely Muslim Germans and Germans whose roots lie outside Europe. Pushing the metaphor even further: like Narcissus, Europe is incapable of seeing anything but its own distorted reflection, however catastrophic the consequences. Instead of adapting the image of Germany to the makeup of its people, vexatious elements are externalized as un/German on the one hand and integrated into German history on the other by linking them to an earlier stage of development that "normal" Germans have long since outgrown. The examples are many, though the most extreme expressions are found in discourse on Muslim antisemitism and "Islamofascism."

The term *Islamofascism*, originating in the anglophone world, spread rapidly across continental Europe in the 1990s. The transnational buzz was not in response solely (if at all) to actual signs of fascist structures in the Islamic world but rather to the death of a system that had dictated global structures since the end of World

---

37. The title of this section is a quote from Eckert, "Gefangen in der Alten Welt."
38. Eckert, "Gefangen in der Alten Welt."

War II. The retooled alliances, borders, and economies that resulted—both within and between nations—rekindled old enmities at the same time as they ushered in new coalitions. The reference to fighting fascism allowed the United States, last superpower standing, to justify the rise in NATO combat missions following the end of the Cold War. This justification went hand in hand with Europe's retrospective exoneration: the fact that a new batch of Nazis was detected in the "Orient," a part of the world whose culture was assumed to be no longer merely antidemocratic but actively fascist, made it possible for Europe to squash or redirect nascent discussions about colonial excesses of violence in these very regions. The narrative surrounding this new fascism was especially powerful in the land of the perpetrators, where it was a discursive marker for Germany having mastered its Nazi past, as we saw in chapter 4. The country needed this symbolic mastery in part to complete its integration into the reunified European community. In other words, both global strategies (like the "war on terror" or "humanitarian" NATO interventions) and intracontinental discourse (namely the focus on Europe's Muslims as a threat to continental stability) contributed to a reinterpretation of World War II. This new reading cast Europe in its entirety as (historically) antifascist and effectively allowed totalitarianism (with its necessary by-product, antisemitism) to be seen as naturally connected to Islam, the perennial enemy of the Judeo-Christian continent.

The problematic but popular metaphor of the "zero hour" reflects the ambiguous role that National Socialism and World War II play in German and other Western cultures of remembrance. Though it represents the nadir of European civilization, firmly situated in the past, this moment also serves as a central reference point in justifying Western dominance: to the United States, it proves that American supremacy following the "Good War" was based on antiracist humanism that liberated the world from the fascist threat.[39] As the United States

---

39. In his foreword to Michael Adams's *The Best War Ever: America and World War II*, historian Stanley Kutler sums up the myth of the "Good War" as follows: "We did not seek the war, so we believed; instead, we responded to the duty and challenge of a great power. We fought the war to preserve democracy; yet, we also envisioned a larger responsibility for protecting humanity. The end of the war decisively fulfilled the

began its postwar ascent to superpower status, Western Europe (via the EC and EU) positioned itself as a judicious middle power without ambitions for global dominance but at the same time obviously predestined to set a good example on the world stage; after all, according to the internalist narrative, the EU epitomizes an advanced, postnational form of society toward which other parts of the world are still working. To legitimize a world order in which the West functions as the model of global development, Western superiority must be accepted as fact (and as a good thing); equally essential is that the West bear no structural responsibility for the conditions that force it to intervene (politically, economically, militarily) outside its borders in efforts to establish systems that correspond to its development model. The end of World War II represents a starting point for Europe's own success story, ambivalent as it may be: the war and decolonization that followed taught (Western) Europe the risks of rampant expansionism. Since then, it has used the qualities that led to its temporary decline for the good of the world: Europe had to process its past guilt in order to assume its place in the new world order, and it accomplished just that. As the French philosopher Pascal Bruckner puts it,

> The entire history of the 20th century attests to the fanaticism of modernity.... No matter that first Nazism and then communism were defeated by democratic regimes inspired by the Enlightenment, human rights, tolerance and pluralism.... Modernity has been self-critical and suspicious of its own ideals for a long time now, denouncing the sacralisation of an insane reason that was blind to its own zeal. In a word, it acquired a certain wisdom and an understanding of its limits. The Enlightenment, in turn, showed itself capable of reviewing its mistakes. Denouncing the excesses of the Enlightenment in the concepts that it forged means being true to its spirit.[40]

In an act characteristic of the limits of hegemonic self-criticism, Bruckner focuses exclusively on European suffering and heroism,

---

war's aims. German fascism and Japanese militarism were utterly crushed and discredited, and after the war American beneficence lifted those nations from the ashes of defeat, reshaped them in our image of democracy, contributed to their prosperity, and encouraged them to resume roles of world responsibility." Adams, *Best War Ever*, xi.

40. Bruckner, "Enlightenment Fundamentalism or Racism?"

represented by fascism, communism, and the fight against both. European colonialism and the millions of victims outside the continent, meanwhile, are omitted from this review: a causal link between Western development and the deliberate underdevelopment of the Global South cannot be established, otherwise the West could no longer function as the global model of development. It also means that such humanitarian catastrophes as the Holocaust (and, less present in Western consciousness, the transatlantic slave trade) cannot be read as an outcome of Western development but must instead appear as anomalous, as temporary regression to a premodern (and ultimately "non-European") barbarism that has no bearing on European postwar society. Achieving this seemingly illogical aim and leaving the West in a state of "already" and the rest of the world in a state of "not yet" (to quote Josef Böröcz[41]) required merging the two elements of Western dominance after the Cold War, namely American military superiority and the European pledge to protect human rights, a trend that could be seen by the early 1990s, at the latest. The United States' "humanitarian" intervention in the Gulf War and in Kosovo, along with the resulting tribunal in The Hague and later the permanent international court, produced a logic in which war and the protection of human rights are no longer mutually exclusive—they now exist in symbiosis. What's more, they reproduce and fortify the dominant historical image described earlier: these military interventions were explicitly presented as a restaging of World War II. Dispensing with subtlety, Saddam Hussein was equated with Hitler, the Serbs with the Nazis.[42]

---

41. Böröcz. "Goodness Is Elsewhere."
42. See Kempf, *Manipulierte Wirklichkeiten*.

6

GERMAN NORMALIZATION, ISLAMOPHOBIA, AND MUSLIM ANTISEMITISM

Hitler's Revenants, or Anthropological Fascism

Although George H. W. Bush was probably the first to liken Saddam Hussein to Hitler in the debate over the Gulf War, the comparison was quickly picked up by elements of a German left wing in crisis after the collapse of European state socialism and German reunification. The putative triumph of capitalism and conservatism as well as discomfort with the new status quo prompted many to evoke the key moment in modern German history—Nazi rule—as one that reflected both the moral superiority of the Left and its greatest failure. The Gulf War thus became the backdrop for the German Left's reorientation and division into two camps, both of which justified their position by referencing National Socialism and projecting it onto modern-day reality and the world outside Europe.[1] Protesters

---

1. Schmid, "Der Nahe Osten."

opposed to US intervention chanted "Nie wieder Krieg!" (Never again war!)—recalling a pacifist tradition from as far back as World War I that was revived in the Easter marches of the 1960s—while those in favor countered with "Nie wieder Auschwitz!" (Never again Auschwitz!). Supporters of the United States ran with the comparison of Saddam to Hitler and identified the destruction of Israel as the actual objective of the invasion of Kuwait.[2] This went well beyond Bush's original intent for the comparison, which was to justify the United States' intervention by referencing Saddam Hussein's war crimes. What it now implied was that Saddam was trying to carry out Hitler's plan to exterminate the Jews.[3]

Intense debates over the legitimacy of the Gulf War fueled the division of the German Left into anti-imperialist and antinationalist camps and popularized the idea that the end of the Cold War and of state socialism had left a vacuum that was in terrible danger of being filled by "new Hitlers," unless the West remained extremely vigilant. The argument was probably delivered most concisely in "Hitlers Wiedergänger" (Hitler's revenants), an essay by Hans Magnus Enzensberger in the February 1991 issue of *Der Spiegel*. Enzensberger, one of postwar Germany's most influential writers, asserted that enshrining the singularity of Nazi crimes was not driven entirely by facts but was morally justified because it helped head off comparisons that ultimately aimed to trivialize the Holocaust. Now here was a situation that not only invited the comparison but demanded it. Applying a narrow set of criteria, Enzensberger argued first that Saddam Hussein was an "enemy of humankind" hell-bent on destroying the entire world if necessary, his own people included. This led to obvious parallels to Hitler, mortal enemy not only of

---

2. Saddam Hussein's threatening gestures toward Israel were aimed primarily at Arab audiences: the 1990 Temple Mount killings, in which Israeli soldiers shot twenty-three Palestinian protesters, provided the perfect opportunity for Iraq to appear less as the occupier of a neighboring Arab country and more as the sole Arab defender of beleaguered Palestinians. This was all the more relevant for Iraq because a number of Arab states had joined the US-led coalition against the country. German discussions, which cannot have held much interest for Saddam, largely ignored this explicit connection, as it did not fit into the Saddam-as-Hitler narrative. See Schmid, "Der Nahe Osten."

3. See Bruhn and Ebermann, "Der Golfkrieg."

Jews, Russians, and Americans but ultimately of Germans too. Enzensberger then came to his second point of comparison, namely equating contemporary Iraqis with the German population between 1933 and 1945. While enemies of humankind exist everywhere, the likes of "a Hitler or a Saddam can only enter into history if an entire people wishes it."[4] Quick to conflate Iraq with the Arab world as a whole, he identified a "death energy" fed by historical grievances in the latter, and concluded, "The new enemy of humankind does not behave differently from its predecessor. Irrespective of their wildly disparate conditions, the emotions of this enemy's admirers are identical to those of our fathers and grandfathers, and they pursue the same goal. This continued existence proves that what we are facing is neither a German nor Arab fact, but rather an anthropological one."[5] Enzensberger follows the internalist narrative to the letter by making modern-day Arabs relive the low point of German history. From that he derives the ability of Germans to know from experience what is best to do in such a case, or more precisely, he identifies the responsibility—borne by a handful of Germans who recognize the historical parallels—to oppose appeasement: "No conceivable policy, however shrewd or prudent, can compete with such an enemy. They always get what they want in the end: war."[6] Almost casually, Enzensberger introduces another idea that quickly gains traction (and that, as we will see, is later applied explicitly to Muslim youth): since the new Hitler has the same objective as the old one, support for the Palestinian cause must be interpreted strictly within this context, namely as another "vestige of fascism" motivated by the desire to eliminate the Jews once and for all. He writes, "If a significant share of German youth identifies with Palestinians more readily than with Israelis, if they prefer to protest against George Bush than against Saddam Hussein, there must be some explanation other than cluelessness."[7] It seems self-evident, then, that world history amounts to European history and that the Palestinians'

---

4. Enzensberger, "Hitlers Wiedergänger," 27.
5. Enzensberger, "Hitlers Wiedergänger," 28.
6. Enzensberger, "Hitlers Wiedergänger," 28.
7. Enzensberger, "Hitlers Wiedergänger," 28.

fate (or the situation in the Middle East in general) can be perceived only through the lens of German history, while also remaining subordinate to it, as the rest of the world necessarily must, from a Eurocentric point of view.

Abandoning the assumption that German transgressions were unique—a move justified by the alleged existence of comparable goings-on (with comparably catastrophic potential, if the Allies failed to respond to the new Hitler, a failure that would be far more reprehensible than in 1938, because this time we know the stakes)—can be seen as another important step toward reunited Germany's normalization within a continental union that had allied itself politically and militarily with the world's one remaining superpower, the United States. It certainly was not the last step, as indicated by NATO's 1999 intervention in Kosovo, the first one in which the German military was involved. Changes in discourse since the Gulf War allowed policymakers such as Joschka Fischer—the first ever Green Party foreign minister, an electoral victory that shows the impact of the West German peace movement of the 1980s—to justify the Bundeswehr's maiden combat deployment by asserting clear ties between World War II, the Holocaust, and Serbian rule in Kosovo. At a special congress of the Greens in May 1999, Fischer alluded to the split in the German Left over the Gulf War: "Auschwitz is beyond comparison. But I believe in two principles: never again war and never again Auschwitz. Never again genocide and never again fascism. Both belong together for me."[8] In this case, according to Fischer, one tenet had to be made subordinate to the other in order to prevent another fascist genocide, as implied in the line, "Auschwitz is beyond comparison. But . . ." The success of this argument was not independent of place: the status of the Balkans as European was always controversial; conflicts around the continental borders, both ideological and military, often played out there. Europe needed to pacify and integrate the Balkans into the European Union (EU) and the West if it wanted to maintain control over its demons and continue projecting them onto a racialized outside.

---

8. Fischer, "Speech at Green Party Congress."

"We Will No Longer Recognize Europe"

Strictly speaking, the former Yugoslavia lay outside the Soviet sphere of influence, yet its disintegration became symptomatic of the danger of "Balkanization" in Eastern Europe after the Soviet Union's collapse, of the threat of chaos lurking just outside Europe's borders—and in its past. The crumbling region in the southeast of the continent represented both to Fischer: "Let me tell you that with the end of the Cold War there has been a return to ethnic warfare and to nationalistic policies that Europe must not accept. If we accept these policies, we will no longer recognize Europe."[9] Those nationalistic policies—the founding of states in which established populations were sorted along ethnonational lines into categories of "belonging" or "foreign"—really should have been recognizable, given that they underlie most European nation-states, Germany included. Equally familiar was the catalyst, the collapse of existing structures of dominance, in this case a European and global order defined by the East-West dichotomy. This familiarity could have—maybe should have—easily provided the basis for a critique of escalating developments in the former Yugoslavia. Instead, the NATO coalition was formed around a different narrative, one that eventually led to the Bundeswehr's first ever foreign deployment: "Balkanization," not as an expression of European deep structures but as a manifestation of that region's un-Europeanness: "As in the case of the Orient, the Balkans have served as a repository of negative characteristics against which a positive and self-congratulatory image of the 'European' and the 'West' has been constructed. With the reemergence of East and orientalism as independent semantic values, the Balkans are left in Europe's thrall, anticivilization, alter ego, the dark side within."[10] Maria Todorova and others have studied the Balkans' perennial role

---

9. Translated from the German original, as the published English version only contains excerpts. The original, "Rede Joschka Fischers auf dem Außerordentlichen Parteitag in Bielefeld, 13.5.99," is accessible via the Internet Archive at https://web.archive.org/web/20170924001517/http://staff-www.uni-marburg.de/~naeser/kos-fisc.htm.

10. Todorova, *Imagining the Balkans*, 188.

as Europe's "inner Orient" and concluded that it quickly became the default explanation for the civil war in the former Yugoslavia.[11] Just as the conflict did not represent a simple relapse into premodern, "non-European" barbarism, the reactivation of the Balkans-as-Orient trope was not merely resorting to pre-(Cold) War explanatory patterns. Rather, it was directly motivated by the postwar justification of Western dominance, now demarcated from "enemies of humankind" by multicultural tolerance:

> Keeping a vigilant eye on the Balkans does not just mean that the West periodically saves the Balkans from the region's never-ending cycles of violence, but that the "Balkans" must be continually reinvented in the Euro-American imaginary in order to redefine the meaning of the "West." In contemporary media, political and legal discourses that maintained and legitimized NATO's military intervention in Serbia and Kosovo, the Balkans were construed as Europe's wild and monstrous geographic limit, whose stability was central to a postsocialist world and a united Europe's security and well-being. By envisaging the ambiguously European Balkans as the point of origin of all twentieth-century European violence, including terrorism and Nazism, and by reducing the Balkans to a space of ethnic conflict and ethnic cleansing, U.S. political and media discourses distanced the civilized West from its own racial thinking and racist violence that have been constitutive of Euro-American modernity. In other words, within the West, racism was produced as a monstrous formation of the past, currently playing itself out in the Balkans.[12]

---

11. See Todorova, *Imagining the Balkans* and Atanasoski, *Humanitarian Violence*. As several other authors have pointed out, the Balkans were not the sole focus of Orientalist discourse within Europe; eastern European Jews, as seen in the responses to Jewish refugees in the Weimar Republic, were often classified as "eternal Orientals." See Shooman, "Zur Debatte," 125–56. For a long time, of course, Muslims have been primary targets of "external" Orientalism, and in debates over European Muslims, the two discourses blend into one. As in the case of colonial racism, racialized structures of dominance were never projected onto non-European spaces alone—they always played out at home, too.

12. Atanasoski, *Humanitarian Violence*, 131. The German press participated as actively as the US media in this production—for instance, by sharing unverified reports on the so-called horseshoe plan, which allegedly evidenced the long-planned expulsion of Kosovo Albanians (thus ruling out NATO bombings as one cause for the incipient mass exodus). See Moritz, "Einsame Zweifler." The construct of an archaic culture, centuries removed from the Western capacity for tolerant multicultural coexistence, quickly came to apply to other parts of the "Second" and "Third" Worlds. During the Cold War, these regions had still been thought "capable of

Controlling the return of a historical moment that had already been overcome (in the West) thus became symptomatic of the new unilateral world order, in which Western capitalist dominance guaranteed stability and peace. The NATO mission in Kosovo seemed an ideal example of the modern American empire's methods and values: surgically precise and therefore "humane" high-tech military operations in defense of civilian multiculturalism (which also represented the transformation of US society over the course of the civil rights movement) against the barbaric protofascism of Serbian "ethnic cleansing."

The interpretation of NATO's first war on European ground as humanitarian and just corresponded with the postwar narrative of a human-rights-oriented Western Europe as well as the higher-level internalist view of history. Both build upon the contrast between modern, civilized, "clean" Western technology and chaotic, brutal, primitive, Eastern-Oriental ethnic violence—in other words, they build upon an image of the Balkans deeply entrenched in Western thinking.[13] This manufactured dichotomy allowed for the discursive presentation of the Kosovo conflict as a repeat of the "Good War," in which the United States and Europe (now no longer divided along Cold War lines) joined forces to oppose a fascist threat that was finally pushed from the heart of Europe to its periphery, where this discursive logic would claim it "naturally" belongs. The war in Kosovo served to affirm current US dominance by linking it to that of its European predecessor while simultaneously distancing it from the same: whereas a mighty twentieth-century Europe sent itself and the world into a devastating war, the United States as a pragmatic superpower nipped such conflicts in the bud, with support from a

---

development"—that is, capable of integration into the capitalist West. Afghanistan is probably the most striking example.

13. See President Bill Clinton's statement at the start of the war: "Kosovo is a small place, but it sits on a major fault line between Europe, Asia and the Middle East, at the meeting place of Islam and both the Western and Orthodox branches of Christianity. . . . All the ingredients for a major war are there: ancient grievances, struggling democracies, and in the center of it all a dictator in Serbia who has done nothing since the Cold War ended but start new wars and pour gasoline on the flames of ethnic and religious division." Clinton, "Statement by the President."

reformed Europe. This was only possible because the Balkans—just like the "Orient"—could be presented both as a place of historical continuity (or stagnation) and as a tabula rasa on which history can be rewritten to reflect the realities of the day. In this way, the war in Kosovo became emblematic of a post/socialist world order shaped by the alliance between reunified Europe and the American superpower, which was allegedly committed to a humanitarian militarism that would prevent a return to those forms of barbarism with which Europe had been stricken under fascism and communism. This noble cause (which, conveniently enough, history has already retroactively confirmed as justified and necessary) thus permits military operations, even without United Nations (UN) authorization; as it is, the latter organization repeatedly failed in its duty to defend human rights around the globe (including in Bosnia in the early 1990s, when the United States and EU still had a radically different stance on the Balkan conflict).[14]

A circular narrative dominates here. History repeats itself, refuting the "end of history" in capitalism proposed by historian Francis Fukuyama after the fall of the Soviet Union: time and again, the Western Allies are found fighting the Islamofascist-communist foe. Modern-day interventions also seem to confirm that Europe has successfully overcome its past. The clearest sign of this is Germany's new and very different position among the allied antifascists, and in an increasingly central role, no less. The Bundeswehr's deployment to Kosovo—the first German military mission since World War II—would have been impossible before reunification and the end of the Cold War, because of provisions in the German Basic Law. As unthinkable as it would have been for Europeans or Americans to provide Germans with the means to undertake another war of aggression in the direct aftermath of World War II, the

---

14. The strategy of targeted, "surgical" attacks has since been refined in the age of drone warfare in Pakistan, Yemen, and Somalia: risk-free for "our" troops, though with an acceptable level of "collateral damage" to non-white, non-Western civilians. Despite media saturation, the public has been kept ignorant of these unofficial wars, sometimes through targeted attacks on neutral forces, like Doctors without Borders hospitals in Yemen and Syria, an approach introduced in the wars of the 1990s, as when the United States bombed the Chinese embassy in Kosovo in 1999.

notion that reunited Germany could pose a serious military threat to Europe was equally inconceivable at this point. Consequently, Germany was granted the right to participate in military action against those who currently embodied that threat. The artless attempt to rewrite Europe's ambivalent response to the rise of Nazism—presenting it as a resolute intervention by Allied (NATO) forces to prevent a humanitarian catastrophe and protect vulnerable minorities—was successful enough to provide a template for a lasting construct in which the West combats "new fascists" that may actually be worse than the old ones.

Islamofascism

It would be obvious to take the growing focus on alleged similarities between fascism (or National Socialism)[15] and Islamism and link it to the September 11 attacks and subsequent war on terror, which was often criticized in Europe—this all the more so because in Bosnia and Kosovo, Muslims were the (European) victims of "new fascist" aggression. (Meanwhile, the German media barely registered the fact that one of the Nazis' main targets, Eastern European Roma, were under attack from both Serbian and Kosovo-Albanian sides; it had little impact on how Roma refugees were treated.) Despite later rhetoric, Europe's response to the genocide in Bosnia was actually very hesitant, and European intellectuals led the charge in characterizing Islam as the fascism of the twenty-first century, points that suggest the situation's complexity and Europe's more central role. The origins of the term *Islamofascism* are not entirely clear; in one of the most influential genealogies of the term, the British journalist Christopher Hitchens traced it back to the Anglo-Irish writer Malise Ruthven, who first used it in 1990.[16] Not

---

15. Whether the comparison is being made to Nazism or fascism is not always methodologically clear, but proponents of the Islamofascism theory emphasize antisemitism as the common characteristic. That alone suggests that the connection is primarily made between Islamism and Nazism, as antisemitism was less central to other forms of fascism.

16. Hitchens, "Defending Islamofascism."

entirely coincidentally, perhaps, French and Dutch intellectuals like Bernard-Henri Lévy and Leon de Winter were quick to adopt the concept. In the late 1990s both France and the Netherlands had gone through the difficult, overdue process of addressing their history of collaboration with German occupiers.[17] These discussions, however, soon gave way to debates about the new fascism allegedly spreading within the Muslim minority, all while hard-right, Islamophobic political parties were gaining ground.[18]

---

17. The Netherlands was facing a major crisis after the role played by Dutchbat, part of the UN's peacekeeping forces, in Srebrenica in 1995 came to light. Dutch troops drove off thousands of Bosniaks who had sought refuge in the UN enclave, sending them straight into the hands of Serb forces, who murdered more than eight thousand men and boys and raped thousands of women and girls. Investigations conducted later by the Dutch government found that not only had the soldiers felt abandoned (the United States, France, and Great Britain had denied requests for air support) but prejudice against the Muslim refugees had also been rampant. (As one Dutch soldier later recounted, "Babies were being born, there weren't any bathrooms, there was shit everywhere, and temperatures were in the mid-80s to mid-90s." (Robinson, "Dutch Still Grapple.") In response to the investigation, the Dutch government stepped down in 2002. The explicitly anti-Muslim Pim Fortuyn List party was hugely successful in the elections that followed. See van der Veer, "Pim Fortuyn" and Robinson, "Dutch Still Grapple." See also Rizvev, "What Does a Victim Look Like?" for details on Šejla Kamerić's public art project *Bosnian Girl*, based on graffiti done by an unknown Dutch soldier in Srebrenica that read: "No teeth . . . ? A mustache . . . ? Smel [sic] like shit . . . ? Bosnian girl!"

18. France's National Rally (formerly National Front), founded by Jean-Marie Le Pen in the early 1970s to protest Algerian independence, is probably the most successful far-right party in western Europe. It now holds the majority in many local constituencies, a position it uses to implement populist measures (like abolishing the use of pork substitutes in public schools), and enjoys growing influence over the national political landscape. With Le Pen's daughter Marine at the helm, the party abandoned its formerly explicit antisemitism but remains extremely Islamophobic. In the Netherlands in the early 2000s, the blatantly anti-Muslim Pim Fortuyn List party gained rapid support (its openly gay founder, Pim Fortuyn, was assassinated by a white environmental activist in 2002). The last decade has seen Geert Wilders's Partij voor de Vrijheid (Party for Freedom; PVV) take over as the leading ethnonationalist party in the Netherlands. The PVV has held seats in Dutch parliament since 2005 (and in European Parliament since 2009) and takes an extreme anti-Islam stance: Wilders supports a ban on Muslim immigration and on the Koran, which he equates with Hitler's *Mein Kampf*. The PVV denies the existence of social issues in the Netherlands and instead sees only a "problem with Moroccans," which allegedly manifests in racism against the white mainstream population. See van der Veer, "Pim Fortuyn" and Quinan, "Hidden Memories."

Those who support the idea of Islamofascism tend to highlight criteria that supposedly prove the fundamental equivalence of radical Islam and fascism, not unlike Enzensberger with his theory of Hitler's revenants. Unlike Enzensberger, though, these adherents do not ascribe this affinity to human nature but rather to the nature of Islam, as in Hitchens's argument:

> Both movements are based on a cult of murderous violence that exalts death and destruction and despises the life of the mind. ("Death to the intellect! Long live death!" as Gen. Francisco Franco's sidekick Gonzalo Queipo de Llano so pithily phrased it.) Both are hostile to modernity (except when it comes to the pursuit of weapons), and both are bitterly nostalgic for past empires and lost glories. Both are obsessed with real and imagined "humiliations" and thirsty for revenge. Both are chronically infected with the toxin of anti-Jewish paranoia (interestingly, also, with its milder cousin, anti-Freemason paranoia). Both are inclined to leader worship and to the exclusive stress on the power of one great book. Both have a strong commitment to sexual repression—especially to the repression of any sexual "deviance"—and to its counterparts the subordination of the female and contempt for the feminine. Both despise art and literature as symptoms of degeneracy and decadence; both burn books and destroy museums and treasures.[19]

This "proof" of a fundamental affinity between fascism and Islam(ism) dismisses as irrelevant the very different role religion plays in both systems as well as the historical fact that fascism has been a (Christian) European phenomenon. It seems far less pressing to examine what it was about European structures that produced fascism, and which of these elements linger, than it does to battle a fascism that has long since quit Europe (and never really belonged there in the first place). Rather, migration from the Islamic world and Muslim Europeans represent the threat of fascism's otherwise unimaginable return to Europe. It's no coincidence that, despite striking differences, political Islamism is equated with fascism, of all systems, and not with other extremist movements (such as the global rise in religiously-fueled nationalist violence).[20] On the

---

19. Hitchens, "Defending Islamofascism."
20. Religious extremism began to take root globally in the early 1980s, around the advent of major neoliberal restructuring, and one of the greatest challenges in

contrary, the equation is part of integrating the US-led Western system of rule, established after the Cold War ended, into the tradition of the antifascist alliance of World War II. Rather than identifying a new enemy, it is always new variations of the old being fought, without having to reestablish why. At the same time, this structure confirms that, despite the growing popularity of far-right parties in Europe, fascism is no longer present on the continent (unless brought in from outside).

For obvious historical reasons, the construct of Islamofascism lands differently in Germany. It could certainly be seen as a specifically German responsibility to monitor modern-day neo-Nazi movements and structures with care. Instead, talk of "Muslim antisemitism" has increasingly overshadowed the neo-Nazi violence that has persisted since reunification more than twenty-five years ago and often targets Muslims—even though the worst terrorist attack in postwar Germany was carried out by (at least) one neo-Nazi; even though an organization called the *National Socialist* Underground (NSU) murdered Muslims for a decade; even though pogroms in this country are still carried out by members of the mainstream population against minorities. Among the hundreds of victims of racist violence since 1981, when Sydi Koparan was murdered by right-wing extremists in Gündelbach, many of those victims' identification as Muslim was reason enough for the perpetrators to take their lives. Why, then, are Muslims in Germany perceived primarily as threatening and not as threatened? The potential for violence among Muslim Germans and right-wing extremist groups is gauged, communicated, and received in drastically different ways, a disparity that cannot (only) be explained by actual potential threats—ISIS is an internationally active terrorist organization, and there is no reason to

---

today's context is understanding why. This extremism—whether Christian, Jewish, Islamic, or Hindu—really does reflect many of the features Hitchens enumerates, which is why it would make sense to question where the commonalities are found, beyond any specific religious doctrine. What makes less sense is to classify these movements as fascist across the board, at least if one cares to preserve the term's analytical and historical specificity. And what strikes me as wholly unjustifiable is to categorize Islamic extremism as the only form of religious extremism that is fascist, as this requires the meta-argument that Islam and fascism are fundamentally akin.

assume that Germans wouldn't be recruited for attacks, but Germany is one target among many (most ISIS targets remain in the Middle East) and not the primary object of violence as Muslims in Germany were for the NSU.

Other factors can help explain the lopsided focus on the Islamist threat, including who is targeted—the NSU investigation and other cases have shown that it matters whether potential victims are members of mainstream society or not; year after year, studies confirm that racist violence in Germany is not consistently prosecuted or even noticed.[21] Another factor is the prevalent perception of Muslims as culturally pathological. Whether the focus is on circumcision, homophobia, or hijabs, the media, politicians, and the public tend to embrace majority practices as the healthy norm, against which Muslim aberration is measured. The obsession with Muslim failures eclipses the necessity for critically examining the truth of one's own purported tolerance. The response was also a means of managing the crisis of universalist humanism unleashed when those who fell under Josef Böröcz's "not yet" category—women, queers, racialized groups—started demanding inclusion in the "human" category. This inclusion process has been uneven, largely guided by the existent racialized space-time model. White Western women and queer folks come across as receptive, whereas others—in this case, Muslims—appear unwilling or unable to adapt to a cosmopolitan, human-rights-oriented system that is at once universal and Western. Since the early 2000s, they have instead been beamed into every chapter of European history imaginable, from the Middle Ages (where they supposedly remain stuck, culturally) to the Nazi era (due to an alleged "eliminationist Muslim anti-Semitism").[22]

As we have seen, the process of pathologizing (young, urban) second- and third-generation Muslim immigrants as criminal and violent began decades ago and has a causal connection to the decline of the social market economy in western Europe. In eastern Europe,

---

21. Amnesty International, "Leben in Unsicherheit."
22. "Eliminationist anti-Semitism" is a concept introduced by Daniel Goldhagen in *Hitler's Willing Executioners* to distinguish between German antisemitism and less lethal European versions.

the tremendous political, social, and economic upheaval following the end of the Cold War manifested in ethnic conflicts and the scapegoating of racialized minorities. Most affected by this were Roma, Black people, and, especially in the former Yugoslavia, Muslims—in other words, the same groups being racialized and marginalized in the West. And for all the verbal lines western Europe drew between itself and eastern Europe, condemning the racist violence there—which was roundly interpreted as a "democratic deficit" and an aftereffect of totalitarian socialist rule—it turns out the exclusion of these groups also helped facilitate the post/socialist transformation in the West. Accordingly, the focus on Muslims has less to do with their supposedly incompatible value system than it does with their marginalized socioeconomic position, useless remnants of labor migration in a postindustrial society.

The historian Volker Ullrich has demonstrated that, starting with the so-called Fischer Controversy in the early 1960s, arguments about Germany's Nazi history have shaped the way the country approaches contemporary conflicts, from the close of the Adenauer years to the end of the social market economy in reunified Germany.[23] The German historians' dispute in the 1980s, referred to as *Historikerstreit*—which Ulrich sees as a response to the end of the social-liberal era—was the first concerted attempt to reassign the origins of fascism to the (Asian) East, represented at the time by the communist Soviet Union. Over the course of the 1990s, fascism became situated as the quasi-anthropological inheritance of the European Orient by way of the Balkans; it now seems to have arrived in the non-European Orient with the turn of the millennium and discussions about Islamofascism. This steady push eastward was compatible with changing images of the enemy, shifting from the totalitarian Soviet Union in Europe's eastern regions to the

---

23. Ullrich's analysis was prompted by the publication of Götz Aly's *Hitler's Beneficiaries*, in which Aly argues that the Nazi state was an "accommodating dictatorship" (*Gefälligkeitsdiktatur*) that bought the people's support by means of generous welfare programs financed by robbing occupied Europe and, above all, the Jewish population. According to Ullrich, the liberal mistrust of the masses implied here found fertile ground in the context of dismantling the German welfare state. See Ullrich, "Goetz Alys Provokation."

Islamofascism of the Middle East. As I have mentioned, this strategy was in part a reaction to the faltering and overdue debate about collaboration in countries occupied by the Nazis during World War II and its roots in widespread European antisemitism. Here too, the shift occurred, with burgeoning interest in collaborations between the Nazis and Muslims. The trope of Muslim antisemitism recasts white Christian Europe as the protector—not persecutor—of the Jewish minority, which strengthens the narrative of a Judeo-Christian European past and unity. European antisemitism thus appears as a historical aberration, long since beat, rather than a persistent structural problem. This perpetuates the narrative of Europe as victimized by external totalitarianism, framing the new internal threat of "Islamofascism" and Muslim antisemitism.

Localizing antisemitism within a population group that is already largely excluded from society allows that society to make symbolic condemnations that absolve the majority of any responsibility and suggest discipline as the only logical countermeasure against the minority. "Muslim culture" is construed as so fundamentally divergent from "European culture" that scarcely any commonalities remain (as few as exist between fascism and European culture). Not only does this negate centuries of shared history, it also sketches a bleak future: in *Eurabia: The Euro-Arab Axis*, which posits that leading European and Arab powers are conspiring against Israel and the United States, Bat Ye'or describes "Europe's evolution from a Judeo-Christian civilization, with important post-Enlightenment secular elements, into a post-Judeo-Christian civilization that is subservient to the ideology of *jihad* and the Islamic powers that propagate it."[24] While European Jews' position as a legitimate part of the continent is undoubtedly less controversial today than it was before World War II, the increasingly frequent reference to the "Judeo-Christian" culture of the West is inseparable from Muslim Europeans' positioning as being outside this constellation, or even endangering it. It is scarcely coincidental that this also trivializes the persecution and oppression of the racialized Jewish minority by the Christian majority that characterizes most of that joint past.

---

24. Ye'or, *Eurabia*, 9.

The categorization of Muslim antisemitism as more aggressive and widespread than both its historical European counterpart and that of today's right-wing extremists influenced reactions to Rabbi Daniel Alter's brutal assault in Berlin in August 2012. The victim later described his assailants as "Arab-looking youths,"[25] a statement media commentators quickly focused on. Anetta Kahane, founder and longtime director of the antiracist Amadeu Antonio Foundation, appeared to have evidence for the breakneck generalizations: "There have been more physical attacks on Jews recently than in past years, particularly in conurbations and big cities. Unfortunately, it's usually young migrants."[26] Although she hastened to add that this did not clear the rest of German society from responsibility regarding antisemitism in the country, Kahane's statement set the tone. (The leftist daily newspaper *taz*, for instance, ran its report on the assault under the headline "Leider sind es meist Migranten" [Unfortunately it's usually migrants].) It helped that, as usual, migratized Germans were subsumed under the term "migrants" in Kahane's statement, which automatically turns racialized people into non-Germans. This regrettably contributed directly to what Kahane herself identifies and criticizes as the "self-exoneration tendency" within (mainstream German) society and provided another example of that society's consistent inability (even on the left) to see how the persistent alienation of racialized groups helps to preserve the very thing Kahane believes she is fighting, namely an ethnonational understanding of Germanness. "Young migrants" (which usually means people born and raised in Germany) were made out to be the driving force behind the problem, ignoring the fact that the vast majority of antisemitic attacks—whether physical, verbal, or symbolic—are carried out by white German right-wing extremists, as confirmed quarterly by statistics provided by the federal government at the request of the Left Party.[27]

---

25. Kopietz and Schütze, "Warnungen vor wachsendem Judenhass."
26. "Leider sind es meist Migranten."
27. These requests can be found here: https://dip.bundestag.de/suche?term=antisemitische%20Straftaten&rows=25, and the government responses here: https://dip.bundestag.de/suche?term=antisemitische%20Straftaten%20antworten&rows=25.

Public response to the violence against Rabbi Alter was not shaped by these facts, though, but by the widespread conviction that Muslim antisemitism was both comparable to and worse than German antisemitism in the early twentieth century—the former because it was fed by the same sources and the latter because it was aware of the Holocaust. Naming modern-day German Muslims the successors of historical German antisemites relieves the German majority of this hereditary guilt as well as any responsibility for antisemitic crimes committed by mainstream Germans today. The most extreme expression of this symbolic self-exoneration was probably the kippah flash mobs organized following the attack against Alter and in response to Gideon Joffe, chairman of the Jewish Community of Berlin, asserting that people who presented as Jewish no longer felt safe in certain (i.e., migrant) neighborhoods.[28] On the surface, the flash mobs—demonstrations at which non-Jewish participants signaled support for Jews by donning a skullcap—were a gesture of solidarity with a minority under threat, a display of tolerance to teach those intolerant foreigners a lesson in humanism. Beneath the surface, however, there is a certain cannibalistic appropriation of victimhood by a mainstream German population that has moved so far past the stigma of the Holocaust that it can stage the embodiment of Jewish identity as an antifascist gesture without feeling a glimmer of shame. This underscores the role of Jews as symbols—not as real people—in German discourse, taken a step further in this instance, with mainstream society ingesting and symbolically enacting Jewish identity.[29]

It comes as no surprise that there haven't been any hijab flash mobs, although it is well known (or should be) that attacks against Muslims in headscarves are part of everyday life in Germany. I am not suggesting that solidarity with Jews who feel unsafe is somehow devalued by the fact that other vulnerable groups do not receive the same support; instead, I am suggesting that this specific

---

28. "Überfall in Berlin."
29. As Katrin Sieg explains, the impersonation of the racialized Other has been a consistent and unthinking act in German postwar society (dressing up as "Indians" has long been a German obsession, and blackface, too, remains popular), one that contains an element of exonerating the perpetrators through their identification with the victims. Sieg, *Ethnic Drag*.

gesture of solidarity through appropriating the victims' identity is rooted in Germans' history as perpetrators, and that to some degree, the act implies a Jewish-Christian equivalence in the face of Muslim antisemitism that does not accurately reflect either historical facts or current constellations but serves primarily to absolve mainstream society: by casting Muslims as Nazis in the ongoing retelling of World War II, mainstream Germans can assume the role of savior and victim simultaneously. Whether accomplished through identifying with Jews or in discourse on migrants' hostility toward Germans, this satisfies the calls from such figures as Martin Walser to put an end to the German "guilt complex."

Muslim Antisemitism

Antisemitism among Muslims in Germany exists, of course, but there is no evidence to suggest it is any more pronounced than among mainstream Germans or non-Muslims.[30] There *is* evidence for the fact that antisemitic crimes are almost all committed by mainstream Germans. So when Muslim antisemitism dominates media debates; when numerous articles claim that "many" or "most" Muslims are antisemitic (then admit that there are a scant few studies on the subject);[31] when the heads of the Jewish Community of Berlin and the Central Council of Jews in Germany specify migrant neighborhoods as those in which Jews are not safe; and when the latter even calls for restrictions on refugees from Arab countries to prevent what he says would otherwise be an unavoidable spike in antisemitism,[32] then what we have on our hands is not just targeted stigma against this community but racism that functions as part of a larger structure. Identifying antisemitism as an "ethnic problem" inherent to Arab societies finalizes its localization in the Middle East, both in the present and the past.[33] And with that, antisemitism has

---

30. Özyürek, "Export-Import Theory."
31. See Wagner, "'Hitler gefällt mir'" and Amira, "Pädagogische Ansätze."
32. "Antisemitismus in Deutschland" and "Pro Asyl weist Äußerung."
33. In a statement, the president of the Central Council of Jews in Germany, Josef Schuster, echoed Enzensberger's theory of anthropological fascism: "When I

become yet another danger introduced to German society by backward Muslim migrants.[34]

This then justifies punitive measures in the name of state antiracism policies that apply only to a group that has already been marginalized and criminalized—in other words, a group that authorities claim can only be reached by means of discipline or penalties, because cultural deficits limit its ability to respond to rational argument.[35] There are, however, educational and deculturization programs for Muslim youth (including state-run "anti-antisemitism" initiatives), to introduce them to Western values and instill in them an appreciation for democracy and tolerance.[36] In the 1990s, programs like these focused on a different at-risk group: East German youth. Over the past decade, however, as discourse has turned to "new" (i.e., migrant/Muslim) antisemitism, so too has the focus of these interventions.[37]

---

consider the places and countries in Europe experiencing the greatest problems, one could conclude that the issue is not religious, but ethnic." "Pro Asyl weist Äußerung." Muslim antisemitism is real but not as constitutive for Muslim societies as it has been for Christian Europe. Contemporary antisemitism in the Islamic world is fueled by ethnoreligious fanaticism and the Israeli-Palestinian conflict, both relatively new and distinct from the antisemitism that has shaped European cultures for thousands of years. This neither renders it a harmless phenomenon nor justifies its discursive construction as an element inherent to Muslim identity. Historical antisemitism in the Islamic world cannot be compared to the centrality of antisemitism in the Christian tradition. Furthermore, the debate completely ignores the connection between Western development narratives, colonialism, racism, and antisemitism, all of which played a role in the dominant dogma of Western superiority, for which an equivalent did not exist in Islamic history.

34. That about captures the tone of the most comprehensive study conducted by the Federal Ministry of the Interior to date, which was published in 2011. In response, Ezra Özyürek writes, "It is noteworthy that the report does not discuss immigration to Germany from other countries with high levels of antisemitic prejudice, including Greece (69 percent), Poland (45 percent), Bulgaria (44 percent), Serbia (42 percent), and Ukraine (38 percent). More importantly, *Antisemitism in Germany* does not address the most significant source of antisemitism in Germany, namely extreme right-wing, mainstream German political organizations and formations." Özyürek, "Export-Import Theory," 51. This flagrant omission further demonstrates that the narrative about "new" antisemitism needs "old" European antisemitism, which is alive and well, to go ignored.

35. Haritaworn, "Queer Injuries."

36. See Amira, "Pädagogische Ansätze"; Patridge, "Holocaust Mahnmal (Memorial)"; and Özyürek, "Export-Import Theory."

37. See Özyürek, "Export-Import Theory."

Whereas addressing the Holocaust has been a central aspect for both groups, the programs for Muslim youths dedicate the most attention to the Israeli-Palestinian conflict; after all, the conflict and the "utter hostility toward Israel" it engenders are a defining element of the "new" antisemitism.[38] Amira (short for Antisemitism in the Context of Migration and Racism), a Berlin-based initiative that ran from 2007 to 2010, a period that included the 2008–9 invasion of Gaza, acknowledged the potential for conflict here, especially for young Muslims and Arab Germans. It did not necessarily equate anti-Zionism with antisemitism, but it did present the former as a misguided ideology that could be corrected by communicating objective facts. For initiatives like Amira, the goal of addressing the conflict in the Middle East is to create understanding for the "other side," which includes teaching the history of Jewish persecution in Europe. One hope is that the young people will tap into their own experiences with ostracism in learning this history, but at the same time, they are accused of competitive victimhood: "For instance, a statement like 'Muslims are always being put down, and Jews are so spoiled'—made by a young man whose self-identification as Muslim amounts to a shield against being defined by others in discriminatory terms—highlights the problems of Muslim negatory self-definition, minorities' subordination

---

38. See Kiefer, "Antisemitismus unter muslimischen Jugendlichen." According to this theory, "new" antisemitism differs from its historical analogue in its focus on Israel as the enemy. This does not necessarily mean that antisemitism and anti-Zionism are inseparable. Theoretically, a distinction is made between a rejection of Israel—because the state represents a group of people, namely Jews, who are denied the right to a state of their own or the right to exist—and criticism of aspects of Israel's ethnonationalist colonial policy toward Palestinians. In practice, however, proponents of the theory of new antisemitism tend to interpret all forms of anti-Zionism as antisemitic. See Küntzel, "In the Straightjacket of Anti-Zionism" and Schellen, "Israel bietet sich." What emerges is a self-fulfilling prophecy, in which new antisemitism is found primarily among Muslims and other people of color, because anti-Zionist attitudes are more widespread in these groups than in mainstream society—however, this is not because antisemitism is more widespread among them but because anticolonialism is. Equally important is Israel's long-standing support of the South African apartheid state; that support isolated the country from the rest of Africa and undoubtedly contributed to the debate on Zionism as racism at the UN World Conference Against Racism, Racial Discrimination, Xenophobia and Related Intolerance, held in Durban, South Africa, in 2001.

in conformity with mainstream society, and the external construct of anti-Jewishness that conjures up competition among minority groups."[39]

The goal is to move past this "competitive victimhood" and teach young people about the Holocaust as well as the circumstances that led to the founding of Israel (but not, as far as I know, about the longer history of German antisemitism). However meaningful this process, the problem is its one-sidedness: organizers do not deem it necessary to coach Jewish youth in understanding the "other side," nor do they question mainstream society's role as neutral facilitator, although the young participants certainly do.[40] For the process to be successful, the Amira report posits, something must be done to overcome this mistrust, and the majority must be open to all reasonable positions (implying that the young people's positions are unreasonable): "For instance, mainstream society accepts people standing up for Palestinian independence as part of a two-state solution. It has a very different effect, though, when someone says 'I'm against Jews' or 'Down with Judaism.'"[41] Based on this example, mainstream society is rational and tolerant, whereas the Muslim youths are clearly in the wrong. But this constellation does not necessarily reflect reality; it simply reflects the construct Amira engages to interact with its wards. More complex constellations—in which viewpoints are not so clearly distributed and mainstream society might be representing irrational or biased stances—remain as unimaginable as the possibility that the various groups' interests may be irreconcilable. The issue, then, is

---

39. Amira, "Pädagogische Ansätze," 12.
40. "Many young people distrust 'German' or 'Western' depictions of the conflict, which differ from media portrayals in their home context." Amira, "Pädagogische Ansätze," 13. The report does not elaborate on what media accounts might look like in these "home contexts." In "Export-Import Theory and the Racialization of Anti-Semitism," Özyürek points out that Amira's first report addressed antisemitism in Turkey, based on the assumption that this was the only way to establish basic knowledge about Muslim antisemitism in Germany. The implications are that (a) when it comes down to it, Turkish Germans truly are Turks; (b) they have imported their antisemitism from Turkey; and (c) Turkey is an antisemitic nation. According to Özyürek, this approach has had such limited success because Turkish German youths *aren't* primarily navigating a Turkish ideological context but rather a German one. Özyürek, "Export-Import Theory."
41. Amira, "Pädagogische Ansätze," 28.

that the stated goal and norms are fixed from the outset and cannot be revisited over the course of the process. The result is renewed emphasis on the young people's cultural deficits, echoing the consensus of the overall debate on Muslims and other racialized groups: they have nothing to offer German society; all they do is hold it back, and it is high time they learned to be more like the majority.[42]

This ignores the fact that tolerant coexistence requires debate on equal ground. Such debate is impossible when mainstream society assumes it already knows what defines these young people, given their background—machismo, homophobia, and antisemitism. Consensus is defined as adopting the dominant position, which in turn is seen as requiring little or no improvement (not perfect, but better than any alternative). Mainstream society's blind spots multiply, rather than being identified by the minority and then resolved collectively. There's no reciprocity; the notion of enrolling mainstream German youths (and adults) in systematic, state-sponsored programs to help them confront their prejudices and understand the "other side" (say, the one that experiences German society as structurally racist) seems beyond utopian, although it would be in line with the logic behind state programs for "at-risk groups." There is an urgent need to educate mainstream Germans about the history of antiziganism and colonialism, for instance. However, attempts made in this direction demonstrate that this is not (only) about knowledge or truth; it is about who wields the power of definition.

In its efforts to shift away from guilt, the reunified Germany has failed to incorporate a minoritized population whose origins actually

---

42. In his ethnography of a program for migrant (that is, Muslim) youths, Damani Patridge observed dismissive attitudes among most of the mainstream German teachers and social workers toward the kids: "Through this experience, it struck me that what was absent in the contemporary German discussion of racism, expressed in terms of immutable 'cultural difference' and the 'failure of integration,' was humility and love. There may have been and may continue to be a lingering anti-Semitism among some of these young people. . . . But such an anti-Semitism might best be overcome by constructing a safe space of care, which not only teaches these young people but also learns from them, in conversation with their contemporary experiences." Patridge, "Holocaust Mahnmal (Memorial)," 847. See Shohat, "Nahostkonflikt und Holocaust" for an approach that avoids mainstream German positions: a school project run by Mohamed Ibrahim, a Palestinian, and Shemi Shabat, an Israeli.

feature the absence of such (biographical, if not historical) guilt. This group could introduce its own, centuries-old tradition of a more peaceful, equal coexistence of Muslims, Jews, and Christians to help unlock constructive new forms of addressing Germany's continued responsibility for the Nazi genocide.[43] Instead, the country's historical guilt is projected onto them. This says quite a lot about mainstream society's inability to see minoritized communities as a (normal, equal) part of the German population. It also reveals that a constructive examination of guilt—of the responsibility for crimes that occurred two generations in the past—never really happened; that guilt was instead reconfigured as belonging to others.

The assumption that antisemitism among young second- and third-generation "migrants" can be traced back to their "foreign" (i.e., Muslim) cultural background, making it an expression of failed integration, disregards antisemitic structures within dominant society and their potential influence on these young people. It also ignores the link between antisemitism and other forms of racism, including those targeting Muslim youth. Positioning Jews and Muslims as antagonists, and mainstream Germans and the state as mediators, negates the common experiences of both groups as non-Christian minorities in the racialization of religion—discursive focus on this process would move the root of the problem from the periphery to the middle of (Christian/ Christian-secular) society. It would also highlight the fact that antisemitism, racism, and Islamophobia are on the rise across Europe and typically emerge in concert. Rather than problematizing the growing normalization of racist attitudes and actions, neoliberalism instead locates the crisis of its multiculturalism within a population group that is already economically

---

43. This is not about idealizing Islamic history, which is as rife with violence and oppression as any other expansionist ideology. That point is as indisputable as the fact that Islamic kingdoms featured far less religious intolerance over the centuries than Christian realms, a tradition that is relevant to this context and should be taught to members of mainstream society as well as Muslims and other minoritized groups—especially because the German media now makes constant reference to allegedly traditional Muslim antisemitism, and especially because admitting that the majority stands to learn something from the minority is as difficult as it is important.

marginalized, politically disenfranchised, and positioned at the edges of German society, if not outside it.

The Third World in World War II

The degree to which historical memory depends on contemporary constellations was on display in *Die Dritte Welt im Zweiten Weltkrieg* (*The Third World in World War II*), an exhibit slated to open in September 2009 at Berlin's Werkstatt der Kulturen (Workshop of Cultures; WdK). In adapting a 2005 book by the Rheinisches JournalistInnenbüro, a collective of journalists based in Cologne, the curators' explicit aim was to shed light on a part of history society had largely ignored, namely (as the title suggests) the effects of World War II on the Global South and people of color. It was new territory for the mainstream German writers, but they quickly discovered that this level of ignorance was culturally specific not global:

> Our research showed that familiarity with this topic is far greater elsewhere, than here at home. Nearly across the board, we found eyewitness accounts, biographical testimonies by veterans, and even studies about the impact of the war on civilian populations in a given region. In West Africa, for instance, most bigger cities have a *Maison des ancients combattants*, a meeting place for veterans who fought for their European colonial powers, and who to this day advocate for recognition of their service as well as equal pension benefits.[44]

Journalist Karl Rössel and his colleagues compiled extensive material from four continents, which they used to illustrate (among other things) Germany's wide-ranging involvement in military and colonial histories outside Europe—from the landmines German troops planted in Libya, which still kill people today, to the situation on Pacific islands formerly colonized by Germany, to battle zones in North Africa and the fate of Black Germans under Nazi rule. The authors do not mince words in explaining why Western

---

44. Rössel, "Die Rolle des globalen Südens."

accounts, whether academic or popular, fail to include this major aspect of what was, after all, known as the *world* war:

> People have balked at addressing this history, because it could—and likely would—have consequences, as in the form of compensation or, in places where war was waged, reparations. Acknowledging what colonized people contributed to the war effort would also change the way they and their descendants are treated today. In reality, however, the EU has established racist isolationist policies that in some cases deny entry to the children and grandchildren of Africans who fought to liberate Europe from fascism.[45]

The book, which is more than four hundred pages long, contains a wealth of visual material, thus lending itself well to the idea of an exhibition. It seemed just as obvious to team up with the WdK, one of Germany's best-known "intercultural centers" thanks to it running the annual Carnival of Cultures in Berlin. Housed in a former brewery in Neukölln, the WdK opened in October 1993 as a "socio-cultural institution funded by the Berlin Senate to promote cross-cultural understanding and to reduce social exclusion and discrimination experienced by ethnic-cultural minorities."[46] In direct response to the uptick in racist violence since reunification, the workshop was conceived as a community center where people could overcome their fear of the unfamiliar by meeting each other. Its initial focus on a mainstream German audience is obvious in the original mission statement:

> The Werkstatt der Kulturen in Berlin is aimed particularly at:
> - Youth and adults from all population groups who would like to join others in discussing and thinking about their fears, reservations, and aggressions toward the "Other," without being ostracized for doing so.
> - Educators, teachers, and coaches who would like to get to know and participate in the center's work and programming with their groups and classes.
> - Multipliers, employees of governmental and non-governmental organizations who are looking for assistance in developing their own action models.

---

45. Rössel, "Die Rolle des globalen Südens."
46. *Werkstatt der Kulturen*, 6.

- Individuals, groups, initiatives, associations, institutes, and organizations with a sense of social responsibility and a wish to get involved by contributing their own knowledge, skills, experience, or services for personal reasons (and not because "xenophobia" is a promising hole in the market).[47]

In the following years, the WdK offered educational programs and event spaces, for example [event spaces] for the Black History Month, organized (since 1991) by the Initiative Schwarze in Deutschland (Initiative for Black People in Germany; ISD); this was my first encounter with the center, as it was for many other Black people from around Germany. Its primary focus, however, was showcasing Berlin's many non-mainstream-German communities. The Carnival of Cultures, which the workshop ran from 1996 to 2014, was by far the most successful event of its kind, a major tourist attraction for Berlin that drew up to 1.5 million spectators annually.[48] A project like *The Third World in World War II*, which attempted to teach the mainstream population about overlooked contributions the "Others" had made to their society, seemed like a perfect fit for the WdK. Nonetheless, shortly before the show was scheduled to open, on September 1, 2009, an altercation between Rössel and workshop administrators resulted in the exhibit moving to a different venue. Although the parties never agreed on the exact reasons, the larger underlying conflict soon came to light, as did the fact that it struck a societal nerve.

According to Rössel, Philippa Ebéné, the director of the WdK, refused to open the show unless three of the ninety-six display panels were removed, namely those on Arab collaboration with the Nazis, especially regarding Mohammed Amin al-Husseini, the mufti of Jerusalem:

That seems to be the panel that bothers Frau Ebéné most. Al-Husseini was a staunch fascist, a fanatical antisemite who

---

47. *Werkstatt der Kulturen*, 11.
48. According to a 2011 study by the Investitionsbank Berlin, the Carnival of Cultures brought in four times the amount of money the city invested in it each year, yet the Senate Department for Integration, Labor and Social Affairs did not increase its subsidies for years despite rising costs, which ultimately led to new organizers taking over the event. See Investitionsbank Berlin, "Karneval der Kulturen"; Kappe, "Karneval der Kulturen"; and Djijaleu, "Die Werkstatt der Kulturen."

congratulated the Nazis for assuming power in 1933, who later helped orchestrate a pro-fascist putsch in Iraq and lived in exile in Germany from 1941 until the end of World War II, whose residence here in Berlin was an "Aryanized" Jewish home, who recruited tens of thousands of Muslim volunteers in the Balkans for the Waffen-SS. And he participated in the Holocaust.[49] Rössel viewed Ebéné's stance as part of a larger problem: There is a frighteningly powerful lobby of people in this country, whom I would describe as international historical revisionists, who simply try to disregard, dismiss, reinterpret, and rewrite a given part of history that they then piece back together in such a way that it cannot negatively affect current debates. After all, that is what people fear when it comes to Palestine.[50] Upon questioning, Rössel clarified that he did not know which panels Ebéné had found objectionable, and that he simply suspected it had been those about Arab collaboration (an

---

49. Beier, "Die Ausstellung gibt es ganz." Amin al-Husseini was born into an influential family in Jerusalem that had produced a number of muftis. His career was typical of local elites, starting first in the Ottoman administration and then continuing in the British colonial apparatus, which named him mufti, or the chief religious authority, in 1921. He used his position for anti-Zionist agitation, culminating in his leadership role in the 1936 Arab revolt. To avoid arrest by the British, al-Husseini fled first to Iraq, then to Italy, and ultimately to Germany. His primary objective was to prevent Jewish immigration into Palestine and to secure the support of Axis powers for an Arab Palestine under his rule. From 1941 to 1945, he prevented various attempts to grant European Jews safe passage to Turkey or Palestine; played a big part in recruiting Bosnian Muslims for the Waffen-SS (two of the three units of Muslim soldiers rebelled in 1943 and 1944, some of whom were deported to Neuengamme concentration camp; see Fava, "Waren eigentlich auch Muslime im KZ?"); and at the same time produced Nazi propaganda in Arabic. After the war ended, al-Husseini fled to France, where the government shielded him from extradition to England for more than a year, because French officials hoped he would help them stifle Arab independence efforts. Upon his return to the Middle East, al-Husseini quickly returned to a position of political power, now under the Egyptian protectorate. However, the Palestinian government-in-exile—installed by Egypt and led by al-Husseini—quickly receded in importance after 1948 and was officially dissolved in 1959, at which point al-Husseini went to Lebanon, but he was isolated from the movement emerging from refugee camps there, and he expressed clear opposition to the Palestine Liberation Organization. By the time he died, in 1974, his political influence had waned almost entirely. See Novick, *Holocaust in American Life*; Wien, "Arab Fascism"; and Nordbruch, "Arab World and National Socialism."

50. Beier, "Die Ausstellung gibt es ganz."

assumption that could easily emerge from his perception of "historical revisionists"),[51] but the media (and then Rössel himself) quickly reported this suspicion as fact (as a result, al-Husseini was the only Nazi collaborator whose role was discussed extensively in the press).[52]

From this perspective, the conflict was clearly between two groups: those who speak frankly about international solidarity (especially with Palestine) and Arab collaboration with the Nazis and those—leftists and Muslims—who wish to prevent that happening.[53] Ebéné, who had assumed the director role at the WdK the year before, painted a very different picture of the conflict: "As far as we were concerned, the plan was to honor all the Black and other non-white people who had contributed to liberation from National Socialism in World War II."[54] She denied claims that she had taken particular issue with the representation of Arab collaboration, or that there had been pressure from the Arab community, and said that she had objected to all eighteen display panels dedicated to collaboration: "This is about people whose contributions have gone unacknowledged for seventy years."[55] Information about collabo-

---

51. As it happens, Rössel had already published a five-part series on the topic of non-European collaboration with the Nazis in *iz3w* magazine in May 2009. Three of the pieces outlined the history of these collaborations, while the other two described German reception, with all five focusing on Arab collaborators. Rössel rightly pointed out that Nazi collaboration outside Europe could not be classified as a purely tactical measure, particularly as the wide range of anticolonial movements' positions indicate the existing scope for decision-making. Then, however, he departs from differentiation, delivering defamatory and historically false statements like "Hitler was considered a 'king of hearts' in Palestine" and explaining that dictatorial power relations in postcolonial nations came about when Nazi sympathizers took over government. See Rössel, "Schwerpunkt: Nazikollaborateure," 26 and 38. Rössel seems to display the very issue his exhibit and book condemned, namely ignorance of and uninterest in non-European realities, which create the perfect conditions for projecting European conflicts outward.

52. See Posener, "Götz Aly platzt der Kragen"; Wierth, "Streit um Ausstellung eskaliert"; and Oehmsen, "Wanderausstellung."

53. Although Rössel did not mention this, various newspapers and the mayor of Neukölln reported that the event was canceled in response to pressure from Arab groups. See "Geschichtsaufarbeitung nach Neuköllner Art."

54. Amadeu Antonio Stiftung, "Auseinandersetzung um Ausstellung."

55. Wierth, "Streit um Ausstellung eskaliert."

ration would relativize that involvement, she argued, and would be better exhibited separately: "It would overwhelm visitors to have victims in the Middle East, Africa, and Asia introduced in the same breath as collaborators and Japanese aggressors."[56] By her own account, Ebéné primarily wanted to highlight what non-European and non-white people had done in the fight against fascism, service that had long been overlooked. She found less support in the mainstream German press, which accused her of historical relativism and even antisemitism, than she did among organizations of racialized groups like ISD, ADEFRA—Schwarze Frauen in Deutschland (Black Women in Germany), the Black media watchdog Der braune Mob (The Brown Mob), the advocacy association Migrationsrat Berlin, and the Amadeu Antonio Foundation, and with the director of the Ballhaus Naunynstrasse theater, Shermin Langhoff.

We can already see that the conflict was less about differing positions on the question of non-white collaborators with the Nazis than about the parties' differing positionalities within German society: on one side is Rössel, other white Germans like the historian Götz Aly, and the writers behind nearly every newspaper article published on the controversy, and on the other side is Ebéné, along with other racialized and migratized people. At the time, Ebéné was the only Black woman, and one of the only people of color, at the helm of a German cultural institution of that size, including those dedicated explicitly to multiculturalism (all Ebéné's predecessors at the WdK were white men). Not only is she aware of this fact but it is at the heart of her work: "What sets us apart from other institutions is that we represent a different perspective than what typically runs through the mainstream. That means that as a rule, Black people, people of color, and migrants take center stage here and shine a light on issues of migration policy from their point of view."[57] This was the case behind the scenes, too, as Ebéné promised it would be (and soon made happen) when she assumed the directorship: "In the future the WdK should be seen as a center of excellence for such

---

56. See Ataman, "Neuköllner Kulturwerkstatt bekräftigt Kritik" and Wierth, "Erinnerung teilen ist schwer."

57. Djijaleu, "Die Werkstatt der Kulturen."

matters as transculturality, migration, and post-migratory work. For that, of course, we need representatives whose personal or professional backgrounds, fields of research, and language skills equip them with the expertise required to complete this kind of repositioning."[58] This was a radical change of tack that drew previously invisible whiteness to the fore: a shift in focus and audience demonstrates that culture and policies produced by white people for white people are neither universal nor neutral but systematically exclusionary. Ebéné's explicit self-positioning, including during the episode with Rössel ("I am the only person with biographical connections to colonialization"),[59] as well as the inferred claim to expertise, was a breach in German debates, which are supposedly always about "historical truth," "facts," and other noble concepts that float above the positionality of those representing them. As I touched upon in the introduction, this "colorblind" stance almost always results in the reproduction of social power structures (which is why, for instance, it is still possible to find debates about racism conducted exclusively by white people).[60] Deviation from the societal norm is usually equated with an inability to speak for the general public (or even oneself): racialized status and what is called "objectivity" in mainstream German debates preclude one another by definition. In canceling the show, Ebéné prioritized the position of racialized people, treating their interests as most relevant, which brought attention to the normalized privileging of white positions.

Contrary to Götz Aly's stance—the historian accused Ebéné of "anti-Enlightenment one-sidedness"[61]—debate on the exhibition brought together two subjective positions equally without claim to truth or objectivity. However, the two were not equally marginalized. Arab collaboration with the Nazis is not exactly unexplored subject matter; since the 1990s, with an added surge following 9/11, interest in Nazi influence over the Arab world has exploded.[62] Most publications have focused on the mufti of Jerusalem; Al-Husseini was

---

58. Wierth, "Montags-Interview mit Philippa Ebéné."
59. Ataman, "Neuköllner Kulturwerkstatt bekräftigt Kritik."
60. See "Hamsterrad der Ignoranz."
61. See Posener, "Götz Aly platzt der Kragen."
62. See Wien, "Arab Fascism."

without a doubt the most important Nazi propagandist and collaborator in the Arab world, but the importance attributed to him depends directly on how much sway he is said to have over Arab and Muslim public opinion and politics during and after World War II.[63] This suggests that his role is evoked not only in reference to historical conflicts but also to make claims about current ones, especially since researchers largely ignore organizations founded by Christian Arabs under Nazi influence in the 1930s, like the Syrian Social Nationalist Party or the Lebanese Phalangists, which are still active today.[64]

The most flagrant leveraging of al-Husseini was found in a 2015 speech by Israeli prime minister Benjamin Netanyahu at the 37th Zionist Congress: "He had a central role in fomenting the final solution. He flew to Berlin. Hitler didn't want to exterminate the Jews at that time, he wanted to expel the Jews. And Haj Amin al-Husseini went to Hitler and said, 'If you expel them, they'll all come here.' 'So what should I do with them?' he asked. He said, 'Burn them.'"[65] Netanyahu's claim was unanimously rejected by historians as false, but it wasn't created in a vacuum; it emerged from the swirl of debates on Islamofascism and their attempt to reconfigure fascism as originally "Oriental" and un-European.[66] This configuration has increasingly been swept up into mainstream debates. It is unclear

---

63. Rössel's own take on Palestine is as follows: "The anti-Zionism seen in such organizations as Hamas and Hezbollah today has the same objective as the antisemitism in Nazi collaborators back then: the expulsion and extermination of the Jews." Rössel, "Zensierte Kontinuität." Generally speaking, it could be said that research specializing in the Arab region attributes far less significance to al-Husseini than Holocaust research does. See Novick, *Holocaust in American Life*; Herf, *Nazi Propaganda*; Wien, "Arab Fascism"; and Nordbruch, "Arab World and National Socialism." The attention he receives in Holocaust research is remarkable: Peter Novick notes that the *Encyclopedia of the Holocaust*, published by the Yad Vashem memorial in 1990, gives al-Husseini "a starring role. The article on the Mufti is more than twice as long as the articles on Goebbels and Göring, longer than the articles on Himmler and Heydrich combined, longer than the article on Eichmann—of all the biographical articles, it is exceeded in length, but only slightly, by the entry for Hitler." Novick, *Holocaust in American Life*, 158. This seems disproportionate, regardless of how great one believes al-Husseini's actual influence to be.
64. See Herf, *Nazi Propaganda*.
65. Netanyahu, "PM Netanyahu's Speech."
66. Achcar, "Blame the Grand Mufti."

how useful it is to overvalue the mufti's role in this way. There should absolutely be open discussion about Palestinian, Arab, or Muslim collaboration in World War II, but until Palestinian, Arab, or Muslim history is understood—even approximately—in its complexity, there is no way that discussion can happen. Until then, this smacks of another disciplining of a group cast as backward and inferior. In 2004, Neuengamme concentration camp featured al-Husseini in its educational materials, characterizing him as the "leader of all Arabs and Muslims," a sloppy and serious error,[67] while such Muslim antifascists as Noor Inayat Khan, who was killed at Dachau in 1944,[68] remain widely unknown. (She did not appear in Rössel's exhibit, either.) Furthermore, this biased focus threatens to overshadow other debates about the impact of Nazism on the Global South, as the ISD stressed in its statement: "The controversy sparked in the media and politics by Philippa Ebéné's resolve and courage indicates that, rather than engaging in objective debate, this is an attempt to construct a polemical and simplistic sweeping connection between Muslims and Nazi crimes. It remains unclear how people of color, who have been ignored in recorded histories of World War II, will receive recognition for their role as liberators under the aforementioned conditions."[69] Germany's position on the Israeli-Palestinian conflict is not neutral—it has been supplying arms to Israel since 1959—nor could it be, given its singular historical responsibility. That puts Palestinian Germans in an especially difficult position, but demonizing them will not solve it. Regarding this conflict, the historian Peter Wien writes, "To ignore an all-important marker of historical consciousness—the Holocaust for Jews and the Nakba for Palestinians—represents an epistemological disconnect that fuels populist and pseudo-scientific debates that conflate the rules of public opinion-making with the historical record."[70]

It can scarcely be considered neutral when the German media presents the commemoration of the expulsion of hundreds of thousands

---

67. Fava, "Muslime im KZ?"
68. See Dalton, "Noor Inayat Khan."
69. ISD/ADEFRA, "Stellungnahme zur abgesagten Ausstellung."
70. Wien, "Arab Fascism," 2.

of Palestinians from their homeland as an expression not of mourning but of the desire to destroy Israel. However, it is equally impossible to transfer the situation in Israel and Palestine onto German realities.[71] Conditions in Germany are instead determined by the fact that debate takes place almost exclusively among members of the majority population, meaning the mainstream German perspective shapes views of the Holocaust and Nakba alike.

Accordingly, as far as Rössel was concerned, the dispute over *The Third World in World War II* was primarily one among white German lefties. The project was, after all, an offshoot of a book on the West German movement for solidarity with the "Third World," and Rössel's assumption about Ebéné's motives was based on his assessment of the movement; it probably didn't occur to him that other, non-mainstream-German positions could even exist, and yet he had described the spark for the World War II project as follows:

> We noticed that all the forms of solidarity work being done here during the postwar period by movements in the so-called "Third World" had been done earlier the other way round by people in "Third World" countries in the fight against fascism and for the liberation of Europe from the terror regime of the German National Socialists: from boycotting German goods, which we saw in Latin America in the thirties, to antifascist cultural events or conferences and brigades that (unlike Nicaraguan solidarity in the eighties) didn't stop at harvesting coffee, but instead (in the Spanish Civil War) took up arms to fight European fascism.[72]

The Rheinisches JournalistInnenbüro wanted to bring attention to this solidarity "the other way round," and this meant that the

---

71. It is worth pointing out that Palestinians are perhaps the only population for whom the symbolic function routinely assigned to Jews is less relevant than the Jewish population's actual presence and actions. In their experience, Jews are not a minority but a majority. In the Israeli-Palestinian context, Jews are not the Other; they are the norm, meaning they hold the social power to create Others. Anti-Jewish resentment among Palestinians tends to be the resentment against a dominant political power and its concrete strategies of dominance and thus resists comparison to European antisemitism directed at a Jewish minority. Anti-Zionism in Germany must be aware of this difference, too, in order to not reinforce existing antisemitic structures.

72. Rössel, "Die Rolle des globalen Südens."

work was geared toward a mainstream German audience. This was the conceptual issue that Ebéné and her supporters took with the exhibit: under her leadership, the WdK's target audience is people whose history is not usually told; unlike when it was run by white directors, the workshop no longer aims to educate a majority German public but instead works to represent positions of people of color. This focus set Ebéné apart, and her outsider status was clear in the language she employed: terms like *people of color* and *transcultural* positioned her outside the German mainstream—which Rössel never left—and marked her as Other: "'people of colour' and ... 'communities' (as these people are wont to say)."[73]

Fuming over the "excessive ethics of conviction," the historian Götz Aly stormed out of a public discussion on the topic hosted by the Amadeu Antonio Foundation, though not before declaring that "not only were Black British and French troops 'involuntary liberators,' but 'every village in southwestern Germany had stories of rape by Black soldiers,' who had not acted 'any differently than the Russians.'"[74] Historian that he is, Aly should be aware of the implications of the racist stereotype of Black rapists;[75] him introducing it to the debate anyway is characteristic of its overall hostile tone, especially on the mainstream German side, and went against Anetta Kahane's suggestion (at the same event) that people "simply listen for a change" to allow the overdue examination of German racism to begin.[76] This listening is still very difficult when it comes to racialized people criticizing their (well-intentioned)

---

73. Posener, "Götz Aly platzt der Kragen."
74. Posener, "Götz Aly platzt der Kragen." A few months later, Aly published an overwrought article in *Berliner Zeitung* (titled "Desecraters of Kreuzberg Streets") in which he blasted the renaming of a stretch along the Spree River, from Gröbenufer to May-Ayim-Ufer, for which Black organizations had fought for decades. He likened it to a loaded display in the tradition of fascist or communist totalitarianism. Aly, "Straßenschänder in Kreuzberg."
75. This stereotype played an important role in German history. It justified the prohibition against "mixed marriages" during the colonial period, helped the Black Horror on the Rhine (*Schwarze Schmach*) campaign after World War I, and fed into the World War II propaganda Aly evoked. See El-Tayeb, *Schwarze Deutsche*.
76. Wierth, "Streit um Ausstellung eskaliert."

representation by members of the majority. Unaccustomed to pushback, the latter quickly perceives this as censorship, which in turn yields righteous anger that activates racist clichés and accusations of (antiwhite) racism or antisemitism.

A similar controversy and response had arisen from a 2002 exhibit on racialized people under Nazi rule titled *Besondere Kennzeichen: Neger. Schwarze im NS-Staat* (Special features: Negro. Blacks in the Nazi state). The show was financed by the United Nations Educational, Scientific and Cultural Organization and created by a group of white researchers led by historian Peter Martin, a recognized expert on Black German history with a notoriously fraught relationship toward his research subjects (whom he views as research objects). The ISD's criticism of the show, even before it opened, addressed the dearth of Black academics among organizers as well as the title; in both, the group saw familiar hegemonic power structures that reduced the Black subjects of the exhibition—and the Black community as a whole—to objects.[77] Martin's overreaction to criticism from the ISD and others was a match for Aly in polemics; he called it "an intellectual form of ethnic cleansing."[78] It might seem as if mainstream German historians were suffering from an especially bad case of competitive victimhood, but the most recent of these debates, regarding racism in children's books, demonstrates that literary critics and culture writers are not far behind. In each case, the same issues emerge: the imbalance of (historical and social) expertise and dominance in discourse; the utter lack of knowledge among the majority about colonial history or the effects of casual racism; and, in short, the lack of "understanding for the sensitivities of Black Germans or people from an

---

77. See Claussen, "Besonderes Kennzeichen: Unversöhnlich." After the show opened at EL-DE House, a Nazi documentation center in Cologne, in November 2002, the presentation itself was criticized for a lack of context (for instance, by excluding German colonial history) and the resulting tendency to reproduce racist stereotypes without sufficient historical classification. Peter Martin distanced himself from the presentation but rejected criticism of the content. See Grosse, "Der Designer war Schuld."

78. Claussen, "Besonderes Kennzeichen: Unversöhnlich," 94.

immigrant background," as the sociologist Mark Terkessidis stated, with notable restraint, at an Amadeu Amadeus Foundation press conference.[79]

---

79. Wierth, "Streit um Ausstellung eskaliert." This understanding could have been based on questions like, Is Nazi collaboration among colonized people the same as that among people in occupied European countries? What is the difference between the way Japanese troops treated the Dutch in Indonesia (under the "exceptional conditions" of occupation) and the way the Dutch treated colonized Indonesians (under the "normal conditions" of colonialism)? What differences did colonized people see between France and England on the one hand, and Germany and Italy on the other? What did "liberation" from fascism mean for people who returned home to colonial exploitation or segregation in the United States or Australia? It would be decades before these democratic Western nations put an end to legal racial segregation, and systematic discrimination, criminalization, and structural racism continue to this day (as a reminder: the postwar plans for continental unification included European colonial territories). For sixty years, the part people of color played in fighting fascism was largely ignored in the West, with no mention made in commemorative events, films, or textbooks. There was no support for former colonial soldiers or the affected nations generally, whether to address the long-term consequences of chemical weapons in Ethiopia or German land mines in Libya. In view of this postwar silence, one has to wonder whether it was really necessary or appropriate to link the *first* event honoring this long-suppressed (not merely forgotten) history with the history of collaboration.

Conclusion

> The fact is that ... Europe is unable to justify itself either before the bar of "reason" or before the bar of "conscience"; and that, increasingly, it takes refuge in a hypocrisy which is all the more odious because it is less and less likely to deceive.
>
> —Aimé Césaire, *Discourse on Colonialism*

> We are born into webs of interlocution or narrative, from familial and gender narratives to linguistic ones and to the macronarratives of collective identity. We become aware of who we are by learning to become conversation partners in these narratives.... Nonetheless, just as the grammatical rules of a language, once acquired, do not exhaust our capacity to build an infinite number of well-formed sentences in a language, so socialization and acculturation do not determine an individual's life story or his or her capacity to initiate new actions and new sentences in conversation.
>
> —Seyla Benhabib, *The Claims of Culture*

> This is the new Germany. It's currently renegotiating itself
> and its national identity in a post-migrant way.
> —Naika Foroutan, Coşkun Canan, and Sina Arnold,
> "Deutschland Postmigrantisch I"

I opened this book with the argument that German identity is defined by regularly recurring "crises" around an Other that itself is constructed, time and again, through these confrontations. Our journey began in 1989, at a moment of what seemed like radical upheaval, when nothing felt certain, old borders—material and immaterial—became permeable, and myriad potential futures suddenly presented themselves. Whereas this moment of potentiality persisted for some, for others it quickly became clear that they would not be granted an active role in shaping this new world and that the future of those establishing themselves as the new norm would allow as little space for plurality as the old orders. The upheaval, rather than producing something radical or even marginally new, brought back a wealth of familiar strategies and concepts of the enemy, in which exclusion of the foreign—the un/German—would continue to play a central role. Since the early 1990s, steady levels of aggression have normalized racist violence, and though pogroms, arson attacks, or deadly assaults have prompted candlelight vigils and other short-lived expressions of solidarity with "foreigners," long-term political consequences such as the tightening of asylum laws have signaled a de facto acceptance of hard-right narratives about the tide of foreignness that threatens to inundate Europe if it does not fight back with all its might.

In the two years since I began this project (2014–2016), that very narrative has rapidly gained traction again. As ever, it is presented as a response to sudden, chaotic, uncontrollable events whose origins lie (as ever) beyond the control of the normalized middle, which remains untouched by the response to the last so-called crisis. And so the same response is repeated again, seemingly without any knowledge of the consequences: ostracizing refugees; discovering the enemy at home in racialized communities; political concessions to growing nationalist and hard-right movements, who use violence to make themselves heard; the shift away from a culture of welcoming outsiders and toward more restrictive laws on asylum and integration that define "foreigners" primarily as a threat; and so on. In other words, Europe appears to have successfully shielded itself from a chaotic outside world again. The internalist narrative has yet again reconstituted the success story of constant continental progress by projecting outward anything that might cast doubt onto that storyline, whether taking aim at those who can't keep up—the Global South or perennially backward racialized groups—or those who don't want to, as in the case of Brexit, which was powered by post/colonial nostalgia for a powerful, white, Christian United Kingdom. For all the European outrage at the UK's decision to leave the European Union (EU), it is all too easy to forget that Europeans vote against Europe whenever they get the chance (as we saw most recently in the Netherlands, when the EU–Ukraine Association Agreement was on the ballot).

One thing these unchanging responses are not doing is tackling the root causes in an effort to stop the cycle of crises. The Office of the United Nations High Commissioner for Refugees recently released its latest numbers: there are more refugees worldwide than ever before, a tiny fraction of whom ever reach Europe. The Mediterranean remains the deadliest border crossing on the planet; the EU agreement with Turkey and its cooperation with such southern Mediterranean nations as Libya, Morocco, and Algeria (now supposedly "safe third countries") are designed to keep refugees out of Europe, not to stop them dying. The EU congratulates itself on having effectively cut off the escape route to Greece; refugees who manage to reach Europe by sea, departing from North Africa, can be classified as "economic migrants," as usual, and legally "fended off."[1] Meanwhile, the news is full of reports about "criminal gangs of human smugglers," as though they were the cause, not the symptom, of a catastrophic situation that neither police nor military measures can stop. At the same time, the German government is authorizing more arms exports than ever before, while the Transatlantic Trade and Investment Partnership ensures the continuation of a policy of escalating economic inequality.[2] In other words, business as usual.

---

1. Saure, "Hilfsorganisationen kritisieren EU-Vorschläge."
2. "Deutschland exportiert."

My attempt at providing an overview of the last twenty-seven years should have made it clear that there is a dynamic at work here that has followed known, explicable patterns since at least 1989 (and further back, as my digressions into the early twentieth century illustrate). This dynamic does not come out of nowhere, nor is it a knee-jerk response to unforeseeable developments; it is instead anchored in the deep structure of European and German societies. When such patterns are visible and predictable, they can also be changed and ideally broken up. For that to happen, however, it will take a deep and honest examination. Instead, Germany still clings to the image of itself as the cradle of civilization and human rights; "crises" are still said to be produced elsewhere, then brought into Europe; racialized and migratized people are still not considered part of the population, let alone part of the *Volk*—they are viewed with distrust, their behavior constantly monitored for any hint of extremism or alterity, with immediate calls for sanctions. All the while, the majority lives in comfortable ignorance, structural racism is denied or glossed over, and societal violence steadily increases. What makes this possible is maintaining the crisis narrative, which allows worsening verbal and physical aggression toward minoritized people to be presented as a (understandable, if not excusable) reaction motivated by panic and fear, not selfishness and hostility.

Attempts at explaining what's behind right-wing movements in Europe often evoke the "insecurity" citizens feel. What insecurity, one has to wonder: Germany is not in a state of crisis—for people in crisis, one need look no further than Syria. This "insecurity" was around in the 1980s, 1990s, and 2000s—if this is going to serve as an explanation, then what we need to talk about is a structural crisis. Discussions about the supposed susceptibility of Islam to totalitarian forms rarely point to the insecurity of Muslim citizens; instead, ethnocultural deficits are to blame. When citizens who are better off than anyone else regularly get caught up in racist crises of their own making, perhaps there is another ethnocultural issue that demands naming: racism as a systemic strategy for dealing with social change.

Concerned Citizens and the Right to Security

The right to feel safe or "secure" is a central element in debates about the future of German society and the challenges of integrating refugees as well as migratized Germans: mainstream Germans do not feel safe due to the arrival of thousands of refugees, who might be sheltered in their own backyard; Jews do not feel safe given the fact that most of these people have fled from Arab countries; women do not feel safe being increasingly exposed to patriarchal Muslim culture. It seems understandable, if not necessary, for the state to respond to this prevalent feeling of insecurity; after all, one of its main functions is to guarantee its citizens' security. As a result, we are now seeing the tightening of laws, compulsory integration, and discussions about deploying the army domestically.[3] The question remains how threats to society are measured—and how the feeling of being threatened. Are there clearly defined limits to what is acceptable?

These questions are feverishly disputed in civil society, with the same blind spots that characterized earlier debates on the topic, for obvious reasons: to this day, influencers and other media figures are nearly all white, Christian (socialized) men.[4] The selective presence of migratized and racialized people, compared to their complete absence twenty years ago, undoubtedly makes some difference, but it is hardly cause for optimism, as the structures have not really changed: Germany is still a heteronormative, segregated society. One thing that the systematic inclusion of other voices in the debate

---

3. See Braun and Hickmann, "Einsatz der Bundeswehr im Inneren."
4. And those calling it out are nearly all racialized journalists (see Sander, "Klassisch Rassistisch"), while the white men being criticized for their dominance immediately make themselves out to be the primary victims of an unchecked global censorship campaign by the politically correct police, or they play the "antiracists' racism" card, which has been popular since the 1990s (see Chervel, "Ausnahmslos Differenz"). The trope is largely meaningless and could be seen as an extreme case of what educators and psychologists refer to (among Muslims) as competitive victimhood: without fail, people are always meanest to the white man and target him with impunity. It's a good thing he still controls the media, at least, so he can complain about it publicly.

would make very clear is that the right to security and the right to feeling secure are not granted to everyone, and the limits of what is acceptable are flexible, depending on who is affected and how far they deviate from the norm. Without looking to dramatize, the notion that I could feel safe in Germany as a Black lesbian woman is absurd, something that has never been part of my reality here—or elsewhere. People like me are reminded on a daily basis that, in the eyes of the majority (however it defines itself at any given moment), our lives are of little worth.[5]

I am not looking to rank individual experiences of violence or to deny my own privilege but rather to point out the mechanisms by

---

5. I am writing this shortly after the mass shooting (on June 12, 2016) at Pulse, a gay nightclub in Orlando, Florida. The perpetrator was an American Muslim man who may have regularly visited the club himself and who claimed in a 911 call he had acted for ISIS. US and European media outlets have largely portrayed it as an attack on "us all," an attack on Western freedom and tolerance by a Muslim fanatic. Mostly queer critics point out that the Pulse nightclub shooting was not really an attack on us all but rather on a specific group that is marginalized in "our" society as well. European media outlets have barely reported on the known and relevant fact that almost everyone at Pulse that night was a person of color, Latinx in particular. The United States is still a highly segregated society, along racial and socioeconomic lines, and not only in the South. The perpetrator knew he was attacking a place frequented by racialized people who existed in a state of precarity, the same group he watched over in his job as a guard in a private prison. In a case like this, why is it so incredibly hard for Western media to get more specific, moving from "us all" to "queer people" to "queer people of color"? It's the same reason people take such pains to differentiate between "Germans" and an endless list of un/German deviations (Muslims, NdHs [*nichtdeutsche Herkunftssprache*, meaning people whose mother tongue is not German], German Africans, citizens with a migrant background): only the norm can stand for the general public; the Other does not evoke solidarity. No one, whether in the United States or Germany, thinks "queer people of color" when they hear talk of "us all." What this reporting simultaneously tries to hide and makes abundantly clear is that the perpetrator—even though he was a Muslim, even though he professed allegiance to ISIS—was as American as apple pie: a racist, sexist, homophobic gun fanatic who would have loved nothing more than to become a police officer. His profile wouldn't have attracted much attention in Florida, one of the centers of political opposition to the gradual increase in LGBTQ rights across the country. None of this makes his crime any better, but it does situate it within a logic that is internal, not external, because "all of us" exist only when an external image of the enemy has to be created—an image that then makes it possible to condemn the crime while carrying on the politics that gave rise to it by constructing identity through norm and deviation.

which these experiences of violence and insecurity become legible—or not, as the case may be. The right to security is structurally unequally distributed, and it is no coincidence that the specifics of my position, for instance, bar me from enjoying this right. The point is also not to explain this to the majority and to show them that we already feel the way they are just starting to feel. The point is this: the security of the majority is structurally bought with the insecurity of those who have never "really" belonged. Privilege tends to be invisible when you have it, unmissable when you do not. Living without certain privileges, like the right to security, also means learning to navigate an environment that is always potentially hostile, in which one's own claim to security is never an obvious and unquestioned priority. Instead, that security depends on the whims of the majority, whose passivity is not neutral but actively contributes to this insecurity. Violence against women becomes intolerable only when perpetrated by racialized people, and violence against racialized people does not count as a threat to the state—on the contrary, state violence against racialized people is the norm.

Anti-Black Racism and the State Monopoly on Violence

Racist police violence, especially against Black men, is a normal occurrence in unified Germany.[6] This is another fact that comes into public view intermittently, only to be forgotten again, meaning that the obvious conclusion—that this violence is structural and not an exception to the rule—is never arrived at. Otherwise, people would need to question the causes and consequences of specifically anti-Black racism, which manifests in these acts and elsewhere. Police violence—the abuse of the state's monopoly on the use of force—is of particular significance when it comes to the question of who is allowed to feel safe and secure, feel as part of the group that this monopoly supposedly serves. The many documented cases

---

6. I have written extensively elsewhere on anti-Black racism and Black German activism. See El-Tayeb, *Schwarze Deutsche* and *Anders Europäisch*.

of police brutality against Black people as well as the way these occurrences are treated by the public reveal the interplay between precarity and a colonial racism that characterizes Black people as more aggressive, hypersexual, physically stronger, and less sensitive to pain, a set of characteristics used to justify abuses against them: African illegalized migrants experience the worst forms of police brutality in Germany.[7]

Here is just one example from the Amnesty International report on a Hamburg police scandal in 1994, the first of its kind to spark a major response:[8]

> [A] Hamburg police officer of 17 years service, the last two at station 11 in Hamburg, [provided evidence] to the prosecuting authorities in connection with their investigations into police abuses. In his testimony the witness alleged that he had seen a fellow police officer make six black African detainees undress, before placing them in a cell. The officer then emptied the contents of a canister of tear gas into the cell and quickly closed the door. In a second incident the witness reported seeing an officer spray a naked detainee with disinfectant. The programme [that made the case public] quoted the manufacturer's warning that the spray could cause serious injury to the skin. The witness also reported hearing other officers boast about how they had subjected an African detainee to a mock execution in the Hamburg harbour area. Reportedly the officers had made the detainee undress and while one of them had held his service revolver against the man's head a colleague fired a shot from his weapon into the air. The officers had allegedly said that the victim had "almost pissed and shit himself" with fear.[9]

Amnesty's follow-up reports in 2004 and 2016 and the 2016 European Network Against Racism report show that anti-Black

---

7. In 2016, a US study showed that the majority of white medical students still assume that there are biological differences in the ways white and Black people feel pain—which explains why white doctors prescribe pain medication more frequently to white patients than to Black patients (which many other studies have documented as well). See Somashekhar, "Disturbing Reason."

8. For one, the senate of Hamburg ordered an internal report, which confirms and documents thousands of pages of allegations. It ultimately led to the resignation of Senator of the Interior Werner Hackmann, a figure we know from his altercation with the Rom und Cinti Union.

9. Amnesty International, "Ausländer als Opfer."

racism remains widespread in Germany and across Europe.[10] One characteristic of this form of racism is the perception that Black people are biologically different from "normal" people. It is a constant that can be traced back through German history and found, for instance, in the usage of the pejorative prefix "*Neger-*," which was commonplace well into the 1970s: *Neger*-waiter, *Neger*-state, *Neger*-song—or *Neger*-work, which is still popular today. Black people have thus been excluded from the greater human collective because of their "*Neger*-ness" (and as mentioned in Chapter 6, when pressure mounted in 2013 to do away with the word in children's books and beyond, it sparked a national crisis, at least as far as the arts pages were concerned). In 1960, a quantitative psychological study of the status of "*farbige Kinder*" ("colored children") surveyed two hundred Black children and their parents, teachers, neighbors, and social workers.[11] The most alarming and consequential finding was that the group demonstrating the most entrenched prejudices was teachers. More than the other groups, they substantiated their derision with "scientific" theories that supposedly proved lesser intelligence, greater primitivity, and unchecked urges in "*Mischlinge*," or "mongrels."[12] This belief, which nearly all two hundred teachers shared, had a concrete impact on the Afro-German children (for instance, only three out of one hundred children were recommended for secondary school), but of course it shaped white children's attitudes, too, meaning that teachers were among the most effective multipliers of racist convictions.

In the 1920s, an international campaign targeted North African colonial troops stationed with the French army in the occupied Rhineland. German propaganda against the *Schwarze Schmach am Rhein* (Black Horror on the Rhine) portrayed the North Africans (already deemed "inferior," at best) as monsters—at the heart of the campaign, which enjoyed international support, was the image of the unfettered Black rapist and his victims, helpless white German women.[13] A

---

10. European Network Against Racism, "Black People in Europe."
11. Eyferth, Brandt, and Hawel, *Farbige Kinder in Deutschland*.
12. Eyferth, Brandt, and Hawel, *Farbige Kinder in Deutschland*, 66.
13. See El-Tayeb, *Schwarze Deutsche*. The Swedish prime minister and French Nobel laureate Romain Rolland joined in the protest, and the pope, too, intervened

decade earlier, the Reichstag had debated the legality of "mixed marriages" in German colonies. Colonial secretary Wilhelm Solf declared,

> I ask you simply to take in the bare facts. You send your sons to the colonies: Is their bringing black daughters-in-law into your home what you wish? Is their tucking woolly-haired grandchildren in the cradle what you wish? But far worse: the German colonial society spends an annual 50,000 marks to send white girls to Southwest Africa. Is these white girls returning with Herero, Hottentot, and bastard husbands what you want? ... The entire German nation will thank you if your considerations are restricted to: we are Germans, we are white, and we want to remain white.[14]

It is true, then, that anti-Black racism does not threaten the state; it hasn't since the state's founding, and it still doesn't—how could excluding, marginalizing, insulting, or attacking racialized people harm German normality? It couldn't, because these things *are* German normality—this does not mean that they could or should remain the norm, but for racism to be deemed a threat to the state, the self-image of the German state and German nation must change. Black Germans occupy a special place in this self-image, by challenging the widely held conceptions of what defines German identity. According to studies such as one on postmigrant German identity recently conducted by the Berlin Institute for Empirical Research on Integration and Migration, "the criteria for Germanness are at once open and exclusive. Germanness today can be learned and acquired, and by contrast, innate features play a lesser role: most important is the ability to speak German (97 percent), as is possessing German citizenship (79 percent). Nevertheless, 37 percent of the population maintains that having German predecessors is important to being able to be

---

with allied governments to arrange the withdrawal of troops. There were initiatives against the "Black Horror" in the Netherlands, France, England, Italy, Sweden, Denmark, Hungary, Czechoslovakia, Poland, Norway, New Zealand, Peru, Argentina, and the United States, with nearly the entire political spectrum represented. Whereas actions in the United States, including a demonstration at Madison Square Garden, were led by conservative Southerners and associations of German Americans, in France the protests were largely powered by the Socialist Party.

14. El-Tayeb, *Schwarze Deutsche*, 128. Stenographic minutes of Reichstag session on May 2, 1912.

German."[15] Most Black Germans meet all three criteria, so really it should not pose any problem for them to be accepted as German. There *is* one, however: Blackness and Germanness are still perceived as incompatible, as the prospect of having German footballer Jérôme Boateng as a neighbor recently showed (not that anyone cared much about whom *he* might want next door).[16] Skin color was not mentioned in the study, nor is it likely the survey included any questions about it; even if it did, many of those surveyed probably would not have realized it was a deciding factor for them—how can one poll for unconscious biases? One approach would be to poll people who are inevitably more aware of these processes. White Germans respond to Black Germans in unthinking, uniform ways ("Where are you from? No, I mean where are you *really* from?"; "Wow, your German is really good"; sharing unsolicited stories about trips to Africa; etc.), and when it is brought to their attention, they do not tend to see this behavior as problematic or symptomatic. Black Germans are better equipped to classify these patterns of behavior, because we encounter them every day: for all our lives, we are involuntary and unpaid statisticians when it comes to matters of Germanness. I have a pretty good sense of whether I'm encountering a response the first, hundredth, or thousandth time, which allows certain conclusions to be drawn about how mainstream Germans define being German.

The news right now is full of reports announcing that casual racism is on the rise in Germany. That may be true, but it all sounds pretty familiar to me. It seems more likely that we are entering

---

15. Foroutan, Canan, and Arnold, "Deutschland Postmigrantisch I," 6.

16. Who plays in the German national team is a question of utmost importance in the soccer-obsessed country. Soccer culture in Germany, and Europe in general, is also notoriously racist, exactly because the sport is seen as an expression of national identity. (See Sloop, "European Soccer.") Black players have long suffered the brunt of the abuse—and not only when they are on the opposing side. This is true for those on the German team, who have long been under particular scrutiny as there was a widespread feeling that they did not "deserve" to represent the nation—unless they were key to the team's success, as was the case with Boateng. The right-wing Alternative für Deutschland party put that sentiment into words when its deputy leader declared that Germans might admire Boateng's skills but still would not want to have him as a neighbor, i.e., still would not accept him as one of their own. See Kroet, "German Far-Right Politician."

another phase in which the mainstream becomes aware of the existence of racism and declares it a reality. A debate might follow, opening with a lengthy discussion about the insecurity citizens experience with regard to foreigners. There will almost certainly be some insights, too, but before a real confrontation with racist deep structures can occur, new issues will demand people's attention, or rather, people will grow tired of the navel-gazing; they will feel unjustly cornered and exploited by the racist antiracists on account of their capacity for self-critical reflection. In ten years' time, German racism will be rediscovered by mainstream Germans, and the process will start all over again, as though for the first time.

"Europe and the Wider Mediterranean Region" Revisited

The fact that what happened twenty years ago is repeating itself today, down to the last detail, indicates that Germany is still clinging to an image of normality that is the result of both artificial compartmentalization and historical misrepresentation: racialized populations, which have been part of Europe for centuries (especially Roma and Jews), have been controlled and marginalized by a system of discriminatory regulations for much of their shared history, without a hint of equality. The same went for colonial populations, whose countries were considered part of Europe as far as their economic exploitation was concerned but not when it came to those same people's freedom of movement. The idealized state of "before"—before refugees began streaming into the country, before Islam became a threat to European core values, before multiculturalism infiltrated the dominant culture—is one in which racialized groups may have been present but certainly did not have equal rights, and in which Europe shielded itself against immigration from outside while at the same time easing its own economic and social tensions through emigration (this applies to Germany in particular, which produced Europe's largest emigrant population until one hundred years ago).

Externalizing the foreseeable negative consequences of its own global power structures has been central to the rise of the modern

West, but now it is not working anymore, not even for those it was meant to benefit; the effects of ecological and economic destruction were projected into a future that has become the present, and while the Global South still bears the brunt of this destruction, Europe has lost the ability to seal itself off from those fleeing this situation, lost the power to pretend that continental borders are real and impenetrable. The fact that European experts and governments were unprepared for what was happening on the other side of the Mediterranean, despite ample indications—from the "Arab Spring" to the "refugee crisis"—reveals the extent to which the internalist narrative still shapes perceptions of reality. It also reveals, however, with increasing intensity, that the narrative is becoming less useful for Europe itself. Instead of perpetual navel-gazing punctuated by acute, haphazard crisis management, Europe's involvement in global developments and its partial responsibility for these crises—present and past—must be acknowledged. Rejecting internalism also reveals that fluid borders have always existed; they have always created alternatives, and they still do. The global financial crisis hit southern Europe especially hard and resulted in economic policy requirements that had otherwise been reserved for nations in the Global South. The latter South—in particular North Africa, which is separated from Spain, Greece, and Italy only by the Mediterranean—provided not only the model of merciless "structural adjustment policies" but also models of resistance to austerity measures. These practices inspired the *Indignados* movement in Spain, Gezi Park protests against neoliberal government policies in Turkey, and the "OPlatz" (Oranienplatz) movement in Germany, involving the refugee-led occupation of a public square in Berlin's Kreuzberg neighborhood.

European support for democracy movements in a part of the world that is considered to have close cultural ties to Europe when it is convenient for the continent has been limited, despite lip service to freedom and democracy. The return of supposedly telltale Oriental conditions—cruel, despotic leaders ruling over oppressed yet fanatical populations[17]—was practically greeted with relief by the

---

17. Edward Said's *Orientalism* (1978) outlines how Western notions of the Orient generated an overarching logic that still largely determines the cultural,

European public and immediately sanctioned by resumed economic and military relations, as such regimes are more reliable partners than wily democracies. In the global order, every region has its part to play, so the Orient has to remain the Orient. This Orientalism is needed to distinguish Europe clearly from its neighbors to the south and east—and in this narrative, southern and eastern European countries (most recently Greece) keep threatening to lapse into Oriental conditions when they fail to adhere strictly to (northwestern) European standards. In fact, this "normal state" of North African and Middle Eastern countries under pro-Western authoritarian rule perpetuates an unequal, neocolonial order that privileges Western interests at the expense of the Global South and makes borders as impermeable as possible.

Europe must face up to the fact that its stable, affluent democracies were bought with the dehumanization and exploitation of colonized and enslaved people, whose lives are still significantly less valuable, less worthy of mourning—more expendable. Colonialism was not only about depriving colonized subjects of their independence in the present and of any hopes for self-determination in the future but also about robbing them of their past, both through literal theft (as in the "non-European" artworks that fill European museums) and in the creation of a rootlessness, a lack of history that stole from the colonized the tools they could have used to question Western evolutionary temporality. This attempt ultimately failed, as it was bound to do, for no system has succeeded in stripping people of all forms of expression, and where there is a possibility for expression, there is resistance. We should not forget, though, that although the cultural, economic, and physical destruction Europe exercised upon its colonies was not total, it was extreme.

It hardly seems coincidental that Belgium and France are at the center of Islamist violence, especially when one does not only ask about the perpetrators' "background" (i.e., where they're "really" from) but where they are at home—namely in the ghettos of Paris and

---

political, and social representations of the regions that fall under this umbrella. For more on German Orientalism, see Zantop, *Colonial Fantasies*; Berman, *Orientalismus, Kolonialismus und Moderne*; and Kontje, *German Orientalisms*.

Brussels, which reflect a system that has never confronted, let alone overcome, colonial hierarchies. Belgium and France maintained intensely brutal colonial regimes that cost millions of people their lives, especially in Congo and Algeria. Just how, exactly, could a system implemented for centuries that necessarily assumed a fundamental inferiority of racialized people and derived from this assumption the right to systematically exploit them to Europe's advantage have prepared Europe to see citizens of Black or Arab descent as equal, or even simply as having equal rights? Especially without a critical examination of this past? The uprisings in French *banlieues* ten years ago illustrated just how hopeless things feel for racialized young people, just how few prospects exist for them, and yet the uprisings did not arouse any constructive responses but rather a new wave of repression (both material and memorial, through intensified surveillance and the framing of the "riots" as unprovoked and unforeseeable, another inexplicable violent outburst by the eternal Others). The new Europe is now nearly a generation old, which means there is a new generation of Europeans of color who, like the generations before them, grew up with the knowledge that they would never be able to become part of the greater collective. (From this perspective, the sudden sensitivity of the continental European media to a form of British racism toward white EU migrants, which is deemed symptomatic of an impending return to pre-EU nationalism, seems cynical in the extreme.) As long as Europe's colonial history goes unexamined, it will continue to define the continent's present-day reality—if Europe ever thought it could ignore this past and its lasting effects, that has now clearly become impossible. It should be equally impossible to see this development as independent of European racism. Europe must confront its colonial past to break the cycle of violence, which means that the European narrative must make space for those Europeans whose history includes colonialization from the perspective of the victims.

Analytical models like theories of totalitarianism systematically disregard that history in advancing a false dichotomy between modern authoritarian regimes (fascism and communism) and Western democracy. If it's not democracy, it's totalitarianism, and vice versa, despite the fact that Hannah Arendt—who more or less laid the groundwork for all future scholars of totalitarianism—explicitly highlighted the significance of colonial rule in the creation of European structures of thought and dominance. The theory was first formulated to capture the specifics of fascism and Bolshevism. Today these systems (especially National Socialism and Stalinism) are increasingly defined as "extreme," or even "exceptional," forms of totalitarian rule, which thus becomes an increasingly vague and all-encompassing counterpart to democracy:

> From the standpoint of liberal democracy, totalitarian regimes represent the same degrees of divergence, but typological classifications of power are mum on the political and ideological purposes of power, which is why one cannot derive the similarity of totalitarian regimes from their common claim to total power. The fact that the concept of totalitarianism is bound up with values is not, however, an analytical weakness, but rather marks the fundamental difference between democracy and dictatorship.[18]

It should therefore come as no surprise that the specific focus changes depending on which system is cast as the antithesis to the democratic West at a given moment; it is similarly unsurprising that attention has now turned to Islamism as a totalitarian form of rule. In his definitive work on the bloodlands—the eastern European territories in which millions of civilians were murdered during World War II—Timothy Snyder defines the ability to deny certain groups of people the right to be considered human as key to understanding both Nazism and Stalinism.[19] What does it mean, though, when the same characteristic can be used to understand European democratic nations? Without racial fanaticism, colonialism is unthinkable; Africans in particular were treated as an inexhaustible resource, without any regard for individual lives. Snyder writes, "In both the Soviet Union and Nazi Germany, utopias were advanced, compromised by reality, and then implemented as mass murder."[20] More than half a century earlier, Aimé Césaire had analyzed the extent to which this also applies to the European utopia of enlightened humanism.[21]

---

18. Vollnhals, "Der Totalitarismusbegriff im Wandel."
19. Snyder, *Bloodlands*, 386.
20. Snyder, *Bloodlands*, 387.
21. More than ten million Congolese people were killed over twenty years of Belgian colonial rule. The German genocide in Namibia is discussed more frequently

Conclusion

Totalitarianism is easy to align with democracy, a fact one can only ignore if racism and racialized people are externalized. Racist terror and democracy can coexist—what's more, to date, democracy has never existed *without* racism. Given that colonialism and transatlantic slavery are inextricable from the West's economic ascent and lasting wealth, the question remains as to whether Western democracy *can* exist without this structural racism. The two systems did not stand in contradiction but were mutually dependent: without colonial exploitation, there would be no European prosperity. Just like the rest of the continent, Germany was part of and continues to benefit from this process, vestiges of which can be found in everyday institutions like the Edeka supermarket chain (its name is based on an abbreviation of Einkaufsgenossenschaft der Kolonialwarenhändler, or Purchasing Cooperative of Colonial Goods Retailers), pharmacies across the country with the word "Moor" in their names (*Mohrenapotheke*), or, as we have seen, the term *Kanake*.

Unified Europe's attempt to establish a post/fascist and post/socialist collective memory consisted of externalizing both fascism and socialism as "un-European." After the Cold War, the theory of totalitarianism in Europe has increasingly functioned to provide absolution, as it establishes the battle between democracy and (fascist) dictatorship as the historical throughline of the last century and situates modern-day political conflicts within this context. This explanatory model again relies on externalization and evolutionary time: fascists are always the Others. At the same time, however, these others are stripped of their own history; who they are and what they do can only ever be seen through the lens of the European past. A theoretical framework of this kind does not explain either the compatibility of internal violence (e.g., racism) with Western democracies or the colonial violence that was in no way inferior to that perpetrated by totalitarian regimes. What is needed is an approach that allows for a critical examination of Western democratic systems

---

(though no less contentiously) these days, whereas the hundreds of thousands who fell victim to a famine deliberately caused by German colonial authorities in East Africa during the same period receive scant mention. The fact that enslaved Africans on Haitian and Jamaican plantations had an average life expectancy of seven years shows that colonialism and slavery were built on subjugation and extermination.

that demonstrates their affinity for structures usually associated with totalitarianism (and therefore thought not to exist in democracies). Post/colonial memory cannot simply be integrated into the existing model of memory; rather, an understanding of Europe as a post/colonial continent demands a reassessment of its fascist and socialist past. An image of what this might look like will emerge only when Europe turns away from its internalist history and evolutionary model of time and starts learning from its "Others."

An Intersectional, Postmigrant Germany

Naturalizing the despotic, primitive Orient as diametrically opposed to the other side of the Mediterranean region goes hand in hand with naturalizing the affinity between Islam and violence. In European discourse, Muslim men (especially those from North Africa) stand for endemic, uncontrollable aggression. They direct this aggression toward their own communities as tyrannical patriarchs, abusive husbands, and brothers who don't think twice about slaying their sisters in honor killings; when their aggression turns outward, toward society as a whole, the men become terrorists, juvenile delinquents, and religious fanatics. In this stereotypical, homogenized take on Muslim communities, female autonomy becomes as impossible as a confrontation with toxic masculinity, which is hardly limited to Islamists; indeed, examples abound in "enlightened" Western powers' interventions in the "Orient," where human collateral damage has long been routine. Meanwhile, the idea that Islam is fundamentally at odds with modern societies becomes normalized, creating a superficial unity among European nations. This applies to the relationships between countries as well as their internal structures, in that they are widely (and unquestioningly) upheld as the desirable norm to which Muslims, flawed in so many ways, must adapt.

The perception of Muslim antisemitism as excessive, even when compared to the much more violent variety among far-right extremists, indicates that the very presence of Muslims is seen as excess. After Rabbi Daniel Alter was assaulted, German society asked if

Jews were still safe here,[22] just as the attacks on New Year's Eve in Cologne made them ask if women were still safe here. This yields a false dichotomy: no Muslims equals no violent antisemitism and sexism, ergo no Muslims equals safety for Jews and women in Germany. That they currently *aren't* safe is not really up for debate; rather, it is debates about the state of mainstream German society that make this externalization so appealing.[23] From problems that exist in society and must be addressed collectively, sexism and antisemitism are simply turned into problems that can be externalized along with Muslims. The debate also exposes the lingering effects of European colonialism and the fatal consequences of dispelling colonialism from collective memory, in that it reveals an inability to communicate about contemporary conflicts that comes down to divergent discourses on memory. Colonial racism and its long-term effects in both formerly colonized nations and European cities are central aspects of life for second- and third-generation "migrants" (i.e., Europeans who are not white and/or socialized Christian, rendering them eternal outsiders); these aspects influence their understanding of their own marginalization as well as their interpretation of international current events, like the Israeli-Palestinian conflict. Majority society's tendency to negate this experience and insist on a European view of history that omits colonialism as unimportant worsens the conflict instead of resolving it.

The primary outcome of debates surrounding the 2015 New Year's Eve attacks in Cologne was not broad societal sensitizing to sexism among Muslims, North Africans, or the population in general; instead, the debates led to societal splintering and pitted marginalized people against each other, which confirmed what the majority

---

22. See Bauer, "Sind Juden hier noch sicher?"
23. Recent surveys show that racist leanings remain widespread among majority populations in the West and East alike, with hard-right extremists increasingly willing to resort to violence. Decker, Kiess, and Brähler, *Die enthemmte Mitte*. Although these extremists identify Muslims, Black people, and Roma as their main enemies, they are also responsible for the vast majority of antisemitic offenses. Economic disparities are growing in Germany too, with the gender pay gap in force and women holding far fewer positions of power than men. See Brinkmann, "Reiche sind viel vermögender" and Heuser, "Die letzte Bastion."

already believed and allowed the dominant group to cement its role upholding law and order. White women pointed out the irony of the fact that white men could thus turn from perpetrators into protectors without having to examine or alter their own behavior (the same could be said about mainstream Germans in the antisemitism debate or heteronormative dominant society in discussions of Muslim homophobia). None of this is new, of course, and one group in particular has analyzed it in great detail, though they are almost entirely ignored in the debate, as if they had nothing to say on the matter: women of color. Debates about what happened in Cologne demonstrated an interaction of racism and sexism in the perception of racialized men as sexually aggressive (and thus a danger to white women, who must be protected/controlled by white men), in the gender hierarchy as a means for racialized men to regain authority, and in the interplay of structural hierarchies that make it impossible for dominant society to imagine racialized women having agency.

Intersectionality is a political analytical framework for examining power structures that aims to both theorize and produce strategies of resistance, all from a situated perspective that addresses power differentials within possible coalitions. This perspective uses the marginalized position of racialized women as its analytic focus. As Angela Davis puts it, "The most exciting potential of women of color formations resides in the possibility of politicizing this identity—basing the identity on politics rather than the politics on identity."[24] The term itself was coined by American legal scholar and philosopher Kimberlé Crenshaw. It gained immediate practical relevance after the abolition of legal racial discrimination in the United States: in certain cases, people could now take legal action against this erstwhile state-sanctioned practice if they could prove discrimination on the basis of race (or, not long after, gender).

Although this cannot have been the legislation's intention, it soon became evident that membership in more than one disadvantaged category made it virtually impossible to secure protection against discrimination: class actions brought by Black women were regularly dismissed because other members of the groups in question (namely

---

24. Davis, "Reflections on Race," 318.

white women and Black men) did not experience discrimination in the same way. This paradoxical situation demonstrated that a conception of group identity based on dominant notions of normativity (white women as representing women in general, Black men as representing Black people in general, etc.) not only made it impossible to prevent discrimination but actually served to reproduce it. According to Crenshaw, what was needed instead was a legal as well as societal approach that acknowledged the fact that group identity is never homogeneous but rather emerges from complex intersections of such societal power vectors as race, class, gender, religion, sexual orientation, and nationality. At the same time, Crenshaw emphasized that the complexity of group identity did not imply the futility of collective action:

> [Intersectionality] might be more broadly useful as a way of mediating the tension between assertions of multiple identity and the ongoing necessity of group politics. . . . But to say that a category such as race or gender is socially constructed is not to say that that category has no significance in our world. On the contrary, a large and continuing project for subordinated people—and indeed, one of the projects for which postmodern theories have been very helpful—is thinking about the way power has clustered around certain categories and is exercised against others. This project attempts to unveil the processes of subordination and the various ways those processes are experienced by people who are subordinated and people who are privileged by them.[25]

Crenshaw's theory synthesized a practice rooted in decades of activism among American feminists of color, a practice as inextricable from the civil rights movements of the 1960s as it was from theoretical frameworks found in postcolonial and critical race studies. German scholarship on intersectionality tends to reference "Demarginalizing the Intersection of Race and Sex" (1989), in which Crenshaw uses the positioning of Black women to illustrate and introduce intersectionality, while her follow-up, "Mapping the Margins: Intersectionality, Identity Politics, and Violence against Women of Color" (1991), provides greater insight into her theory.

---

25. Crenshaw, "Mapping the Margins," 1296–97.

The text also refutes a number of common points of criticism, such as the argument that in its original form, intersectionality was fixated on the Black-white dichotomy in the United States. In reality, Crenshaw places "women of color" at the heart of her text, which is itself a category characterized by numerous, at times incompatible positionalities (she uses residency status as an example). With this group as her focus, Crenshaw analyzes the complicated and frustrating yet necessary process of coalition-building in racialized and marginalized communities, which is also happening in Germany. Intersectionality addresses multiple nonbinary identity constructs and power structures and their interdependence (meaning that any "interdependence theory" based on Crenshaw's work merely reproduces what's already there).

In contrast to majority German reception of intersectionality, which did not occur until the first decade of the 2000s and remains superficial, the framework is part of a broader political and intellectual discourse in the United States. For instance, writers like Michael Rothberg have incorporated it into Holocaust research; Rothberg's notion of "multidirectional memory" outlines connections between the Holocaust and colonialism in the works of such twentieth-century thinkers as Aimé Césaire, Hannah Arendt, and W. E. B. Du Bois, and he argues that "Holocaust memory emerged in dialogue with the dynamic transformations and multifaceted struggles that define the era of decolonization."[26] His approach situates the historical events with particular focus on the forms of their remembrance as multidirectional and intersectional; in this way he attempts to dismantle dichotomies that are constructed by means of binary comparative and hierarchical perspectives, such as those found in totalitarianism research.

The point is not to expose European colonialism as a further example of totalitarian rule; instead, it's about challenging the dichotomy of (Western) democracy and (Eastern/Oriental) totalitarianism. The assertion that fascism is compatible with any system other than democracy immediately shuts down uncomfortable conversations and important historical analyses. Democracy, meanwhile, is

---

26. Rothberg, *Multidirectional Memory*, 7.

understood as fundamentally Western, an original Western value that courses through Europeans' veins but that "migrants" must work hard to acquire (as in compulsory integration programs). This dichotomy must be taken apart to reveal a more complex relationship that most certainly does not contend that democracy and totalitarianism are interchangeable but that *does* make it impossible to present such totalitarian elements as structural racism as a priori incompatible with democratic systems. Instead, here too what we need is an intersectional approach that articulates the connections between post/fascism, post/socialism, and post/colonialism. We also need the involvement of people whose careers are built on examining these structures, but too often these experts contribute to the defense of dominant, internalist positions, as we have seen among members of my own guild—historians like Eberhard Jäckel, who lectured Roma and Sinti when they objected to being called "Gypsies" on the first national monument to them as victims of Nazi genocide; Hans-Ulrich Wehler, who advanced the construct of the *Türkenproblem* and the categorial exclusion of Islam from Europe's past, present, and future; and Götz Aly, whose tirade against Black rapists was delivered in the same breath as his assessment of forced sterilization of Black Germans under Nazism as a "bagatelle."[27]

The failures of so-called experts reflect a wider problem: the lack of knowledge among the majority and associated refusal to learn from minoritized groups also indicate that there is no excuse for ignorance; it is willful and artificially created, time and again. In contrast we have the decades' long activism of refugee initiatives like The Voice, Black initiatives like Initiative Schwarze in Deutschland and ADEFRA—Schwarze Frauen in Deutschland (which have been around for more than thirty years now), the Rom und Cinti Union, and IniRromnja, as well as racialized academics, whose work is used—but not acknowledged—in the mainstream.[28] Not only does the mainstream usually ignore these counterdiscourses but whenever the messages do get through, they are presented in a

---

27. Posener, "Götz Aly platzt der Kragen."
28. For a discussion of the use and origin of the term "citational violence" see Nash, "Citational Desires."

filtered form that makes them easier to digest for the majority and that precludes openness or challenges to established discourses, whether through activism or such disciplines as critical race studies. Instead, critical information is selectively integrated into the majority discourse, thereby reestablishing it as the single relevant instance. Despite valuable work done by mainstream German critics, like those behind the *Third World in World War II* project, they too must accept this criticism and question their own positioning, practicing the art of stepping back and listening—an almost unthinkable stance for a mainstream German Left that still does not see itself as part of the problem.[29]

The response one often encounters instead is defensiveness; the feeling of being overly criticized, rather than recognized for good work; and an insistence on defending "the truth" against particularist interests. Routine reactions to competing interpretations of the past—enforcing hegemonic discourses as normative and neutral by ignoring and delegitimizing the experiences of marginalized groups—locate the cause of communication crises within the latter groups and pass the consequences on to them as well. Surely this is not always the intention, as insistence on Eurocentrism is often powered by the belief in its objectivity, in Eurocentrism as a universalist representation of a kind of humanism that has room for everyone, provided they want it. Thus, the goal is to integrate marginalized or "foreign" people into this comprehensive model, and when issues arise, it is not the sustainability of the model that is called into question but the motivation of the "unintegratable." Here too, we

---

29. The *Third World in World War II* project was undeniably important, caring work, but it largely ignored the work of people of color. Karl Rössel stated in his interview with Simon Inou that "a serious examination of this suppressed and silenced aspect of history did not begin in Germany—with exhibitions and historical research projects—until six decades after the war ended," but the Black community had of course begun this examination long before that. I already knew about Moroccan colonial troops, the forced sterilization of Black Germans, and French troops murdering tens of thousands of Algerian civilians on May 8, 1945, because independent discourse and scholarship addressing events long ignored by mainstream Germans (leftists among them) have existed for a long time—because it is our history. Rössel, "Die Rolle des globalen Südens."

are increasingly seeing that such repressive approaches can only serve to worsen conflicts.

One question asked far too rarely is what insights a "subjective" perspective could provide, one that centers on the experience and research of marginalized people. Nevertheless, debates about a past that does not allow for clear separation between the familiar and the foreign—whether the memorial for murdered Roma and Sinti, the exhibition on the "Third World" during World War II, or the Humboldt Forum—can also be seen as a sign of progress, as a necessarily loaded confrontation with changing images of history and of models of the present and future. Attempts to suppress these confrontations are not only counterproductive but pointless. Spaces like the Werkstatt der Kulturen (WdK) represent a departure from the old paradigm of multicultural community centers, and its success demonstrates that a growing segment of society is no longer (completely) resistant to these debates, even as mainstream society regularly regresses when the pressure to change becomes too great. One of this book's goals is to expose these patterns of regression, opening them up to attack. Such patterns are evident in funding cuts to the WdK, which the Berlin Senate justified by claiming that the workshop's programming and audience did not adequately reflect the diversity of the city's population. If this standard were applied to all state-sponsored institutions, 90 percent of them would probably have to close, including the Museum Island—except in these cases, the pendulum swings in the other, perennially accepted direction toward mainstream German whiteness. The attempt to defund the WdK shows "real" Germans in one of their favorite roles after that of the concerned citizen, namely that of the taxpayer. Receiving state funding carries with it the expectation that something will be produced for the *Volk*: criticism of the WdK demonstrates yet again that certain groups are not deemed truly German; they fit the bill occasionally, at best, only to fall out of line again.

On the other hand, repression is required most when resistance becomes visible and effective. The model of Germanness embodied by the WdK is dangerous, because it represents a decidedly "new German," post/migrant position. Understood this way, "post/migrant" is both the recognition of a reality and a call to action, a call to engage with the new Germany, the "fundamental negotiation of rights, of belonging, of participation, and of positions."[30] This includes breaking the destructive cycle of exclusion and denial described in these pages, which is currently threatening to regain control.

---

30. Widmann, "Naika Foroutan."

Acknowledgments

Finally, my sincere thanks to all those whose knowledge, helpfulness, time, patience, and inspiration made it possible for me to write this book. Special thanks to Angelina Maccarone and Peggy Piesche for reading; Eunsong Kim for the invaluable introduction to museum politics; Leslie Adelson and the Institute for German Cultural Studies Colloquium at Cornell University and Anna Younes and the Berlin Colloquium of Color for their generous and important feedback; Sara Johnson for the writing partnership; and Tara Javidi for everything.

Bibliography

Accalmie. "Decolorize the Color Line?" https://stoptalk.wordpress.com/2012/10/11/decolorize-the-color-line

Achcar, Gilbert. "Blame the Grand Mufti." *Le Monde Diplomatique*, May 14, 2010. https://mondediplo.com/2010/05/14blamethemufti.

Adams, Michael C. C. *The Best War Ever: America and World War II*. Baltimore: Johns Hopkins University Press, 1994.

Admoni, Yoav, Abigail Akavia, Hila Amit, Yael Attia, Maja Avnat, Lyu Azbel, Gilad Baram et al. "Freedom for the One Who Thinks Differently: An Open Letter from a Group of Jewish Artists, Writers, and Scholars in Germany." *n+1 Magazine*, October 22, 2023. https://www.nplusonemag.com/online-only/online-only/freedom-for-the-one-who-thinks-differently.

Aidi, Hishaam D. "The Interference of Al-Andalus: Spain, Islam, and the West." *Social Text* 24, no. 2 (Summer 2006): 67–88.

Al Jazeera Staff. "'Double Standards': Western Coverage of Ukraine War Criticized." *Al Jazeera*, February 27, 2022. https://www.aljazeera.com/news/2022/2/27/western-media-coverage-ukraine-russia-invasion-criticism.

Aly, Götz. *Rasse und Klasse: Nachforschungen zum deutschen Wesen*. Frankfurt: Fischer Verlag, 2003.

———. "Straßenschänder in Kreuzberg." *Berliner Zeitung*, February 2, 2010. https://www.berliner-zeitung.de/archiv/von-goetz-aly-historiker-strassenschaender-in-kreuzberg-li.971672.
Amadeu Antonio Stiftung. "Auseinandersetzung um Ausstellung 'Die Dritte Welt im Zweiten Weltkrieg': Rassismusdebatte gefordert." 2009. https://web.archive.org/web/20140528050339/https://www.amadeu-antonio-stiftung.de/aktuelles/ausstellung-die-dritte-welt-im-zweiten-weltkrieg-rassismusdebatte-gefordert.
Amira. "Pädagogische Ansätze zur Bearbeitung von Antisemitismus in der Jugendarbeit: Die Ergebnisse des Modellprojekts 'Amira—Antisemitismus im Kontext von Migration und Rassismus.'" Berlin: amira—Antisemitismus im Kontext von Migration und Rassismus c/o Verein für demokratische Kultur in Berlin e.V., 2010.
Amnesty International. "Ausländer als Opfer: Polizeiliche Misshandlungen in der Bundesrepublik Deutschland." London: Amnesty International, 1995. English version available at https://www.amnesty.org/es/wp-content/uploads/2021/06/eur230061995en.pdf.
———. "Erneut im Fokus: Vorwürfe über polizeiliche Misshandlungen und den Einsatz unverhältnismäßiger Gewalt in Deutschland." London: Amnesty International, 2004.
———. "Leben in Unsicherheit: Wie Deutschland die Opfer rassistischer Gewalt im Stich lässt." London: Amnesty International, 2016.
———. "Solidarity on Trial: People in Europe Are Being Targeted for Helping Refugees and Migrants." March 3, 2020. https://www.amnesty.org/en/latest/campaigns/2020/03/free-to-help.
"Antiken-Schmuggel: Irak, Syrien, Türkei: So läuft das Geschäft mit der Raubkunst." *Focus*, June 3, 2015. https://www.focus.de/wissen/konflikte-antiken-schmuggel-das-geschaeft-mit-der-raubkunst_id_4724996.html.
"Antisemitismus in Deutschland: Zentralrat der Juden rät vom Tragen der Kippa ab." *Der Spiegel*, February 26, 2015. https://www.spiegel.de/politik/deutschland/zentralrat-der-juden-raet-von-der-kippa-in-problemvierteln-ab-a-1020593.html.
Ash, Timothy Garton. "Germans, More or Less." *New York Review*, February 24, 2011. https://www.nybooks.com/articles/2011/02/24/germans-more-or-less.
Ataman, Ferda. "Neuköllner Kulturwerkstatt bekräftigt Kritik." *Der Tagesspiegel*, September 4, 2009. https://www.tagesspiegel.de/berlin/neukollner-kulturwerkstatt-bekraftigt-kritik-4511098.html.
Atanasoski, Neda. *Humanitarian Violence: The U.S. Deployment of Diversity*. Minneapolis: University of Minnesota Press, 2013.
"Auch Sarkozy erklärt Multikulturalismus für gescheitert." *Der Standard*, February 11, 2011. https://www.derstandard.at/story/1297216081044/nach-merkel-auch-sarkozy-erklaert-multikulturalismus-fuer-gescheitert.
"Ausländer: 'Das Volk hat es satt.'" *Der Spiegel*, May 2, 1982. http://www.spiegel.de/spiegel/print/d-14348246.html.

Bade, Klaus J. *Deutsche im Ausland—Fremde in Deutschland: Migration in Geschichte und Gegenwart*. Munich: Verlag C. H. Beck, 1992.
Baeck, Jean-Philipp. "'Verfolgung geht von der Polizei aus': Ein Urteil bestätigt politische Verfolgung einer Romni in Mazedonien. Für Pro Asyl ein Beleg für die Unsicherheit 'sicherer Herkunftsländer.'" *die tageszeitung*, November 11, 2015. https://taz.de/!5247855.
Bakirdögen, Ayhan. "Streit um Text auf Mahnmal für Sinti und Roma." *Berliner Morgenpost*, October 6, 2003. https://www.morgenpost.de/printarchiv/berlin/article102461867/Streit-um-Text-auf-Mahnmal-fuer-Sinti-und-Roma.html.
Balibar, Etienne, and Immanuel Wallerstein. *Race, Nation, Class: Ambiguous Identities*. London: Verso, 1991.
Barkin, Noah. "Europe's Sleeping Giant Awakes." *The Atlantic*, March 1, 2022. https://www.theatlantic.com/international/archive/2022/03/germany-putin-ukraine-invasion/623322.
Barth, Ariane. "'Hier steigt eine Giftsuppe auf.'" *Der Spiegel*, October 13, 1991. http://www.spiegel.de/spiegel/print/d-13491498.html.
Battiste, Marie, ed. *Reclaiming Indigenous Voice and Vision*. Vancouver: University of British Columbia Press, 2000.
Bauer, Elisabeth. "Sind Juden hier noch sicher?" *die tageszeitung*, August 5, 2014. https://taz.de/!5036158.
Bax, Daniel. "Debatte Mauerfall und Migranten: Geteilte Erinnerung: Ostdeutsche und Migranten haben vieles gemein. Aber Einwanderer und ihre Kinder waren die eigentlichen Wendeverlierer." *die tageszeitung*, November 8, 2014. https://taz.de/!5029206.
———. "Neuer Radikalenerlass befürchtet. Der Berliner Senat will eine umstrittene 'Antisemitismusklausel' einführen. Verfassungsrechtler fürchten einen Dammbruch." *die tageszeitung*, May 6, 2024. https://taz.de/Meinungsfreiheit-in-Deutschland/!6008173.
Behrens, Paul. "Nur geduldet, nicht respektiert." *Die Zeit*, March 21, 1986. https://www.zeit.de/1986/13/nur-geduldet-nicht-respektiert.
———. "'Vollzigeuner' und 'Mischlinge': Die ehemalige Rassenforscherin Ruth Kellermann verteidigt ihren Ruf." *Die Zeit*, February 7, 1986. https://www.zeit.de/1986/07/vollzigeuner-und-mischlinge.
Beier, Bernd. "'Die Ausstellung gibt es ganz oder gar nicht.'" *Jungle World*, September 3, 2009. https://jungle.world/artikel/2009/36/die-ausstellung-gibt-es-ganz-oder-gar-nicht.
Benhabib, Seyla. *The Claims of Culture: Equality and Diversity in the Global Era*. Princeton: Princeton University Press, 2002.
Bensmann, Marcus, Justus von Daniels, Anette Dowideit, Jean Peters, and Gabriela Keller. "Secret Plan against Germany." *Correctiv*, January 15, 2024. https://correctiv.org/en/top-stories/2024/01/15/secret-plan-against-germany.
Bentzien, Hans. "Möwengrillen in einer Einraumwohnung." *Norddeutsche Neueste Nachrichten* July 14, 1992, 3.

Berman, Nina. *Orientalismus, Kolonialismus und Moderne: Zum Bild des Orients in der deutschsprachigen Kultur um 1900*. Stuttgart: J. B. Metzler Verlag, 1997.
Blumer, Nadine. "From Victim Hierarchies to Memorial Networks: Berlin's Holocaust Memorial to Sinti and Roma Victims of National Socialism." PhD Dissertation, University of Toronto, 2012. https://tspace.library.utoronto.ca/handle/1807/31694.
Boddien, Wilhelm von, and Hartmut Engel, eds. *Die Berliner Schlossdebatte—Pro und Contra*. Berlin: Berliner Wissenschafts-Verlag, 2000.
Böröcz, Josef. "Goodness Is Elsewhere: The Rule of European Difference." *Comparative Studies in Society and History* 48, no. 2 (2006): 110–37. http://dx.doi.org/10.1017/s0010417506000053.
Brakebusch, Lydia. "Schulwahl: Flucht vor Multikulti." *Zitty*, August 25, 2010. http://www.zitty.de/flucht-vor-multikulti.
Braun, Stefan, and Christoph Hickmann. "Einsatz der Bundeswehr im Inneren soll erleichtert werden." *Süddeutsche Zeitung*, April 12, 2016. https://www.sueddeutsche.de/politik/sicherheit-einsatz-der-bundeswehr-im-inneren-soll-erleichtert-werden-1.2945279.
Bravo, David. "'Volkspalast': Experimental Cultural Centre." Public Space, n.d. https://www.publicspace.org/works/-/project/d208-volkspalast-experimental-cultural-centre.
Breitz, Candice, and Michael Rothberg. "We Still Need to Talk/A Letter to the Symposium Community." Michael Rothberg's official website, October 31, 2023. https://michaelrothberg.weebly.com/uploads/5/4/6/8/5468139/letter__documents_breitz-rothberg_31.10.23.pdf.
Brinkmann, Bastian. "Reiche sind viel vermögender als gedacht." *Die Zeit*, October 23, 2014. https://www.sueddeutsche.de/wirtschaft/gewerkschaftsnahe-studie-reiche-sind-viel-vermoegender-als-bisher-gedacht-1.2186716.
Bristow, Tom. "South Africa Lukewarm over 'Mandela Square.'" *The Local Germany*, December 17, 2013. https://www.thelocal.de/20131217/bid-to-name-mandela-square-sparks-row.
Brubaker, Rogers. *Citizenship and Nationhood in France and Germany*. Cambridge, MA: Harvard University Press, 1992.
Bruckner, Pascal. "Enlightenment Fundamentalism or Racism of the Anti-Racists?" Translated by John Lambert. *Sign and Sight*, January 24, 2007. http://www.signandsight.com/features/1146.html.
Bruenig, Matt. "The Racial Wealth Gap." *Demos* (blog), November 5, 2013. https://web.archive.org/web/20141006191000/http://www.demos.org/blog/11/5/13/racial-wealth-gap.
Bruhn, Jochen, and Thomas Ebermann. "Der Golfkrieg, die Linke und der Tod." *Arbeiterkampf*, no. 331 (1991): 34–36.
Brumlik, Micha. *Post-Colonial Antisemitism? Achille Mbembe, the Palestinian BDS Movement and Other Controversies*. Translated by Carla Welch. Berlin: Rosa-Luxemburg-Stfitung, 2022.

Bundesamt für Verfassungsschutz. "'Rechtsextremisten,' 'Reichsbürger' und 'Selbstverwalter' in Sicherheitsbehörden." Berlin: Bundesamt für Verfassungsschutz, 2022.
Bundesministerium des Innern. "Anti-Semitismus in Deutschland: Erscheinungsformen, Bedingungen, Präventionsansätze. Bericht des unabhängigen Expertenkreises Anti-Semitismus." Berlin: Bundesministerium des Innern, 2011.
——. "Gesellschaft und Verfassung: Nationale Minderheiten. Dänische Minderheit." Berlin: Bundesministerium des Innern, March 20, 2014. https://www.bmi.bund.de/DE/Themen/Gesellschaft-Verfassung/Nationale-Minderheiten/Nationale-Minderheiten-Deutschland/DaenischeMinderheit/daenischeMinderheit_node.html.
Bundeszentrale für politische Bildung. "Verfassung der Europäischen Union: Artikel I-2: Die Werte der Union." Bonn: Bundeszentrale für politische Bildung, 2005.
Bunzl, Matti. "Between Anti-Semitism and Islamophobia: Some Thoughts on the New Europe." *American Ethnologist* 32, no. 4 (2008): 14–25.
Bush, George W. "Address to a Joint Session of Congress and the American People." September 20, 2001. https://georgewbush-whitehouse.archives.gov/news/releases/2001/09/20010920-8.html.
Byrd, Jodi A. *The Transit of Empire: Indigenous Critiques of Colonialism*. Minneapolis: University of Minnesota Press, 2011.
CARICOM. "Remarks by Dr. Carla N. Barnett, Secretary-General, Caribbean Community (CARICOM) for the Opening Ceremony of the Accra Reparations Conference," November 14 2023, https://caricom.org/35409-2/.
CARICOM Reparations Commission. "Press Statement." University of the West Indies: CARICOM Reparations Commission, 2013.
Casanova, José. "Der Ort der Religion im säkularen Europa." *Eurozine*, July 19, 2004. https://www.eurozine.com/religion-european-secular-identities-and-european-integration.
Caspari, Lisa. "Muss Deutschland den Nazi-Kredit zurückzahlen?" *Die Zeit*, February 2, 2015. https://www.zeit.de/politik/ausland/2015-02/griechenland-reparationsleistungen-kredit-hintergrund.
Césaire, Aimé. *Discourse on Colonialism*. New York: Monthly Review Press, 1972.
Chakrabarty, Dipesh. *Provincializing Europe: Postcolonial Thought and Historical Difference*. Princeton: Princeton University Press, 2000.
Chandler, Nuham. "The Possible Form of an Interlocution: W. E. B. Du Bois and Max Weber in Correspondence, 1904–1905." *The New Centennial Review* 6, no. 3 (Winter 2006): 193–239. http://dx.doi.org/10.1353/ncr.2007.0015.
Chervel, Thierry. "Ausnahmslos Differenz." *Perlentaucher* (blog), January 13, 2016. https://www.perlentaucher.de/blog/2016/01/13/ausnahmslos-differenz.html.
Childs, Dennis. *Slaves of the State: Black Incarceration from the Chain Gang to the Penitentiary*. Minneapolis: University of Minnesota Press, 2015.

Chow, Rey. *The Protestant Ethnic and the Spirit of Capitalism.* New York: Columbia University Press, 2002.
Claussen, Philip. "Besonderes Kennzeichen: Unversöhnlich. Zur Debatte um die Ausstellung '"Besondere Kennzeichen: Neger"—Schwarze Im NS-Staat.'" *Stichproben—Wiener Zeitschrift für Kritische Afrikastudien* 10 (2006): 85–103.
Clinton, William J. "Statement by the President to the Nation." March 24, 1999. William J. Clinton Presidential Library and Museum. https://www.clintonlibrary.gov/sites/default/files/documents/kosovo-press-1999.pdf.
Connolly, Kate. "Alleged Far-Right Plotters on Trial in Germany Accused of Plan to Overthrow State." *The Guardian*, April 29, 2024. https://www.theguardian.com/world/2024/apr/29/alleged-far-right-plotters-on-trial-in-germany-accused-of-plan-to-overthrow-state.
Connor, Philip, and Matthias König. "Explaining the Muslim Employment Gap in Western Europe: Individual-Level Effects and Ethno-religious Penalties." *Social Science Research* 49 (January 2015): 191–201.
Crenshaw, Kimberlé. "Demarginalizing the Intersection of Race and Sex: A Black Feminist Critique of Antidiscrimination Doctrine, Feminist Theory and Antiracist Politics." *University of Chicago Legal Forum* 140 (1989): 139–67.
———. "Mapping the Margins: Intersectionality, Identity Politics, and Violence against Women of Color." *Stanford Law Review* 43, no. 6 (July 1991): 1241–99. http://dx.doi.org/10.2307/1229039.
Cuno, James. "Culture War: The Case against Repatriating Museum Artifacts." *Foreign Affairs*, December 2014. https://www.foreignaffairs.com/articles/africa/culture-war.
———. *Museums Matter: In Praise of the Encyclopedic Museum.* Chicago: University of Chicago Press, 2011.
———. *Who Owns Antiquity? Museums and the Battle over Our Ancient Heritage.* Princeton: Princeton University Press, 2011.
Dalton, Samantha. "Noor Inayat Khan: The Indian Princess Who Spied for Britain." *BBC News*, November 12, 2012. https://www.bbc.com/news/uk-20240693.
"Das zweite geheime Gesicht der Nofretete." *Die Welt*, March 31, 2009. https://www.welt.de/wissenschaft/article3477870/Das-zweite-geheime-Gesicht-der-Nofretete.html.
Davis, Angela. "Angela Davis: Reflections on Race, Class, and Gender in the USA." In *The Politics of Culture in the Shadow of Capital*, edited by Lisa Lowe and David Lloyd, 303–23. Durham, NC: Duke University Press, 1995.
Decker, Oliver, Johannes Kiess, and Elmar Brähler, eds. *Die enthemmte Mitte: Autoritäre und rechtsextreme Einstellung in Deutschland.* Giessen: Psychosozial-Verlag, 2016.
"De Maizière will Dank und Gehorsam." *die tageszeitung*, October 2, 2015. http://taz.de/!5238316.
"Der Fall Mohamed erinnert an die NSU-Ermittlungen." *Migazin*, November 2, 2015. https://www.migazin.de/2015/11/02/der-fall-mohamed-nsu-ermittlungen.

"Der totgeschwiegene Anschlag in Schwandorf." *Augsburger Allgemeine*, December 5, 2011. http://www.augsburger-allgemeine.de/bayern/Dertotgeschwiegene-Anschlag-in-Schwandorf-id17816096.html.

Deutscher Bundestag. *Aus dem Zweiten Weltkrieg herrührende mögliche Ansprüche Griechenlands auf Reparationen und Rückzahlung einer Zwangsleihe.* February 6, 2015. http://dip21.bundestag.de/dip21/btd/18/004/180 0451.pdf.

———. *Bundestag beschließt Einführung eines nationalen Veteranentages.* April 25, 2024. https://www.bundestag.de/dokumente/textarchiv/2024/kw17-de-veteranentag-993234.

"Deutschland exportiert 2016 noch mehr Waffen." *Die Zeit*, July 5, 2016. https://www.zeit.de/wirtschaft/2016-07/ruestungsexporte-waffenindustrie-deutschand-ausfuhren-steigerung.

Djijaleu, Dominik. "Die Werkstatt der Kulturen—ein Interview mit Geschäftsführerin Philippa Ebéné." *030 Magazin*, May 17, 2016. https://berlin030.de/die-werkstatt-der-kulturen-ein-interview-mit-geschaeftsfuehrerin-philippa-ebene.

Donadio, Rachel. "Berlin's Museum Tours in Arabic Forge a Bridge to Refugees." *The New York Times*, February 28, 2016. https://www.nytimes.com/2016/02/29/arts/design/berlins-museum-tours-in-arabic-forge-a-bridge-to-refugees.html.

Dostal, Jörg Michael. "The Pegida Movement and German Political Culture: Is Right-Wing Populism Here to Stay?" *The Political Quarterly* 86, no. 4 (2015): 523–31.

Eckert, Andreas. "Gefangen in der Alten Welt." *Die Zeit*, September 26, 2002. https://www.zeit.de/2002/40/Gefangen_in_der_Alten_Welt.

El-Tayeb, Fatima. *European Others: Queering Ethnicity in Postnational Europe.* Minneapolis: University of Minnesota Press, 2011.

———. "'Gays Who Cannot Properly Be Gay': Queer Muslims in the Neoliberal European City." *European Journal of Women's Studies* 19, no. 1 (2012): 79–95. http://dx.doi.org/10.1177/1350506811426388.

———. *Schwarze Deutsche: "Rasse" und nationale Identität 1890–1933.* Frankfurt: Campus Verlag, 2001.

———. "Undisciplined Knowledge: Intersectional Black European Studies." *New German Critique* 50, no. 3 (2023): 37–49.

Endres, Alexandra. "Der Wassermangel hat die Konflikte in Nahost verschärft." *Zeit Magazin*, September 3, 2014. https://www.zeit.de/wirtschaft/2014-09/wasser-ressource-knappheit/komplettansicht.

"Entzug der deutschen Staatsbürgerschaft wider Willen: SVR empfiehlt Aussetzen der Optionspflicht." Deutsch Türkische Nachrichten, January 11, 2013. http://www.deutsch-tuerkische-nachrichten.de/2013/01/465683/entzug-der-deutschen-staatsbuergerschaft-wider-willen-svr-empfiehltaussetzen-der-optionspflicht.

Enzensberger, Hans Magnus. "Hitlers Wiedergänger." *Der Spiegel*, February 4, 1991. https://www.spiegel.de/politik/hitlers-wiedergaenger-a-2cd62036-0002-0001-0000-000013487378.

European Network Against Racism. "Black People in Europe Report Widespread Racism in Anti-Immigration Context." March 21, 2016. https://www.enar-eu.org/Black-people-in-Europe-report-widespread-racism-in-anti-immigration-context.

———. *Recycling Hatred: Racism(s) in Europe Today. A Dialogue Between Academics, Equality Experts and Civil Society Activists*. Brussels: European Network Against Racism, 2012. https://www.enar-eu.org/wp-content/uploads/symposiumreport_lr_final_final.pdf.

European Network Against Racism and European Roma Information Office. *Debunking Myth & Revealing Truth about the Roma*. Brussels: European Network Against Racism and European Roma Information Office, 2018. https://www.enar-eu.org/wp-content/uploads/roma_final_pdf.pdf.

European Union. "Council Directive 2001/55/EC of 20 July 2001 on Minimum Standards for Giving Temporary Protection in the Event of a Mass Influx of Displaced Persons and on Measures Promoting a Balance of Efforts between Member States in Receiving Such Persons and Bearing the Consequences Thereof." July 20, 2001. https://eur-lex.europa.eu/legal-content/EN/TXT/HTML/?uri=CELEX:32001L0055&from=DE.

Eyferth, Klaus, Ursula Brandt, and Wolfgang Hawel. *Farbige Kinder in Deutschland und die Aufgaben ihrer Eingliederung*. Munich: Juventa Verlag, 1960.

Fabian, Johannes. *Time and the Other: How Anthropology Makes Its Object*. New York: Columbia University Press, 1983.

Fava, Rosa. "Waren eigentlich auch Muslime im KZ?" In *Dokumentation der Tagung in der KZ-Gedenkstätte Neuengamme*, 13–15. Neuengamme Concentration Camp Memorial: Umdenken e.V. and Heinrich Böll Stiftung Hamburg e.V., 2007.

Federal Ministry of the Interior and Community. "National Minorities." January 29, 2024. https://www.bmi.bund.de/EN/topics/community-and-integration/national-minorities/national-minorities-node.html.

Feldmann, Hans-Christian. "Denkmalwert oder Denkmalsturz: Der Palast der Republik in Berlin." DenkmalDebatten, October 2010. https://web.archive.org/web/20140808035439/http://denkmaldebatten.de/kontroversen/palast-der-republik.

Feminist Frequency. "The Smurfette Principle (Tropes vs. Women)," April 21, 2011. https://feministfrequency.com/video/tropes-vs-women-3-the-smurfette-principle.

Fioretti, Julia. "European Commission Cuts Fish Quotas for 10 Countries for Over-Fishing." *Reuters*, August 11, 2014. https://www.reuters.com/article/2014/08/11/us-eu-fisheries-quotas-idUSKBN0GB1B120140811.

Fischer, Hilke. "TTIP Talks—Africa Remains Left Out." *Deutsche Welle*, February 6, 2015. https://www.dw.com/en/ttip-talks-africa-remains-left-out/a-18241309.

Fischer, Joschka. "Speech at the Green Party Congress in Bielefeld (May 13, 1999)." Translated by Allison Brown. *German History Intersections*,

November 29, 2023. https://germanhistory-intersections.org/en/germanness/ghis:document-241.

"Flüchtlinge—Italien beendet Rettungsaktion 'Mare Nostrum.'" *Deutschlandfunk*, October 10, 2014. https://www.deutschlandfunk.de/fluechtlinge-italien-beendet-rettungsaktion-mare-nostrum-100.html.

Fontevecchia, Agustino. "The Getty Family: A Cautionary Tale of Oil, Adultery, and Death." *Forbes*, April 23, 2015. https://www.forbes.com/sites/afontevecchia/2015/04/23/the-getty-family-a-cautionary-tale-of-oil-adultery-and-death/?sh=23bdde527eee.

Foroutan, Naika, Coşkun Canan, and Sina Arnold, eds. "Deutschland Postmigrantisch I: Gesellschaft, Religion, Identität—Erste Ergebnisse." Junge Islambezogene Themen in Deutschland (JUNITED). Berlin: Berlin Institute for Empirical Integration and Migration Research, Humboldt University of Berlin, 2014. https://www.projekte.hu-berlin.de/de/junited/deutschland-post migrantisch.

Förster, Larissa. "Nichts gewagt, nichts gewonnen: Die Ausstellung 'Anders zur Welt kommen. Das Humboldt-Forum im Schloss. Ein Werkstattblick.'" *Paideuma: Mitteilungen zur Kulturkunde* 56 (2010): 241–61.

"48.000 Türkischstämmige mit zwei Pässen." *Frankfurter Allgemeine Zeitung*, February 7, 2005.

Fritz, Philipp. "Projekt 'Multaka' in Berlin: Wenn Flüchtlinge die Berliner Museen entdecken." *Berliner Zeitung*, December 19, 2015. https://www.berliner-zeitung.de/kultur-vergnuegen/projekt-multaka-in-berlin-wenn-fluechtlinge-die-berliner-museen-entdecken-li.31036.

"Für jeden dritten Bürger gehört der Islam zu Deutschland." *Migazin*, May 13, 2016. https://www.migazin.de/2016/05/13/fuer-jeden-dritten-buerger-gehoert-der-islam-zu-deutschland.

Garbe, Detlef, ed. *Konzentrationslager Neuengamme: Geschichte, Nachgeschichte, Erinnerungen*. Bremen: Edition Temmen, 2014.

Gelbin, Cathy S., Kader Konuk, and Peggy Piesche, eds. *AufBrüche: Kulturelle Produktionen von Migrantinnen, Schwarzen und jüdischen Frauen in Deutschland*. Königstein: U. Helmer, 1999.

Gerhardt, Christina. "Transnational Germany: Hito Steyerl's Film *Die leere Mitte* and Two Hundred Years of Border Crossings." *Women in German Yearbook: Feminist Studies in German Literature & Culture* 23 (2007): 205–33.

"Geschichtsaufarbeitung nach Neuköllner Art." *Der Tagesspiegel*, August 27, 2009. https://www.tagesspiegel.de/berlin/geschichtsaufarbeitung-nach-neukollner-art-1781938.html.

Gessen, Masha. "In the Shadow of the Holocaust." *The New Yorker*. December 9, 2023. https://www.newyorker.com/news/the-weekend-essay/in-the-shadow-of-the-holocaust.

Goldhagen, Daniel. *Hitler's Willing Executioners: Ordinary Germans and the Holocaust*. New York: Alfred A. Knopf, 1996.

Grosse, Julia. "Der Designer war Schuld." *die tageszeitung*, November 16, 2002. https://taz.de/!1077797.
Guerrilla Girls. *The Guerrilla Girls' Bedside Companion to the History of Western Art*. London: Penguin, 1998.
Ha, Kien Nghi. *Ethnizität und Migration*. Münster: Verlag Westfälisches Dampfboot, 1999.
Hage, Ghassan. "Terrorism, Brussels, etc. . . . Think Before You Hunt." Critical Legal Thinking, March 24, 2016. https://criticallegalthinking.com/2016/03/24/terrorism-brussels-think-hunt.
Hagestedt, Lutz. "Der Streitverlauf in Stimmen und Zitaten." literaturkritik.de, February 1, 1999. https://literaturkritik.de/public/rezension.php?rez_id=20.
Halberstam, Jack. *In a Queer Time and Place: Transgender Bodies, Subcultural Lives*. New York: New York University Press, 2005.
Hall, Stuart. "Europe's Other Self." *Marxism Today*, August 1991.
"Hamsterrad der Ignoranz—Wenn Weiße mit sich selber über Rassismus reden." Mädchenmannschaft, March 29, 2013. https://maedchenmannschaft.net/hamsterrad-der-ignoranz-wenn-weisse-mit-sich-selber-ueber-rassismus-reden.
Hansen, Georg. "Deutschsein als Schicksal: Ein aktueller Rückblick. Das Reichs- und Staatsangehörigkeitsgesetz von 1912/13." *Frankfurter Rundschau*, February 10, 1999.
Hansen, Peo, and Stefan Jönsson. "EU Migration Policy towards Africa: Demographic Logics and Colonial Legacies." In *Postcolonial Transitions in Europe: Contexts, Practices and Politics*, edited by Sandra Ponzanesi and Gianmaria Colpani, 47–66. London: Rowman & Littlefield, 2015.
Haritaworn, Jin. "Queer Injuries: The Racial Politics of 'Homophobic Hate Crime' in Germany." *Social Justice* 37, no. 1 (2010): 69–89.
Hassel, Florian. "Durchhalten bis zur Abschiebung." *Die Zeit*, September 15, 1989. https://www.zeit.de/1989/38/durchhalten-bis-zur-abschiebung.
Hasselbach, Christoph. "Europe Is the Main Focus for Weapons Exporters." *Deutsche Welle*. March 14, 2022. https://www.dw.com/en/sipri-europe-is-the-main-focus-for-weapons-exporters/a-61101019.
Hauenstein, Hanno. "Germany Is Known for Its Heavily Funded, Thriving Art Scene. But a Slew of Cancellations Is Threatening That Reputation." *ArtNet*, December 12, 2023. https://news.artnet.com/art-world/germany-cancellations-2407316.
Hay, Mark. "Why France Should Pay Haiti $18+ Billion Immediately." *Modern Notion*, June 19, 2015. https://web.archive.org/web/20161012173057/http://modernnotion.com:80/france-pay-haiti-18-billion-immediately.
Herf, Jeffrey. *Nazi Propaganda for the Arab World*. New Haven, CT: Yale University Press, 2009.
Hering, Rainer. *Konstruierte Nation: Der Alldeutsche Verband 1890 bis 1939*. Hamburg: Christians Verlag, 2003.
Herold, Kathrin, and Yvonne Robel. "Zwischen Boxring und Stolperstein: Johann Trollmann in der gegenwärtigen Erinnerung." In *Die Verfolgung der*

Sinti und Roma im Nationalsozialismus, edited by KZ-Gedenkstätte Neuengamme, 144–55. Bremen: Edition Temmen, 2012.
Heuser, Uwe Jean. "Die letzte Bastion: Unsere Konzernchefs sind schuld daran, dass es in Deutschland kaum Frauen an der Spitze gibt." *Die Zeit*, November 22, 2014. https://www.zeit.de/2014/45/frauenquote-management.
Hielscher, Monika, and Matthias Herder, dir. *Gelem, Gelem—Wir gehen einen langen Weg*. Hamburg: Rhizomfilm 1991. Documentary.
Hitchens, Christopher. "Defending Islamofascism." *Slate*, October 2, 2007. https://slate.com/news-and-politics/2007/10/defending-the-term-islamofascism.html.
Horowitz, Noah. *Art of the Deal: Contemporary Art in a Global Financial Market*. Princeton, NJ: Princeton University Press, 2014.
Horvath, Gilda-Nancy. "Report Details Anti-Roma Discrimination in Germany." *Deutsche Welle*, June 7, 2021. https://www.dw.com/en/independent-report-details-anti-roma-discrimination-in-germany/a-58178331.
Huyssen, Andreas. "Present Pasts: Media, Politics, Amnesia." *Public Culture* 12, no. 1 (2000): 21–38.
Ibrahim, Aida, Juliane Karakayalı, Serhat Karakayalı, and Vassilis S. Tsianos. "Decolorise It!" *ak*, September 21, 2012. https://www.akweb.de/bewegung/diskussion-um-critical-whiteness-und-antirassismus-decolorise-it.
Initiative Schwarze in Deutschland/ADEFRA. "Stellungnahme zur abgesagten Ausstellung 'Die Dritte Welt im Zweiten Weltkrieg' in der Werkstatt der Kulturen in Berlin," August 30, 2009. http://isdonline.de/stellungnahme-zur-abgesagten-ausstellung-die-dritte-welt-im-zweiten-weltkrieg-in-der-werkstatt-der-kulturen-in-berlin.
Investitionsbank Berlin. "Karneval der Kulturen: Jeder investierte Euro bringt das Fünffache an Einnahmen," June 9, 2011. https://web.archive.org/web/20131021043924/http://www.ibb.de/desktopdefault.aspx/tabid-62/216_read-5273.
Jäckel, Eberhard. "An alle und jeden erinnern?" *Die Zeit*, April 7, 1989. https://www.zeit.de/1989/15/an-alle-und-jeden-erinnern.
———. "Sinti, Roma oder Zigeuner?" *Frankfurter Allgemeine Zeitung*, February 7, 2005. https://www.faz.net/aktuell/feuilleton/denkmal-streit-sinti-roma-oder-zigeuner-1213650.html.
Jakob, Christian. "Europas blutige Außengrenze: Die Berliner Menschenfalle." *die tageszeitung*, March 5, 2014. https://taz.de/!5047592.
Jansen, Frank, Heike Kleffner, Johannes Radke, and Toralf Staud. "Todesopfer rechter Gewalt seit 1990: 156 Schicksale." *Die Zeit*, June 30, 2015. https://www.zeit.de/gesellschaft/zeitgeschehen/2010-09/todesopfer-rechte-gewalt.
Janssen, Michel, Robert Schulmann, József Illy, Christoph Lehner, and Diana Kormos Buchwald, eds. *The Collected Papers of Albert Einstein*. Vol. 7, *The Berlin Years: Writings, 1918–1921*. Princeton: Princeton University Press, 2002.
"'Jeder streichelt seinen Bimbo.'" *Der Spiegel*, December 29, 1991. http://www.spiegel.de/spiegel/print/d-9272170.html.

Jegic, Denijal. "Germany's Relentless Campaign to Silence Pro-Palestinian Voices." *Al Jazeera*, May 22, 2019. https://www.aljazeera.com/opinions/2019/3/22/germanys-relentless-campaign-to-silence-pro-palestinian-voices.
Kappe, Nikolas. "Karneval der Kulturen 2015 findet statt." *Der Tagesspiegel*, December 15, 2014. https://www.tagesspiegel.de/berlin/karneval-der-kulturen-2015-findet-statt-8128231.html.
Karnitschnig, Matthew. "Merkel's Three Little Words: 'Wir schaffen das!'" *Politico*, August 21, 2020. https://www.politico.eu/article/angela-merkel-wir-schaffen-das-5-years-on.
Kawczynski, Rudko, and Werner Hackmann. "Sie haben mich reingelegt." Interview by *Der Spiegel*, November 13, 1989. https://web.archive.org/web/20240225043038/https://www.spiegel.de/politik/sie-haben-mich-reingelegt-a-826a7854-0002-0001-0000-000013497190?context=issue.
Kehaulani, Kauanui. *Hawaiian Blood: Colonialism and the Politics of Sovereignty and Indigeneity*. Durham, NC: Duke University Press, 2008.
Kempf, Wilhelm, ed. *Manipulierte Wirklichkeiten: Medienpsychologische Untersuchungen der bundesdeutschen Berichterstattung im Golfkrieg*. Münster: LIT-Verlag, 1994.
Kiefer, Michael. "Antisemitismus unter muslimischen Jugendlichen—Randphänomen oder Problem?" Bundeszentrale für politische Bildung, October 24, 2012. http://www.bpb.de/politik/extremismus/antisemitismus/145728/antisemitismus-unter-muslimischen-jugendlichen-randphaenomen-oder-problem.
Kim, Eunsong, and Gelare Khoshgozaran. "Politics as Currency and the Souvenirs of War: Reflections on Rijin Sahakian's Statement on the Closing of Sada for Iraqi Art." *Contemptorary*, April 18, 2016. https://contemptorary.org/politics-as-currency-and-the-souvenirs-of-war-reflections-on-rijin-sahakians-statement-on-the-closing-of-sada-for-iraqi-art.
Kirsch, Jan-Holger. *Nationaler Mythos oder historische Trauer? Der Streit um ein zentrales "Holocaust-Mahnmal" für die Berliner Republik*. Cologne: Böhlau Verlag, 2003.
Klärner, Andreas. *Aufstand der Ressentiments: Einwanderungsdiskurs, völkischer Nationalismus und die Kampagne der CDU/CSU gegen die doppelte Staatsbürgerschaft*. Cologne: PapyRossa, 2000.
Koch, Katharina, and Nora Jasmin Ragab. *Mapping and Study of the Palestinian Diaspora in Germany*. Bonn: Deutsche Gesellschaft für Internationale Zusammenarbeit, 2018.
Kompisch, Kathrin. *Täterinnen: Frauen im Nationalsozialismus*. Cologne: Böhlau Verlag, 2008.
Kontje, Todd. *German Orientalisms*. Ann Arbor: University of Michigan Press, 2004.
Kopietz, Andreas, and Elmar Schütze. "Warnungen vor wachsendem Judenhass." *Frankfurter Rundschau*, August 30, 2012. https://www.fr.de/politik/warnungen-wachsendem-judenhass-11310981.html.

Kopp, Christian, and Marius Krohn. "Blues in Schwarzweiss: Die Black Community im Widerstand gegen kolonialrassistische Straßennamen in Berlin-Mitte." Berlin Postkolonial, April 16, 2016. https://web.archive.org/web/20160416184814/www.berlin-postkolonial.de/cms/index.php/orte/78-afrikanisches-viertel.

Krake, Rolf. "The European Initiative 'Cities against Islamization.'" *Gates of Vienna* (blog), January 25, 2008. https://gatesofvienna.blogspot.com/2008/01/european-initiative-cities-against.html.

Kranz, Matt. "Russia's War on Ukraine Makes Defense Investors $49 Billion Richer." *Investors Business Daily*, September 3, 2022. https://www.investors.com/etfs-and-funds/sectors/sp500-investors-gain-69-billion-dollars-off-russia-war-and-upside-remains.

Kravagna, Christian. "Konserven des Kolonialismus: Die Welt im Museum." *transversal*, June 2008. https://transversal.at/transversal/0708/kravagna/de.

Kroet, Cynthia. "German Far-Right Politician Wouldn't Have Jérôme Boateng as Neighbor." *Politico*, May 29, 2016. https://www.politico.eu/article/german-far-right-politician-wouldnt-have-jerome-boateng-as-neighbor.

Kundnani, Arun. "Violence Comes Home: An Interview with Arun Kundnani." open democracy, November 22, 2015. https://www.opendemocracy.net/en/violence-comes-home-interview-with-arun-kundnani.

Küntzel, Matthias. "In the Straightjacket of Anti-Zionism: A Critical Review of Gilbert Achcar's 'The Arabs and the Holocaust.'" *Canadian Institute for the Study of Antisemitism* (blog), December 21, 2011. https://canisa.org/blog/review-of-gilbert-achcars-the-arabs-and-the-holocaust.

Küpper, Beate, and Andreas Zick. "Gruppenbezogene Menschenfeindlichkeit." *Bundeszentrale für politische Bildung* (Federal Agency for Civil Education). October 20, 2015. www.bpb.de/themen/rechtsextremismus/dossier-rechtsextremismus/214192/gruppenbezogene-menschenfeindlichkeit/.

"Leider sind es meist Migranten." *die tageszeitung*, August 30, 2012. https://taz.de/!5085212.

"Lob und Empörung: Merkels Multikulti-Absage sorgt für weltweites Aufsehen." *Der Spiegel*, October 19, 2010. https://www.spiegel.de/politik/deutschland/lob-und-empoerung-merkels-multikulti-absage-sorgt-fuer-weltweites-aufsehen-a-723993.html.

Maak, Niklas. "Die Tempel der Isis." *Frankfurter Allgemeine Zeitung*, October 26, 2014. http://www.faz.net/aktuell/feuilleton/kunst/kunstraub-und-terror-die-tempel-der-isis-13229696.html.

Maksan, Oliver, and Marc Felix Serrao. "Friedrich Merz: 'Deutschland kann nicht noch mehr Flüchtlinge aufnehmen. Wir haben genug antisemitische junge Männer im Land.'" *Neue Züricher Zeitung*, October 21, 2023. https://www.nzz.ch/international/friedrich-merz-wir-haben-genug-antisemitische-junge-maenner-im-land-ld.1761710.

Marzocchi, Ottavio. *The Protection of Article 2 TEU Values in the EU*. European Parliament Fact Sheets on the European Union, June 13, 2024.

https://www.europarl.europa.eu/factsheets/en/sheet/146/der-schutz-der-werte-gema%C3%9F-artikel-2-euv-in-der-eu.

Mbembe, Achille. "Necropolitics." *Public Culture* 15, no. 1 (2003): 11–40. https://doi.org/dx.doi.org/10.1215/08992363-15-1-11.

McClintock, Anne, and Amir Mufti, eds. *Dangerous Liaisons: Gender, Nation, and Postcolonial Perspectives*. Minneapolis: University of Minnesota Press, 1997.

MDR Sachsen-Anhalt. "Die wichtigsten Fragen und Antworten zum Attentat von Halle." *MDR*, February 13, 2023. https://www.mdr.de/nachrichten/sachsen-anhalt/halle/halle/faq-anschlag-synagoge-opfer-taeter-prozess-urteil-100.html.

Mignolo, Walter. *The Darker Side of Western Modernity: Global Futures, Decolonial Options*. Durham, NC: Duke University Press, 2011.

Missing Migrants Project. "Migration within the Mediterranean." International Organization for Migration, April 29, 2024. https://missingmigrants.iom.int/region/mediterranean.

Moritz, Tino. "Einsame Zweifler." *die tageszeitung*, April 6, 2001. https://taz.de/!1178748.

Motte, Jan, Rainer Ohliger, and Anne von Oswald, eds. *50 Jahre Bundesrepublik—50 Jahre Einwanderung: Nachkriegsgeschichte als Migrationsgeschichte*. Frankfurt: Campus Verlag, 1999.

Muñoz, José Esteban. *Cruising Utopia: The Then and There of Queer Futurity*. New York: New York University Press, 2007.

Museum for Islamic Art. "Multaka: Treffpunkt Museum—Geflüchtete als Guides in Berliner Museen." Staatliche Museen zu Berlin, 2015. https://www.smb.museum/en/museums-institutions/skulpturensammlung/online-offers/detail/multaka-museum-as-meeting-point-refugees-as-guides-in-museums-in-berlin.

Nash, Jennifer C. "Citational Desires: On Black Feminism's Institutional Longings." Diacritics 48, no. 3 (2020): 76–91. https://dx.doi.org/10.1353/dia.2020.0020.

Nederveen Pieterse, Jan. *White on Black: Images of Africa and Blacks in Western Popular Culture*. New Haven: Yale University Press, 1992.

Nelson, Arthur. "EU Dropped Climate Policies after BP Threat of Oil Industry 'Exodus.'" *The Guardian*, April 20, 2016. https://www.theguardian.com/environment/2016/apr/20/eu-dropped-climate-policies-after-bp-threat-oil-industry-exodus.

Netanyahu, Benjamin. "PM Netanyahu's Speech at the 37th Zionist Congress." Israel Government website, October 20, 2015. https://www.gov.il/en/departments/news/speechcongress201015.

No Humboldt 21! "Mandela ist kein Preußischer Kulturbesitz." News release, December 16, 2013. http://www.no-humboldt21.de/wp-content/uploads/2013/12/PM-NoHumboldt21_ISD.pdf.

———. "Stop the Planned Construction of the Humboldt Forum in the Berlin Palace!" June 3, 2013. http://www.no-humboldt21.de/resolution/english.

Nordbruch, Götz. "The Arab World and National Socialism." In *Rethinking Totalitarianism and Its Arab Readings*, edited by Manfred Sing. Beirut: Orient Institute Studies, 2010. https://perspectivia.net//publikationen/orient-institut-studies/1-2012/nordbruch_arab-world.

Novick, Peter. *The Holocaust in American Life*. New York: Houghton Mifflin Co., 1999.

Oehmsen, Heinrich. "Wanderausstellung: Die 'weiße Sicht' des Krieges." *Hamburger Abendblatt*, April 17, 2013. https://www.abendblatt.de/kultur-live/article115351192/Wanderausstellung-Die-weisse-Sicht-des-Krieges.html.

Oguntoye, Katharina, and May Ayim. *Farbe bekennen: Afrodeutsche Frauen auf den Spuren ihrer Geschichte*. Berlin: Orlanda-Frauenverlag, 1986.

Oltermann, Philip. "Berlin Museums' Refugee Guides Scheme Fosters Meeting of Minds." *The Guardian*, February 27, 2016. https://www.theguardian.com/world/2016/feb/27/berlin-museums-refugee-guides-scheme-fosters-meeting-of-minds.

———. "German Rightwing Party Apologises for Jérôme Boateng Comments." *The Guardian*, May 29, 2016. https://www.theguardian.com/world/2016/may/29/german-far-right-party-row-jerome-boateng-neighbour-comments.

Oltmer, Jochen. "'Verbotswidrige Einwanderung nach Deutschland': Osteuropäische Juden im Kaiserreich und in der Weimarer Republik." *ASCHKENAS—Zeitschrift für Geschichte und Kultur der Juden* 17 (2007): 97–121.

Opoku, Kwame. "Looted/Stolen Artifacts Declared 'Shared Heritage.'" No Humboldt 21!, 2015. https://www.no-humboldt21.de/wp-content/uploads/2015/08/Opoku_SHARED_HERITA GE-4.pdf.

Özyürek, Ezra. "Export-Import Theory and the Racialization of Anti-Semitism: Turkish- and Arab-Only Prevention Programs in Germany." *Comparative Studies in Society and History* 58, no. 1 (2016): 40–65. http://dx.doi.org/10.1017/S0010417515000560.

Patridge, Damani. "Holocaust Mahnmal (Memorial): Monumental Memory amidst Contemporary Race." *Comparative Studies in Society and History* 52, no. 4 (2010): 820–50. http://dx.doi.org/10.1017/S0010417510000472.

Penders, Christian. *West New Guinea Debacle: Dutch Decolonisation and Indonesia, 1945–1962*. Honolulu: University of Hawaii Press, 2002.

Pfeil, Joachim Friedrich von. *Studien und Beobachtungen aus der Südsee*. Braunschweig: Friedrich Vieweg Verlag, 1899.

Pollitt, Katha. "Hers; The Smurfette Principle." *The New York Times*, April 7, 1991. http://www.nytimes.com/1991/04/07/magazine/hers-the-smurfette-principle.html.

Posener, Alan. "Götz Aly platzt im Faschismus-Streit der Kragen." *Die Welt*, September 4, 2009. https://www.welt.de/kultur/article4455182/Goetz-Aly-platzt-im-Faschismus-Streit-der-Kragen.html.

Prenzel, Thomas, ed. *20 Jahre Rostock-Lichtenhagen: Kontext, Dimensionen und Folgen der rassistischen Gewalt*. Rostocker Informationen zu Politik und Verwaltung 32. Rostock: University of Rostock, 2012. https://www.ipv.uni

-rostock.de/storages/uni-rostock/Alle_WSF/IPV/Forschung/Graue_Reihe/grauereihe32.pdf.

Presse- und Informationsamt der Bundesregierung. "Kulturstaatsminister Bernd Neumann eröffnet Ausstellung 'Im Licht von Amarna: 100 Jahre Fund der Nofretete.'" Presse- und Informationsamt der Bundesregierung, December 5, 2012. https://politische-reden.eu/BR/t/1939.html.

"Pro Asyl weist Äußerung des Zentralrats der Juden zurück." *Die Zeit*, November 23, 2015. https://www.zeit.de/politik/deutschland/2015-11/deutschland-zentralrat-der-juden-fluechtlingszahlen.

Pusca, Anca, ed. *Eastern European Roma in the EU: Mobility, Discrimination, Solutions*. New York: International Debate Education Association, 2012.

Quinan, Christine. "Hidden Memories: October 17, 1961, *Charlie Hebdo*, and Postcolonial Forgetting." In *Postcolonial Transitions in Europe: Contexts, Practices and Politics*, edited by Sandra Ponzanesi and Gianmaria Colpani, 99–118. London: Rowman & Littlefield International, 2015.

Randow, Gero von. "Unter Polizeischutz: Ein Einwanderungsland ist entsetzt wegen seiner Probleme: Berlin-Neukölln ist kein Einzelfall. Eine Nachrichtenanalyse." *Die Zeit*, March 31, 2006. https://www.zeit.de/online/2006/14/ruetlischule.

"The Recognition of the Nazi Genocide of the Sinti and Roma." European Holocaust Memorial Day for Sinti and Roma, September 7, 2020. https://www.roma-sinti-holocaust-memorial-day.eu/recognition/the-recognition-of-the-nazi-genocide-of-the-sinti-and-roma.

Repplinger, Roger. *Leg dich, Zigeuner: Die Geschichte von Johann Trollmann und Tull Harder*. Munich: Piper Verlag, 2012.

Rheinisches JournalistInnenbüro and Recherche International e.V., eds. *"Unsere Opfer zählen nicht": Die Dritte Welt im Zweiten Weltkrieg*. Hamburg: Verlag Assoziation A., 2005.

Rizvev, Seila. "What Does a Victim Look Like? An Interview with Šejla Kamerić on the Legacy of 'Bosnian Girl.'" *Balkanist*, July 7, 2015. https://balkanist.net/what-does-a-victim-look-like-sejla-kameric.

Robinson, Cedric J. *Black Marxism: The Making of the Black Radical Tradition*. Chapel Hill, NC: University of North Carolina Press, 2000.Robinson, Duncan. "Dutch Still Grapple with the Shame of Srebrenica." *The Financial Times*, July 10, 2015. https://www.ft.com/content/93a5c67a-26d2-11e5-9c4e-a775d2b173ca#axzz4ABc69TQe.

Roma National Congress. "Fluchtburg Konzentrationslager." *Fluchschrift*, May 5, 1993. http://www.fluchschrift.net/archiv/progpog.htm.

Romano Jekipe Ano Hamburg. "Romano Jekipe Ano Hamburg erhält Schutzraum vor Abschiebung und fordert weiterhin ein Bleiberecht." *Romano Jekipe Ano Hamburg* (blog), September 21, 2015. https://romas-in-hamburg.blogspot.com.

Roma Union Frankfurt am Main, Ellen Leidgeb, and Nicole Horn, eds. *Opre Roma! Erhebt Euch! Eine Einführung in die Geschichte und Situation der Roma*. Munich: AG SPAK Bücher, 1994.

Rose, Romani. "Ein Mahnmal für alle Opfer." *Die Zeit*, April 28, 1989. https://www.zeit.de/1989/18/ein-mahnmal-fuer-alle-opfer.
Rössel, Karl. "Die Rolle des globalen Südens im Zweiten Weltkrieg." Interview by Simon Inou, June 21, 2007. BlackAustria.info. Posted on December 6, 2023. https://www.blackaustria.info/2023/12/06/hintergrundgespraech-zur-rolle-der-dritten-welt-im-zweiten-weltkrieg-hintergrundgespraech.
———. "Schwerpunkt: Nazikollaborateure in der Dritten Welt." *iz3w*, May/June 2009. http://www.3www2.de/images/stories/Freiburg/iz3w_312_Themenschwerpunkt.pdf.
———. "Zensierte Kontinuität." *Jungle World*, October 1, 2009. https://jungle.world/artikel/2009/40/zensierte-kontinuitaet.
Roth, Joseph. *The Wandering Jews*. Translated by Michael Hofmann. New York: W. W. Norton, 2001.
Rothberg, Michael. *Multidirectional Memory: Remembering the Holocaust in the Age of Decolonization*. Stanford: Stanford University Press, 2009.
Saget, Joel. "'Race' Out, Gender Equality in as France Updates Constitution." *France24*, June 28, 2018. https://www.france24.com/en/20180628-race-out-gender-equality-france-updates-constitution.
Sahakian, Rijin. "On the Closing of Sada for Iraqi Art." *Warscapes* (blog), April 6, 2015. http://www.warscapes.com/blog/closing-sada-iraqi-art.
Samatar, Abdi Ismail, Mark Lindberg, and Basil Mahayni. "The Dialectics of Piracy in Somalia: The Rich versus the Poor." *Third World Quarterly* 31, no. 8 (2010): 1377–94.
Sander, Lalon. "Klassisch Rassistisch." *die tageszeitung*, June 6, 2016. http://www.taz.de/!5310135.
Sarkeesian, Anita. "Tropes vs. Women: #3 The Smurfette Principle." Feminist Frequency. YouTube video, 7:09. Uploaded April 21, 2011. https://feministfrequency.com/video/tropes-vs-women-3-the-smurfette-principle.
Saure, Philip. "Hilfsorganisationen kritisieren EU-Vorschläge zur Migrationsabwehr." *Migazin*, June 28, 2016. https://www.migazin.de/2016/06/28/erste-abkommen-jahresende-hilfsorganisationen-eu.
Schellen, Petra. "Israel bietet sich als Feindbild an." *die tageszeitung*, July 21, 2014. http://www.taz.de/!5037156.
Schirrmacher, Frank. "Junge Männer auf Feindfahrt." *Frankfurter Allgemeine Zeitung*, January 15, 2008. https://www.faz.net/aktuell/feuilleton/debatten/jugendgewalt-junge-maenner-auf-feindfahrt-1512153.html.
Schmemann, Serge. "Gypsy Protesters Driven from a Nazi Camp." *The New York Times*, October 4, 1989. https://timesmachine.nytimes.com/timesmachine/1989/10/04/617589.html?pageNumber=12.
Schmid, Bernhard. "Der Nahe Osten als Projektionsfläche." LabourNet, August 19, 2006. https://archiv.labournet.de/krieg/nahost/projektion.html.
Schmidt, Michael. "Türken waren Kanzler Kohl fremd." *Die Zeit*, August 2, 2013. https://www.zeit.de/politik/deutschland/2013-08/kohl-gastarbeiter-gespraechsprotokoll.

Schönwälder, Karen. "Why Germany's Guestworkers Were Largely Europeans: The Selective Principles of Post-War Labour Recruitment Policy." *Ethnic and Racial Studies* 27, no. 2 (2004): 248–65. https://doi.org/10.1080/014198 7042000177324.

Schroeder, Robin. "Rechtsextreme Anschläge—Alles bloß kein Terrorismus." *Migazin*, December 17, 2015. https://www.migazin.de/2015/12/17/rechtsex tremismus-alles-bloss-kein-terrorismus.

Schuster, Peter-Klaus. "Das universale Museum: Europa und die Welt—vom Betenden Knaben über Nofretete zum Humboldt-Forum." *Der Tagesspiegel*, August 12, 2005. https://www.berlin.de/aktuell/ausgaben/2005/dezember /ereignisse/artikel.230267.php.

Sharma, Gouri. "'Complete Censorship': Germany's Palestinian Diaspora Fights Crackdown." *Al Jazeera*, October 23, 2023. https://www.aljazeera.com /features/2023/10/26/complete-censorship-germanys-palestinian-diaspora -fights-crackdown.

Shohat, Ella, and Robert Stam. *Unthinking Eurocentrism: Multiculturalism and the Media*. London: Routledge, 1994.

Shohat, Gil. "Nahostkonflikt und Holocaust an Schulen: 'Wenn ein Jude kommt, ist was los.'" *die tageszeitung*, September 14, 2014. http://www.taz .de/!5033577.

Shooman, Yasemin. "Zur Debatte über das Verhältnis von Antisemitismus, Rassismus und Islamfeindlichkeit." In *Antisemitismus und andere Feindseligkeiten: Interaktionen von Ressentiments*, edited by Katharina Rauschenberger and Werner Konitzer, 125–56. Frankfurt: Campus Verlag, 2015.

Sieg, Katrin. *Ethnic Drag: Performing Race, Nation, Sexuality in West Germany*. Ann Arbor: University of Michigan Press, 2002.

Sloop, John M. "European Soccer Is Having Another Reckoning over Racism—Is It Time to Accept the Problem Goes Beyond Bad Fans?" *The Conversation*, May 26, 2023. https://theconversation.com/european-soccer-is -having-another-reckoning-over-racism-is-it-time-to-accept-the-problem -goes-beyond-bad-fans-206391.

Smith, Paul Chaat. *Everything You Know about Indians Is Wrong*. Minneapolis: University of Minnesota Press, 2009.

Snyder, Timothy. *Bloodlands: Europe between Hitler and Stalin*. New York: Basic Books, 2012.

Somashekhar, Sandhya. "The Disturbing Reason Some African American Patients May Be Undertreated for Pain." *The Washington Post*, April 4, 2016. https://www.washingtonpost.com/news/to-your-health/wp/2016/04/04/do -blacks-feel-less-pain-than-whites-their-doctors-may-think-so.

Southern Poverty Law Center. "The Racist 'Great Replacement' Conspiracy Theory Explained." May 17, 2022. https://www.splcenter.org/hatewatch /2022/05/17/racist-great-replacement-conspiracy-theory-explained.

Staatliche Museen zu Berlin. "Museumsinsel—Profil." 2016. https://www.smb .museum/museen-einrichtungen/museumsinsel-berlin/ueber-uns/profil.

Statistisches Bundesamt. "Pressemitteilung No. 158." April 20, 2023. https://www.destatis.de/DE/Presse/Pressemitteilungen/2023/04/PD23_158_125.html.
Stavans, Ilam. "Repatriating Spain's Jews." *The New York Times*, April 1, 2014. https://www.nytimes.com/2014/04/02/opinion/repatriating-spains-jews.html?_r=0.
Stiftung Denkmal für die ermordeten Juden Europas. "Memorial to the Murdered Jews of Europe—Stiftung Denkmal für die ermordeten Juden Europas." January 12, 2024. https://www.stiftung-denkmal.de/en/memorials/memorial-to-the-murdered-jews-of-europe.
Stiftung Preußischer Kulturbesitz. *Jahrespressekonferenz der Stiftung Preußischer Kulturbesitz: Anhang: Besucher-, Nutzer- und Bestandszahlen im Jahr 2015*. Berlin: Stiftung Preußischer Kulturbesitz, 2016. https://www.preussischer-kulturbesitz.de/fileadmin/user_upload_SPK/documents/presse/pressemitteilungen/2016/160126_JPK_02_Zahlen.pdf.
Tagesschau. "Bericht aus Berlin." ARD, March 6, 2022. Video, 30:34. https://www.tagesschau.de/multimedia/video/video-998931~_bab-sendung-773.html.
———. "Tagesschau vor 20 Jahren, 09.11.1989." ARD, November 9, 1989. Video, 14:42. https://www.tagesschau.de/multimedia/video/video-ts-134790.html.
Terkessidis, Mark. *Interkultur*. Berlin: Suhrkamp, 2010.
Tharoor, Ishaan. "Is It Time for France to Pay Its Real Debt to Haiti?" *The Washington Post*, May 13, 2015. https://www.washingtonpost.com/news/worldviews/wp/2015/05/13/does-france-owe-haiti-reparations.
Ther, Philipp. *Die dunkle Seite der Nationalstaaten: "Ethnische Säuberungen" im modernen Europa*. Göttingen: Vandenhoeck und Ruprecht Verlag, 2011.
Todorova, Maria. *Imagining the Balkans*. New York: Oxford University Press, 1997.
Tolmein, Oliver. "Die rassende Reporterin." In *Rechts durch die Mitte: Reportagen und Gespräche über die Ordnung der Verhältnisse*, edited by Oliver Tolmein, 20–25. Hamburg: Konkret Verlag, 1998.
Trilling, Daniel. "Dark Things Are Happening on Europe's Borders: Are They a Sign of Worse to Come?" *The Guardian*, November 8, 2021. https://www.theguardian.com/commentisfree/2021/nov/08/dark-europe-border-migrants-climate-displacement.
Trost, Gabriele. "Woher stammt das Wort Kanake?" *Planet Wissen*. https://www.planet-wissen.de/geschichte/deutsche_geschichte/geschichte_der_gastarbeiter/pwiewissensfrage550.html.
Trouillot, Michel-Rolph. *Silencing the Past: Power and the Production of History*. Boston: Beacon Press, 1995.
Tsianos, Vassilis. "'Die deutsche Linke wurde längst migrantisiert.'" Interview by Christian Jakob. *Jungle World*, August 9, 2012. https://jungle.world/artikel/2012/32/die-deutsche-linke-wurde-laengst-migrantisiert.
Tudor, Alyosxa. *From [al'mania] with Love: Trans_feministische Positionierungen zu Rassismus und Migratismus*. Frankfurt: Brandes & Apsel, 2014.

"Überfall in Berlin: Jüdisches Kolleg rät Studenten vom Kippa-Tragen ab." *Der Spiegel*, August 30, 2012. https://www.spiegel.de/panorama/justiz/ueberfall-in-berlin-juedisches-kolleg-raet-rabbinern-vom-kippa-tragen-ab-a-853054.html.

Ullrich, Volker. "Goetz Alys Provokation: Steht ein neuer Historikerstreit ins Haus?" *Die Zeit*, May 4, 2005. https://www.zeit.de/2005/19/Goetz_Alys_Provokation.

"Unterschriftenaktion zur Ausländerpolitik: Union macht gegen Bonn mobil. Stoiber: Doppelte Staatsbürgerschaft gefährlicher als RAF." *Süddeutsche Zeitung*, January 4, 1999.

Veer, Peter van der. "Pim Fortuyn, Theo van Gogh, and the Politics of Tolerance in the Netherlands." *Public Culture* 18, no. 1 (2006): 111–24.

Vidal, John. "Is the EU Taking Its Over-Fishing Habits to West African Waters?" *The Guardian*, April 2, 2012. https://www.theguardian.com/environment/2012/apr/02/eu-fishing-west-africa-mauritania.

Vollnhals, Clemens. "Der Totalitarismusbegriff im Wandel." *Aus Politik und Zeitgeschichte*, September 21, 2006. https://www.bpb.de/shop/zeitschriften/apuz/29513/der-totalitarismusbegriff-im-wandel.

Wagner, Joachim. "'Hitler gefällt mir': Viele muslimische Jugendliche in Deutschland denken antisemitisch. Und ihre Gewaltbereitschaft wächst." *Die Zeit*, June 10, 2007. https://www.zeit.de/2007/24/Muslim-Antisemitismus.

Wahlrecht.de. "Sonntagsfrage Bundestagswahl." May 2, 2024. https://www.wahlrecht.de/umfragen/index.htm.

Waldman, Peter, and Hugh Pope. "'Crusade' Reference Reinforces Fears War on Terrorism Is against Muslims." *The Wall Street Journal*, September 21, 2001. https://www.wsj.com/articles/SB1001020294332922160.

Weber, Beverly. "The German Refugee 'Crisis' after Cologne: The Race of Refugee Rights." *English Language Notes* 54, no. 2 (Fall/Winter 2016): 77–92.

Wehler, Hans-Ulrich. "Das Türkenproblem: Der Westen braucht die Türkei—etwa als Frontstaat gegen den Irak. Aber in die EU darf das muslimische Land niemals." *Die Zeit*, September 12, 2002. https://www.zeit.de/2002/38/Das_Tuerkenproblem.

Werkstatt der Kulturen. Berlin: Werkstatt der Kulturen, 1993. Brochure.

Widmann, Arno. "Naika Foroutan: Was heißt postmigrantisch?" *Berliner Zeitung*, December 12, 2014. https://www.berliner-zeitung.de/naika-foroutan-was-heisst-postmigrantisch-li.27572.

Wiedemann, Charlotte. "Angeblich von der Mauer gefallen: Gibt es im Hamburger Polizeihochhaus immer noch eine 'Zigeuner-Kartei'?" *Die Zeit*, December 4, 1981. https://www.zeit.de/1981/50/angeblich-von-der-mauer-gefallen.

Wien, Peter. "Arab Fascism—Arabs and Fascism: Empirical and Theoretical Perspectives." In *Rethinking Totalitarianism and Its Arab Readings*, edited by Manfred Sing. Beirut: Orient Institute Studies, 2010. https://perspectivia.net//publikationen/orient-institut-studies/1-2012/wien_fascism.

Wierth, Alke. "Erinnerung teilen ist schwer." *die tageszeitung*, September 3, 2009. https://taz.de/!592280.

———. "Montags-Interview mit Philippa Ebéné: 'Wir brauchen für Vielfalt eine Quote.'" *die tageszeitung*, October 20, 2008. http://www.taz.de/!5174132.

———. "Streit um Ausstellung eskaliert." *die tageszeitung*, August 28, 2009. http://www.taz.de/!5157195.
Will, Anne-Kathrin. "Migrationshintergrund—wieso, woher, wohin?" Bundeszentrale für politische Bildung, February 5, 2020. https://www.bpb.de/themen/migration-integration/laenderprofile/deutschland/304523/migrationshintergrund-wieso-woher-wohin.
Winckel, Ännecke. *Antiziganismus: Rassismus gegen Roma und Sinti im vereinigten Deutschland*. Münster: Unrast Verlag, 2002.
Witting, Volker. "Germany's Heated Debate over 'Race' in the Constitution." *Deutsche Welle*, June 6, 2020. https://www.dw.com/en/race-has-no-place-in-the-german-constitution-or-does-it/a-53790056.
Wright, Oliver, and Jerome Taylor. "Cameron: My War on Multiculturalism." *The Independent*, February 5, 2011. https://www.independent.co.uk/news/uk/politics/cameron-my-war-on-multiculturalism-2205074.html.
Wrochem, Oliver von. *Das KZ Neuengamme und seine Außenlager: Geschichte, Nachgeschichte, Erinnerung, Bildung*. Berlin: Metropol, 2010.
Wünsche, Viviane, Uwe Lohalm, Michael Zimmermann, and Heinrich Erdmann. *Die nationalsozialistische Verfolgung Hamburger Roma und Sinti*. Hamburg: Landeszentrale für politische Bildung, 2006.
Ye'or, Bat. *Eurabia: The Euro-Arab Axis*. Madison, NJ: Fairleigh Dickinson University Press, 2005.
Yücel, Deniz. "Mal eben ausgebürgert." *Jungle World*, February 2, 2005. https://jungle.world/artikel/2005/05/mal-eben-ausgebuergert.
Zanden, Jan van. *The Economic History of the Netherlands 1914–1995: A Small Open Economy in the "Long" Twentieth Century*. London: Routledge, 1997.
Zantop, Susanne. *Colonial Fantasies: Conquest, Family, and Nation in Precolonial Germany, 1770–1870*. Durham, NC: Duke University Press, 1997.
ZDF Magazin Royale. "Davor, währenddessen, danach: Das deutsche Versagen beim rassistischen Anschlag von Hanau." *ZDF*, April 26, 2024. YouTube video, 24:04. https://www.youtube.com/watch?v=jXf9d1xHO34.
Zekri, Sonja. "Wiedersehen." *Süddeutsche Zeitung*, April 7, 2016. https://www.sueddeutsche.de/kultur/fluechtlinge-wiedersehen-1.2939406.
Zentralrat Deutscher Sinti und Roma. "Stellungnahme des Zentralrats Deutscher Sinti und Roma zum Artikel von Eberhard Jäckel 'Denkmal-Streit—Sinti und Roma oder Zigeuner?' in der Frankfurter Allgemeinen Zeitung vom 7. Februar 2005." News release, 2005. http://zentralrat.sintiundroma.de/wp-content/uploads/presse/59.pdf.
Ziegler, Jean. "Europas Gier ist Afrikas Hunger." *Le Monde Diplomatique*, March 14, 2008. Translated into German by Sabine Jainski. AG Friedensforschung. http://www.ag-friedensforschung.de/themen/Armut/europa.html.
"Zigeuner: Die Erben der Opfer." *Der Spiegel*, November 13, 1989.
Zimmerer, Jürgen. "Humboldt-Forum: Das koloniale Vergessen." *Blätter für deutsche und internationale Politik* 7 (July 2015): 13–16.
Zimmerman, Andrew. *Anthropology and Antihumanism in Imperial Germany*. Chicago: University of Chicago Press, 2001.

Index

ADEFRA—Schwarze Frauen in Deutschland (Black Women in Germany), 7n4, 9, 188, 218
Afghanistan, xxii, xxiv, 11, 40n15, 166n12
African countries, 39–41, 53, 55, 211n21. *See also* colonialism; East Africa; North Africa; *specific countries*
African migrants and refugees, xix, 35, 47, 49, 120n55, 123–25, 141, 154–55. *See also* Black Europeans
Algeria, xxii, 30n5, 77n48, 153, 198
al-Husseini, Mohammed Amin, 185–87, 189–91
Alter, Daniel, 175–76, 213
Alternative for Germany (AfD), ix, xii, 72, 127, 147, 206n16
Aly, Götz, 91n11, 173n23, 188–89, 193–94, 218

Amadeu Antonio Foundation, 175, 188, 193, 195
Amira initiative, 179–80
anthropology, 44–45, 58–59
anti-Black racism, 57n5, 122–23, 193–95, 202–7, 218
anticolonial liberation movements, xviii, 10, 30n5, 77, 186n49, 187n51
anticommunism, 158–59, 167
antifascism, 20, 97n18, 112, 119, 130, 135, 156–63, 166–77, 183–95
antiracism, ix–x, 7n4, 34, 178, 193
antisemitism: anti-Zionism and, x, xv, xvii, 56, 179, 190n63, 192n71; historical European, xiv–xv, xviii, 31–32, 76n47, 88–90, 137, 174; Muslim, xiv–xvii, xxiv, 76n47, 130–31, 156–57, 168n15, 171–72, 174–83, 185–86, 213–14
antiziganism, 35, 181

Index

anti-Zionism, x, xv, xvii, 56, 179, 186n49, 190n63, 192n71
Arbeiter-Samariter-Bund (ASB), 102
Arendt, Hannah, 85, 210, 217
assimilation, 3–4, 9, 21, 28–29, 88. *See also* integration
asylum laws, 8, 48–49, 101, 104, 112, 120–22, 197–98
asylum seekers, 8, 27, 100–101, 103–4, 112–14, 116–21, 117n34, 121
Auschwitz, 95–96, 105, 122n61
austerity measures, 26, 36, 39–40, 53, 208
Austria, 87, 140

Babylon, 62, 66, 71
Bade, Klaus J., 147n24
Balkans, 54, 163–68, 173
Barth, Ariane, 117–19, 122–23, 129
Bax, Daniel, 7n4
Beck, Anton, 142
Belgium, 209–10, 211n21
Benhabib, Seyla, 196
Benin Bronzes, 73n44
Berlin Conference (1884–85), 44, 87, 92n11
Berlin Ethnological Museum, 73n44
Berlin Palace, 78
Berlin State Museums, 72–74
Black Europeans, 35, 49, 173. *See also* African migrants and refugees
Black Germans, 57n5, 122–23, 125, 139, 183, 188–89, 193–95, 202–7
Black History Month, 185
Black Horror on the Rhine, 193n75, 204
Blunck, Max Andreas, 143
Boateng, Jérôme, 206
Borchardt, Ludwig, 67
borders. *See* European identity
Böröcz, Josef, 51, 159, 172
Bosnia, xxii, 104, 167–68
Böttcher, Hans-Georg, 111
Breivik, Anders, 21n15
Brexit, vii, 36, 198
The Brown Mob, 188
Bruckner, Pascal, 158–59
Bubis, Ignatz, 107

Bunzl, Matti, 137n3
Bush, George H. W., 150, 162
Bush, George W., 148–49

Cameron, David, 146
Camus, Renaud, ix*n*5
Caribbean Community (CARICOM), 55–56, 69–70
Carnival of Cultures (event), 184–85
Casanova, José, 150, 153
Central Council of German Sinti and Roma, 97–98, 107–9, 120
Central Council of Jews in Germany, 107, 177
Central Gypsy Collection Camp (Hamburg), 94
Central Reception Center for Asylum Seekers (ZASt), 113–14, 120
Césaire, Aimé, 17, 85, 196, 211, 217
Ceuta, 37, 48
Charlie Hebdo, 5
Christian Democrat Union (CDU), ix*n*5, x, 143n15, 148, 150
Christianity, 91, 149–52, 154. *See also* European identity; German identity
Christian Social Union (CSU), 143n15, 148
Churchill, Winston, xx
citizenship laws, 96n17, 138–45, 147
civilization, 12, 18, 53, 56, 74–75, 84, 198–99. *See also* evolutionary time; internalist narrative
Clinton, Bill, 166n13
Cold War, vii, 26, 28, 135–36, 160–61, 164
colonialism: in collective memory, xv–xix, 85, 91n11, 159, 181, 194, 207, 209–10, 214; European prosperity and, 39–42, 51–53, 55, 68, 69n33, 212; German, 52, 55–67, 183; legacies of, xxiv, 10–13, 30, 32–35, 51, 55–60, 69n33, 209–10, 214 (*see also* post/colonialism); museums and, 61–80; reparations for, 55–56, 68–70; World War II and, 183–95. *See also* anticolonial liberation movements

colorblind approach, xviii, 2, 10–11, 14n9, 16, 83–84, 189
communism, 78, 83, 85, 135, 173, 193n74, 210
COVID-19 pandemic, xxiv
Crenshaw, Kimberlé, 215–17
critical race theory, xxiv–xxv, 11–12, 14n9
Cuno, James, 67–68

Dachau, 98–99, 191
Danish minority in Northern Germany, 137, 142–43
Davis, Angela, 215
decolonization, 13, 158, 217
democracy, xix, 135, 152–54, 178, 208–12, 217–18
deportation: of minoritized groups, 87, 137; of refugees and migrants, ix, xxiin23, xxiii, 14n10, 48, 113, 155; of Roma and Sinti, 20, 37, 87, 94, 96, 100–105, 112n22, 113, 128
development, 40–47, 51, 55–56, 74–75, 158–59
de Winter, Leon, 169
dominance, structures of, 20, 33–34, 164, 183–95, 219–20
Du Bois, W. E. B., 17, 85, 217

East Africa, 59, 212n21
Eastern Europe, xii, 85, 88–90, 100, 165n11, 173
East Germans, 7–8, 32–33, 77–78, 104, 114–16, 130, 135, 178. *See also* German Democratic Republic (GDR)
Ebéné, Philippa, 185–89, 191–93
Eckert, Andreas, 156
economic inequality, 46, 198, 214n23; economic migrants/refugees, 37, 49–50, 198. *See also* poverty
Egypt, 65, 67, 73–74, 153, 186n49
Egyptian Museum (Berlin), 66–67
Einstein, Albert, 88–90
The Empty Center, 78n52
Enlightenment humanism, 12, 64, 71–72, 75, 152

Enzensberger, Hans Magnus, 161–62, 170, 177n33
ethnology, 44, 73, 75n46
ethnonationalism, xxvi, 86, 90–93, 115, 136–37, 145, 148, 154–55, 164, 175
European identity, viii, 2, 18, 21, 35–54; Balkans-as-Orient and, 163–68; borders and, 43, 74–75, 103–4, 150–55, 163, 208; as multiethnic and multireligious, xiii, 90–93; as superior, 12, 18, 43, 45–46, 51, 53, 56, 74–75, 158, 163, 178n33, 219; as white and Christian, xvii–xix, xx–xxvi, 85, 91, 136–39, 149–52, 154, 174; wider Mediterranean region and, 30n5, 53–57, 207–13. *See also* evolutionary time; internalist narrative
European Others (El-Tayeb), 1–3
European racism, xviii, 2, 5, 11–13, 14n10, 165; analysis of, 34–36, 84–85; antisemitism and, 182 (*see also* antisemitism); democracy and, 212, 218; history of, 30–31, 83–86; national identity and, 28–31. *See also* German racism
European Union (EU), viii, xxiv, 36–37, 47–52, 198; expansion of, 136, 147, 150–52, 163; Germany's role in, 26, 54–55, 151
European values, viii, xix, 12, 51, 54, 145–46
evolutionary time, 35, 42–47, 56, 58, 70, 74, 84, 213
exclusion. *See* racialized groups, exclusion of
exhibits, xiii, 60. *See also* museums
expulsions, xiii, 90–92, 154

Fabian, Johannes, 35, 42–43, 45, 47
fascism, xiv, 19–20, 21n15, 76n47, 162, 173, 190, 210–12. *See also* antifascism; Islamofascism; post/fascism
Federal Republic of Germany, xiv, 26, 32, 76–77, 80, 104, 114–15, 135–36, 143n15

feminism, 11, 14n10; women-of-color feminism, 11, 13, 16, 215–17
Ferguson, Rod, 17
Fichte, Johann Gottlieb, 140
Fischer, Eugen, 59n8
Fischer, Joschka, 163–64
foreigners, 6, 8–9, 57, 92; hostility toward, 112, 129 (*see also* xenophobia); as un/German, 129. *See also* guest workers; migratized groups; refugee crisis
France, xviii, 54, 139; collaboration with Nazis, 76n47, 169; colonialism, 30n5, 69n33, 77n48, 186n49; Islamist violence in, 209–10
Friedrich Wilhelm II, 64
Frontex, xxiii, 48n27
Fukuyama, Francis, 167
futurity, 19, 77–78, 123, 130, 136, 155, 174, 197, 200, 208–9, 218–21

Gaza, xxi, xxv, 50, 179
genocide, xvi, 56, 211n21. *See also* Holocaust
German Colonial Exhibition (1896), 60
German Colonial Museum (Berlin), 60
German colonial rule, 52, 55–67, 183. *See also* colonialism
German Democratic Republic (GDR), 97, 103, 143n15; memory and German identity, 76–80. *See also* East Germans
German Empire, 79, 87, 140
German Historical Museum (Berlin), 61–62, 64
German identity, xiii, xiv–xv, 18–19, 25–27; biologistic definitions of, 139–44, 148; ethnonational understanding of, 115, 148, 175; plural experience of, 72, 80; racialization and, 8, 29–31 (*see also* racialized groups); as white and Christian, xi, 2–9, 21, 57, 86, 124–26, 129, 149–52, 200, 205, 220
German New Guinea Company, 59
German racism, 5–7, 127; anti-Black, 57n5, 122–23, 193–95, 202–7, 218; in mainstream society, xn6, 117–18, 122–31, 145, 171, 175–76, 207; selective racist amnesia, 8–10, 20–21, 112; as strategy for dealing with social change, 199–221; white scholarship and, 15–18. *See also* European racism
German South West Africa (present-day Namibia), 59, 59n8
Germany: crisis narrative and, viii–xii, 25–27, 197–99; dominance in EU, 26, 54–55, 151; emigration, 207; European status of, 54; founding of nation-state, 45n23; immigration history, 147–48; militarization and Bundeswehr, viii, xxiii, 163–64, 167–68; postmigrant, 4, 6, 10, 17–22, 124, 205, 213–21; reunification, 18–20, 26–28, 64, 76–80, 93, 103–4, 111–14, 122–23, 136, 160–61, 184, 197–99; Turkey and, 149–55; welcoming culture, 4, 8–9, 112, 197. *See also* German identity
Gilroy, Paul, 85n2
global financial crisis (2008), 26, 208
Global South, 12; austerity measures in, 208; development in, 40–45, 51, 55, 159; human rights and, 50, 52; World War II and, 183–95
Goldberg, David Theo, 85n2
Goldhagen, Daniel, 172n22
Görlitzer Park (Berlin), 120n55
"great replacement" conspiracy theory, ixn5
Greece, 67n28, 75, 91, 135; economic crisis and austerity, 27, 36–37, 39, 53–55, 209; refugee crisis and, 47, 198
Grexit, 36, 55
guest workers, xiin11, 3, 32, 54, 116, 138, 144–45, 154–55
Gulf War, 159–61

Hackmann, Werner, 101, 106, 110, 203n8
Hage, Ghassan, 50–51, 63, 72
Haitian Revolution, 41n19, 69n33

Index 251

Hall, Stuart, 13, 25, 31, 34–36, 38, 43, 85n2, 115, 156
Hamas, xiv, xxv, 190n63
Hamburg, 93–101
Hamburg List for Halting Foreigners (HLA), 116
Harris, Cheryl, 85n2
Hasse, Ernst, 141
hegemonic self-critique, limits of, 12–15, 84, 158–59
Heissmeyer, Kurt, 94
Herero genocide, xvi, 56
Herzog, Roman, 108
Hezbollah, 190n63
hierarchies, 16, 21; of Europeanness, 54, 136; gender, 29n2; racial, 59–60, 75; of value of human lives, xxi, 43–46, 48, 50–51, 72, 209–11
hijab, 29n2, 176
historical memory. *See* public memory
Hitchens, Christopher, 168, 170, 171n20
Hitler, Adolf, ixn5, 170, 190; Saddam Hussein compared to, 159–62
Höch, Hannah, 64
Hollande, François, 69n33
Holocaust, xvi, xix, 13, 78, 85, 122n61, 159, 176, 190n63, 191–92, 217; genocide of Jews (*see* Shoah); genocide of Roma and Sinti (*see* Porajmos); use of term, 22. *See also* Auschwitz; Dachau; Neuengamme
homophobia, 120n55, 181, 201n5
Honecker, Erich, 103
Hong, Grace, 17
"Hottentots," 60
Hoyerswerda pogroms, 113, 122
Huber, Sasha, 64n21
human rights, xix, 12, 26, 30n5, 47, 50, 52, 159, 199. *See also* asylum laws
human rights violations, xxiv, 91n11; in Turkey, 150, 152, 155
Humboldt Forum (Berlin), 20, 72–80, 220
Hungary, xxiii, 155
Hussein, Saddam, 159–62
Huyssen, Andreas, 19n14

Ibrahim, Mohamed, 181n42
identity politics, 14n9, 58, 123n63
immigration laws, xi–xii, 14n10, 87
Indigenous groups, 83–84
Indonesia, 69n33
IniRromnja, 218
Initiative Schwarze in Deutschland (Initiative for Black People in Germany; ISD), 7n4, 9, 185, 188, 191, 194, 218
insecurity, 199–202, 207, 214
integration, viii, xxiin23, 3–4, 7, 20, 28–30, 63, 145, 181n42, 182, 219–20. *See also* assimilation
internalist narrative, xvii, 28, 32, 35–42, 47, 51, 56–57, 74, 79–80, 136, 156–58, 162–63, 166–67, 198, 208, 213
International Monetary Fund, 40, 46
intersectionality, 13, 14n9, 16, 215–18
Iran, 40
Iraq, xi, xiinn23–24, xiv, 40, 65–67, 70–71, 74, 153
Ishtar Gate, 66–67, 75
ISIS (Islamic State), 27, 70–71, 171–72, 201n5
Islam: fundamentalism, 45n24, 150; as incompatible with Europe, 149–55; terrorism and, 5, 50, 148–49; violence and, 213. *See also* Muslims
Islamofascism, xiv, xvii, 156–57, 167–77, 190
Islamophobia, 20, 21n15, 31–32, 137n3, 182. *See also* Muslims, racism against
Israel, 137, 161, 179n38
Israeli-Palestinian conflict, xvii, xxi, xxiv–xxv, 56, 161n2, 162–63, 167n14, 178n33, 179–80, 186–87, 190n63, 191–92, 214
Italy, 47–48, 65, 67n28

Jäckel, Eberhard, 106–7, 109–10, 218
Januzi, Mohamed, 112n22
Jewish Community of Berlin, 177
Jewish Germans, 31, 88, 107, 177. *See also* Shoah

Joffe, Gideon, 176
Justice and Development Party (AKP), 153, 155

Kahane, Anetta, 175, 193
Kanak Attak (activist group), 57–58
Kanake, 57–60, 67, 72, 212
Karolinenviertel (Hamburg neighborhood), 117–19, 127
Kawczynski, Rudko, 99–100, 101n25, 102–6
Kellermann, Ruth, 99–100
Kerry, John, 70–71
Khan, Noor Inayat, 191
Klein, Suleika, 95
Koch, Roland, 143n15
Kohl, Helmut, 104, 116, 138, 145–46
Köhler, Gundolf, 115–16
Koparan, Sydi, 171
Kosovo, xvn12, 151, 159, 163, 165–68
Kravagna, Christian, 64n21
Kreuzberg (Berlin neighborhood), 120n55, 124, 127, 208
Kupfer, Lothar, 120–21
Kurdish minorities, xv, 152, 155
Kutler, Stanley, 157n39
Kuwait, invasion of. *See* Gulf War

Lampedusa, 4, 37
Langhoff, Shermin, 188
League of Nations, 91
Lebanon, xxiv, 186n49, 190
leftists, German, 7n4, 8, 160–61, 163, 175, 187, 192, 219
Le Pen, Jean-Marie, 169n18
Le Pen, Marine, 169n18
Lévy, Bernard-Henri, 169
Libya, 48, 183, 198
Lowe, Lisa, 17

Macedonia, 104
Magdanz, Peter, 114
mainstream Germans: antisemitism, 177, 179n38, 215; encounters with racialized groups, 3–6, 8–9, 11–12, 115, 148, 200, 206–7, 215, 220; as mediators, 11, 31, 180–82; positioned as experts, 106–7, 109–10, 218–19; public memory and, 18–20, 34, 92–93, 183–85, 188–94, 214; as victims, 121–31, 172, 194. *See also* German racism
Maizière, Thomas de, 47n27, 121
Malta, 37
Mandela, Nelson, 79n56
marginalized groups, 11–12, 14n10, 18, 207, 214, 218–21; collective panic about, 123–31. *See also* un/German
Martelly, Michel, 69n33
Martin, Peter, 194
Martin Walser, 122n61
Marxist theory, 12
Mbembe, Achille, 36n9, 40
McClintock, Anne, 44
medical experimentation, 59n8, 94–95
Mediterranean region, 53–57, 65–66, 207–13. *See also specific countries*
Melilla, 48
memorials to Nazi victims, 92–93, 106–10, 122n61, 218, 220
memory. *See* public memory
Merkel, Angela, x, xin8, 146–47
Merz, Friedrich, x
Metropolitan Museum of Art (New York), 70–71
Middle East, xix, xxiii, 65–66. *See also* Israeli-Palestinian conflict; *specific countries*
migrant crisis, 37; Germans as victims of, 123–24; during interwar period, 86–88. *See also* refugee crisis
migrant laborers. *See* guest workers
Migrationsrat Berlin, 188
migratism, 4n1, 57n5
migratized groups, 2–13, 17–22, 45, 49, 57, 80, 175, 199, 214
miscegenation, 59n8, 141n8
mixed marriages, 143, 193n75, 205
modernity, 38, 158–59
"Moors," 151, 212
Morocco, xxiv, 37, 48, 91n10, 198
Morsi, Mohamed, 153
Multaka project, 61–66, 72

multiculturalism, 10–11, 14n10, 20, 112, 122–25, 155, 188; declared a "failure," 10, 20, 128, 144–47; neoliberal, 11, 32, 145, 182–83
Museum Island (Berlin), 20, 64–66, 68n31, 72–74, 220
museums, xiii, 61–80, 209
Muslims, xii, xix, 3, 27, 49, 54n1, 120n55, 149; antisemitism and (see antisemitism); expulsions of, xviii, 90–92, 154; as Nazi collaborators, 174, 185–92; perceived cultural deficits, 172–74, 177–83, 199; racism against, viii, x, 11–12, 31–32, 123–24, 127, 129, 165n11, 171–72, 182 (see also Islamophobia); in Turkey, 149–55. See also Islam

Nakba, xxin21, 191–92
Nama people, xvi, 60
Namibia, 55, 73, 211n21
National Liberal Party, 142
National Rally (formerly National Front), 169n18
National Socialist Underground (NSU), xvi, 4, 15, 130, 171–72
Native Americans, 84, 91
NATO, viii, xiv, xxiii–xxiv, 153, 157, 163–68
Nazi Germany: collaborators, 76n47, 169, 174, 185–92; German guilt and responsibility, xn6, 20, 54–55, 122, 129–30, 145, 175–77, 181–82; public memory of, xiv–xv, xxv, 11, 76, 78, 122–23, 157, 159–61, 173, 179–82 (see also memorials to Nazi victims). See also Holocaust
Nefertiti, 67, 68n30, 74–75
neocolonialism, xviii–xix, 30n5, 34, 49n29, 52, 209
neoliberalism, 11, 32, 37n9, 40, 120, 127, 145, 182–83
neo-Nazism, ixn5, 111, 115–16, 130, 159, 171
Netanyahu, Benjamin, xxv, 190
Netherlands, xviii, 54, 69n33, 76n47, 169, 169n18, 198

Neuengamme, 94–96, 191
Neuengamme Concentration Camp Memorial, 95; Roma and Sinti activism at, 93, 97n20, 99, 101–3, 105–6, 110n18, 121
Neukölln (Berlin neighborhood), xviin16, xxin21, 117, 120n55, 123–27
Neumann, Bernd, 67n27
nichtdeutsche Herkunftssprache (NdH), 2, 123–24, 201n5
North Africa, ix, 27, 65, 183, 193, 204, 213
Northern Ireland, 138
Novick, Peter, 190n63

objectivity, 189, 219
Opoku, Kwame, 73n44
Orientalism, 164–67, 208–9
Otherness, xii, 18, 20, 29, 33, 35, 45, 49, 73–75, 80, 90, 128, 148, 176–77, 192n71, 193, 201n5
Ottoman Empire, 87, 151
Özyürek, Ezra, 178n34, 180n40

Pacific islands, 58–59, 183
Palace of the Republic, 75–80
Palestine Liberation Organization, 186n49
Palestinians: expulsion of (Nakba), xxin21, 191–92; in Germany, xviin16, 191. See also Israeli-Palestinian conflict
Pan-German League (AV), 141
Papua New Guinea, 58
Partridge, Damani, 181n42
Party for Freedom (PVV), 169n18
Pegida movement, xn6, 15, 21, 127–28, 145, 147, 149, 151
Pergamon Museum (Berlin), 64, 66–67, 75
Perspektive Berlin (organization), 106–7
Peters, Carl, 141n8
Phalangists (Lebanon), 190
Pim Fortuyn List, 169nn17–18
piracy, 39–40

pogroms, xviin15, 87, 93, 100, 105, 111, 113–14, 120–22, 128, 171, 197
Poland, xxiii, 87, 89, 94, 100, 152
Poles, 137, 140–41
police violence, 202–7
Pollitt, Katha, 17n13
Porajmos (Nazi genocide of Roma and Sinti), xvii, xix, 22, 86, 105–11, 121; memorials to, 92–103, 218, 220
post/colonialism, xiii, 18–20, 33, 40, 48–49, 213, 218. *See also* colonialism
postcolonial studies, xxiv–xxv, 11–13
post/fascism, xiii, 18–20, 33, 48, 212, 218. *See also* fascism
postmigrant Germany, 4, 6, 10, 17–22, 124, 205, 213–21
postracial narratives, 6, 10–11, 17
post/socialism, xiii, 18–20, 32–33, 48, 51, 173, 212, 218
poverty, 49–50, 52–54, 69n33, 127
primitiveness, 44, 58–59, 74, 204
privilege, 7, 21, 85, 150, 189, 201–2, 209, 216
Prussia, 137, 139–40
public memory, xiii–xiv; European discourse on, 76; German identity and, 25–26, 76–80; hegemonic, xiv, xix, xxiv–xxv, 20–21, 76, 80, 93, 218–21; limits of hegemonic self-critique, 12–15, 84, 158–59; marginalized groups and, 218–21; public sphere and, 19–22; totalitarianism and, xvii–xviii. *See also* colonialism; Nazi Germany
Puerto Rico, 37n9
Putin, Vladimir, xix

Rabels, Niklas, 119
racial capitalism, 11–13
racialization, defined, viiin4, xix, 28–29
racialized groups, 2–12, 57; connections between, 35–36 (*see also* intersectionality); crisis moments and, viii, xii; exclusion of, xviii, xxii, 18, 20–21, 28, 35, 45, 49, 57, 84, 86, 100, 136–39, 145–46, 175, 197, 199, 207 (*see also* European racism;

German racism); expertise and, 189; in Germany, 8, 29–31; immobilization of, 3–4, 49; insecurity and, 200–202; as new Nazis, 129–31; theoretical frameworks on, 12–14; as threat to European identity, 136–39. *See also* assimilation; integration; un/German
racist violence, 4–5, 7–9, 31–32; after German reunification, 111–14, 122–23, 184, 197–99; crisis narrative and, xii, 199; in East Germany, 114–16, 178; by extreme right, xv–xvi, 178n34, 213; against German majority, 128–30; against Jewish minority, 175–76; against Muslims, 171–72; neo-Nazi, 115–16, 130; reporting of, xvin14, 117n34. *See also* pogroms
Ramberg, Lars, 77n49
Ravensbrück, 95
Reconquista, xviii
"Red Hamburg" (labor movement), 94
refugee crisis, vii–xii, 4–9, 47–52, 198–99, 208; German identity and, 27; German security and, 199–202; immobilization and, 49; internalist narrative on, 37–38, 51; mass casualties, xix, 21, 35, 37, 47–48; sexual violence and, 14n10; Turkey and, 155, 198. *See also* asylum seekers; deportation
Rehoboth Bastards, 59n8
Reker, Henriette, 5
religion, xv, 170, 182. *See also* Christianity; Islam
remigration, ix, xxiv
reparations, 54–56, 68–70, 96
resistance, xxvi, 209, 220–21
Rheinisches JournalistInnenbüro, 183, 192
right-wing extremists, ix, xv, xv–xvi, 116, 122, 145n20, 149n27, 169n18, 171, 175, 178n34, 197, 213. *See also* neo-Nazism
Robinson, Cedric, 11, 17
Rolland, Romain, 204n13

Roma and Sinti, xvii*n*15, xix, 20, 22, 27, 34–37, 87; activism, 93, 97n20, 99, 101–6, 110n18, 121; contemporary racism against, xii, 83–86, 97–121, 127, 155, 173, 218; as "gypsies," 36, 84, 109–11; Nazi persecution of, 93–97, 168; racialization of, 49, 92, 112, 114, 129–30
Roma and Sinti Union (RCU), 97–101, 106, 108, 218
Roma National Congress (RNC), 99, 105, 108
Romania, xxii, 104–5, 113–14, 155
Rose, Romani, 107, 110, 120
Rosh, Lea, 106
Rössel, Karl, 183, 185–93, 219n29
Rostock-Lichtenhagen pogroms, 93, 105, 113–14, 120–21, 128
Roth, Joseph, 1
Rothberg, Michael, xxi*n*21, 217
Russia, 136
Russian Empire, 87
Ruthven, Malise, 168

Sachsenhausen, 94
Sada (art project), 71–72
Sahakian, Rijin, 70–71
Said, Edward, 75n46, 208n17
Samoa, 58, 67
Sarkozy, Nicolas, 146
Sarrazin, Thilo, 45n24, 154
Saudi Arabia, 67n28, 72, 153
scapegoating, xv, 112, 136, 173
Schanzenviertel (Hamburg neighborhood), 117, 120n55, 127
Schäuble, Wolfgang, 104
Scheunenviertel (Berlin neighborhood), 88
Schirrmacher, Frank, 123, 128–31
Schmidt, Harald, 123n63
Scholz, Olaf, x*n*6
Schönwälder, Karin, 154
Schroeder, Robin, 5n2
Schuster, Josef, 177n33
Schuster, Peter Klaus, 72–74
security, right to, 199–202, 207, 214

Seite, Berndt, 114
Senegal, 48
September 11 attacks (9/11), 148–49, 168, 189
Serbia, xiv, 104, 151, 159, 165–66, 168
settler colonialism, xxiv, 35, 83, 85. *See also* colonialism
sexism and sexual harassment, 14, 117, 214–15
Shabat, Shemi, 181n42
Shoah (Nazi genocide of Jews), 22, 86, 106–10
Sieg, Katrin, 176n29
Sinti. *See* Roma and Sinti
Sinti Alliance, 109
slave revolts, 41n19, 69n33
slavery, 36, 49n29, 55, 68–69, 125n65, 159, 212
Snyder, Timothy, 211
Social Democrats, 103, 141n8, 142
socialism, 160, 212. *See also* post/ socialism
Social Nationalist Party (Syria), 190
Solf, Wilhelm, 205
Somalia, 39–40, 167n14
South Africa, 79n56, 179n38
Soviet Union, 26, 76, 94–95, 115, 136, 152, 164, 173. *See also* Stalinism
space-time models, 35, 45n24, 46, 60. *See also* evolutionary time
Spain, xviii, 37, 47, 65, 91n10, 135, 138, 208
Special features: Negro. Blacks in the Nazi state, 20, 194–95
Stalinism, xiv, 76n47, 77, 211
stateless people, 34, 98–99, 142
state of exception, 9–10, 49
Steinbach, Giovanna, 96, 99
Steyerl, Hito, 78n52
Stoiber, Edmund, 148
street names, 60n10, 79n56, 193n74
structural adjustment policies, 40, 46, 208. *See also* austerity measures
Syria, x, xi, xii*nn*23–24, 49, 65–66, 71n38, 74, 153, 190, 199

Terkessidis, Mark, 195
terrorism, 5, 50, 116, 148–49. *See also* war on terror
The Third World in World War II, 20, 183–95, 219–20
Todorova, Maria, 164
tolerance, 21n15, 66, 122, 124, 145–46, 158, 165, 172, 176, 178, 180–82, 201n5
Tolmein, Oliver, 117
Torres Strait Islander peoples, 84
totalitarianism, xiv, xvii–xviii, 157, 174, 210–12, 217–18
Transatlantic Trade and Investment Partnership, 37n9, 41, 46, 198
Treaty of Lausanne, 90–91
Trollmann, Heinrich, 96
Trollmann, Johann Wilhelm "Rukeli," 95–96
Trouillot, Michel-Rolph, 41
Trump, Donald, ix*n*5, xxiii
Tubman Network, xxiii*n*25
Tunisia, xxiv
Türkenproblem, 27, 154, 156, 218
Turkey, xxiv, 74, 91, 136, 180n40, 198, 208; EU membership, 147, 150–52; as Muslim-secular nation, 149–55
Turkish Germans, 3, 27, 116, 124–26, 129–30, 138, 145, 147, 154–55. *See also* Turkey

Ukraine, 198; Russian invasion of, viii, xix–xxiii
Ullrich, Volker, 173
un/German, xvi, 57, 96, 114, 129, 137, 139, 156, 201n5; as category of normalization, 28–31; as different than (white, Christian) Germans, xi, 86, 129 (*see also* German identity); racialized Germans as, xiii (*see also* racialized groups). *See also* Otherness
United Nations, 19, 64, 167, 198
United States, xxiv–xxvi, 68, 125, 201n5; Europe and, 26, 51, 69n33, 91, 163; racism in, 6, 10–11, 13, 49n29, 83–84, 215–17; superpower status, 11–12, 157–59, 166–67
universalism, viii, 12, 16, 34, 43–44, 56, 66–70, 72–75

victims: competitive victimhood, 179–80, 194, 200n4; expert-victim dichotomy, 107, 109–11; Germans as, 121–31, 172; good vs. bad, 106, 111
violence: antisemitic, xv, 88, 177–78; economic, 50; homophobic, 201n5; state monopoly on, 202–7; against women, 202. *See also* pogroms; racist violence
The Voice (refugee initiative), 9, 218
von Dohnanyi, Klaus, 99
von Luschan, Felix, 73n44
von Münch, Ingo, 101
von Pfeil, Joachim Friedrich, 59, 67, 73

Walser, Martin, 177
war on terror, 46, 148–49, 157, 168
Weber, Max, 85n2
Weems, Carrie Mae, 64n21
Wehler, Hans-Ulrich, 151–54, 156, 218
Weimar Republic, xii, 87–88, 165n11
Weiss, Christina, 105, 110n18
Werkstatt der Kulturen (Workshop of Cultures; WdK), 183–88, 193, 220
Western dominance: postwar justification of, 135, 157, 159, 165–66. *See also* European identity
West Germany. *See* Federal Republic of Germany
whiteness: hegemonic, xxiv–xxv, 15–18, 189, 194, 200, 218–21. *See also* European identity; German identity
Wien, Peter, 191
Wilders, Geert, 169n18
Williams, Eric, 17
Wilson, Fred, 64n21
Winant, Howard, 85n2
women-of-color feminism, 11, 13, 16, 215–17

World Bank, 40, 46
World War II, xix–xx, 64, 76n47, 78, 94–95, 137–38, 157, 211; effects on Global South and people of color, 183–95. *See also* Nazi Germany
Wynter, Sylvia, 17, 85n2

xenophobia, 5, 8, 31–32, 92, 112, 116, 129

Yemen, 40, 72, 153, 167n14
Ye'or, Bat, 21, 174
Yücel, Deniz, 123n63
Yugoslavia, 100, 101n25, 102, 155, 164, 173

Zelensky, Volodymyr, xx
Zionism, opposition to. *See* anti-Zionism

www.ingramcontent.com/pod-product-compliance
Lightning Source LLC
Chambersburg PA
CBHW031346230426
43670CB00006B/450